Praise for Kandace DeLain Davis

A searing, soul-baring, yet heartwarming memoir, about a mother's desperate efforts to heal and a grandmother who never gave up. It is a must read for anyone who loves someone with a mental illness.

— Steve Sanders, WGN News Chicago

Out of the Night that Covers Me

A Family Memoir

Kandace DeLain Davis

For Gram

Heroes inspire us by the matter-of-factness of their sacrifice.

~Henry Kissinger

Contents

Author's Note

This is a true story. However, some scenes in this nonfiction book do include an element of speculation, and some characters have been created for dramatic purposes.

Some real characters have been given an alias in order to protect their privacy.

Prologue

My parents met at a hospital for so-called "crazy" people. Then, when I was six, Mother killed herself. It wasn't in a normal way.

The truth was so ugly that protecting me was the kindest option. The only option. Compassionate Omission. A Sympathetic Lie. Had I known how sick my mother was, I would've understood all along.

This book is about my family, in hopes that other struggling families will have a better outcome.

Chapter 1

Things I Can't Throw Away

For seventy years, my grandmother, Mrs. Faire Stein, kept every newspaper clipping that mentioned the name of anyone in our entire family. Every postcard and article smelled like her long-familiar black steamer trunk.

In the winter of 2015, with time off from work, I tackled boxes inherited when we sold my grandmother's house in the fall of 2000. Busy with life, I had put the boxes aside, expecting in time to carefully sift through the artifacts. I knew the items were safely stored and going through them wasn't high on my list. I thought I knew what was there.

I didn't.

Decades-old cigar boxes crafted of hefty cardboard held white envelopes of negatives, Polaroids, and slides, sorted by year. A wood-fronted scrapbook, with paper edges torn from turning, contained some of my mother's silly kindergarten take-homes. An article about how Aunt Helen won the White County spelling bee despite having the chickenpox. A copy of a letter from Gram to the editor of the *Evansville* [Indiana] *Courier* regarding the improper use of a semicolon. My mother saved her ticket stub from the 1964 World Series when the Cardinals, with the star power of Bob Gibson and Lou Brock, defeated the Yankees in seven games. Cards from three daughters, seven grandchildren, and an extra helping from the first grandchild, Doug.

Gram kept any card, note, or clipping that brought her a giggle but also ones which were unfortunate reminders of rotten times.

In an envelope labeled *1959—Things I Can't Throw Away*, Gram stored a letter from my half-brother, Doug, to our mother, written when she was hospitalized after a suicide attempt.

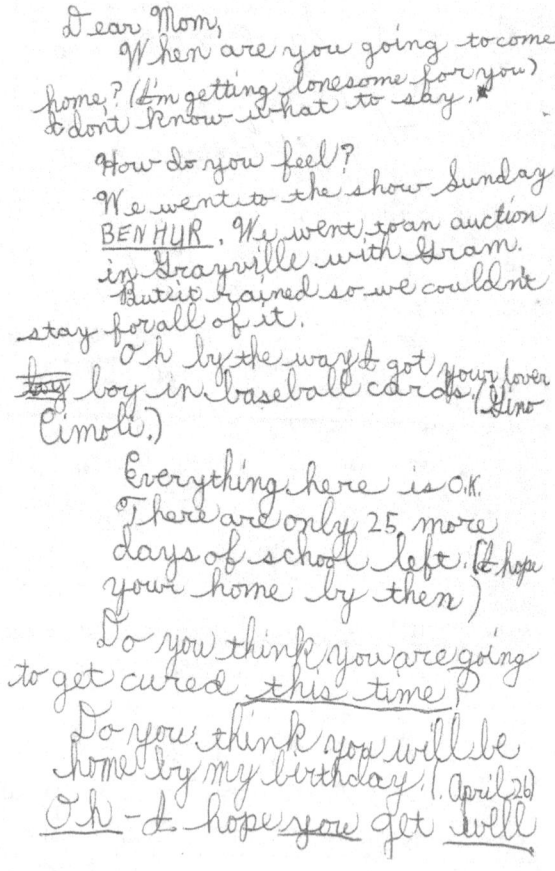

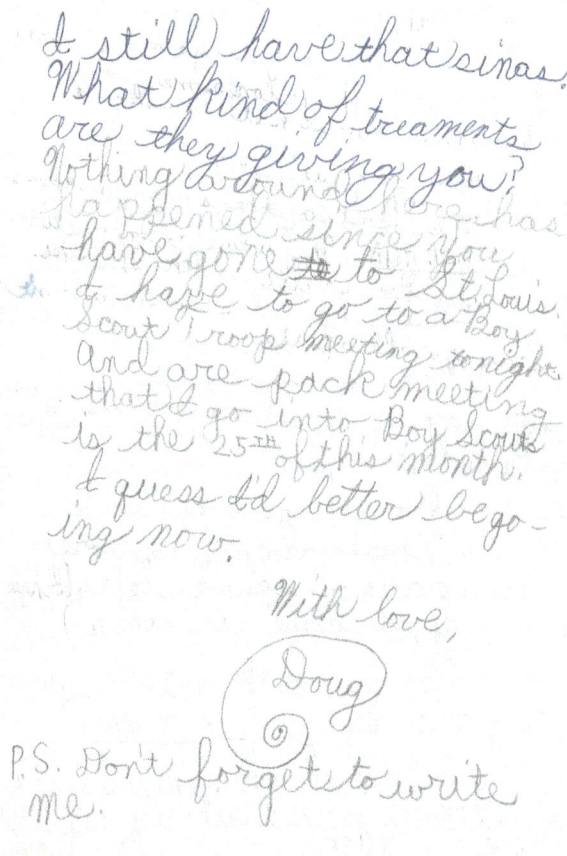

I HAD NEVER SEEN this letter before. I was wrought with pity for Doug, recalling his famous elementary school picture with one front tooth missing after a playground duel. Here on the page, Doug's longing for Mom was so raw. Our Mom. Thirty-six, twenty-four, thirty-six. A perfect figure. Beautiful, bright, a musical prodigy.

Doug hoped for her rehabilitation with all his might. I stopped reading to search on my phone for a picture of Mom's Gino Cimoli. Cute, but I was getting bogged down.

Pulling myself away from my phone, I noticed all the other things I needed to worry about in our 1890 Victorian basement. The white-washed limestone walls made crumbly messes covering the basement floor. I was eager to power up the shop vac, but the boxes needed some attention, too, and sorting memorabilia sounded like more fun.

The women in my family are bound by a yet-undiscovered gene that propels us into a state of locomotion. Movement is our therapy. I reached my forties, and the gene took hold of me hard. Getting through the papers would take hours, but I needed to stay knuckled down on the boxes. I would have no time once food-truck season started up again. I'd be back to my usual sweaty, chefy self. I had finally made a start, holding up each piece and sorting them into piles: pitch, keep, Aunt Helen, Aunt Rita.

Family protocol was that extra-special documents were photocopied and mailed out. Each family member received an account of the great tornado of March 18, 1925, which killed 127 people in White County, Illinois. A total of 613 deaths were recorded across Southern Illinois in the deadliest single tornado in U.S. history. Gram was a junior in high school.

All fifty or so students of Crossville High cowered in the halls and must have wondered, after hours of kneeling, what would await them going home. Gram walked her friend Laura down the gravel road of Main Street and up Vinegar Hill into the lush farmland. Word spread, and before leaving school, they had already learned Laura's mother was dead. The epic wind force snapped the life out of her. Remarkably, Laura's infant sister was found in a field, blown many yards away from their family home, unharmed.

I heard Gram retell this story many times and always with great remorse. Gram didn't know what to say to her friend, she told me, and they walked much of the way in silence.

The tornado wasn't the only disaster Crossville survived. In these relics was the original article documenting the great gas tank explosion.

Witness Edna Rawlinson later recounted the catastrophe in detail: "On Sunday evening, the thirteenth of January, 1952, I witnessed the most terrible disaster in the history of Crossville. The whole world, so far as we could see, was engulfed with fire."

A 500-gallon tank exploded near the yard of May Slankard who was killed. It caromed off a nearby car, went through the home of Myrtle DeLain, my great-grandmother, and continued its trail of tears. Aunt Helen and Aunt Rita had just stepped out of the kitchen to walk one block to United Methodist Youth Fellowship when the massive steel capsule crashed through the house, completely cutting the kitchen off from the rest of the home. Our family got lucky that time.

So I expected that this minuscule article in a small, white envelope would be more of the same. It was just another white envelope in a lifetime's worth of neatly cataloged archives. The article weighed barely a fraction more than the envelope itself. The *Carmi Times* printed this run of sentences on May 20, 1976:

Davis Inquest Set
An inquest into the death of Mary E. Davis, found dead at her home in Crossville Wednesday morning, has been scheduled for 7 p.m., May 28 at the White County Courthouse in Carmi.

White County Coroner Tom Wilson said the inquest into what has been assumed to be a suicide was called after some questions were raised in connection with the case.

I read the words again, wondering if maybe I'd misunderstood. It was a moment of validation that I had never wanted. A moment that showed me that I wasn't the only one who thought Mom's manner of death to be inconceivable. Once again, I was learning critical information about my own mother that no one had thought to share with me. This sentiment from the coroner gave teeth to a theory I'd never allowed myself to consider. I'd had enough of learning things in my aloneness and never asking questions, of being so afraid of the answer that I wouldn't even open my mouth. Shocking and sickening things that ripped me to pieces emotionally. For too many years, I went about my business, being grateful for what I did have, just as I'd been taught. I knew that this ... all of these years of grief ... was not how I wished to feel for the next forty years.

* * *

"LEAVE ME ALONE!" The words were a daily drumbeat in my head. In August of 1987, I was ready to start my freshman year of college. I couldn't wait to get out of Crossville. It was a weighty burden living at Gram's.

I was the remaining thing Gram had to do, to keep track of, to clean up after, to snoopervise. I didn't realize then that I was her busy work — vital to her survival. That week in 1987, Gram was fixated on a set of papers she'd brought home from the bank.

Days before, she placed on her kitchen desk a shallow, gray, metal safety-deposit box stamped with First National Bank of Crossville. The kitchen desk was her domain, and the items on or near it told everything one needed to know about Faire Stein.

A Cubs banner was affixed to light wood paneling above the desk. Next to the box sat her trusty, black adding machine with the pull-down lever and a desk set holding mail, and various booklets, including, "Relieving Constipation." Mortified at the booklet, I frequently moved it to the back of the desk set. It perpetually reappeared. Gram must've thought no one noticed it. I thought everyone noticed it.

Gram sat at the 1960s-era kitchen table topped with a green vinyl tablecloth that my mom's sisters, Aunt Helen or Aunt Rita, had sewed for Gram during one summer visit.

Looking down at a crossword, she said, "You need to go through those papers today. There are things of your mother's in there I need you to look at." The box was just the item of the month. We were constantly going through my mother's things. Maybe it was to declutter, or maybe Gram didn't want me to forget my mother.

Gram moved the deposit box to the table, and I moved it back to the desk. There was so much heaviness inside that box. I was about to be free. College life. I knew I could be happy if I could just get away. Eventually, I succumbed to teenage boredom, moved the box to the table, and sat down alone to do the task. Gram was watching the Cubs in her bedroom ten feet away.

Every item was neatly folded, each in a dated and labeled white envelope: will, savings bonds, life insurance. Then, death certificate.

Skimming the will, then passing over the savings bonds and insurance papers, I pulled out a thicker envelope labeled: "May 20th, 1976. Doug's Statement to Police."

The mention of the word, police, put me on guard. I held a stack of lined notebook pages with edges neatly trimmed. It was a hand-written story I had never heard. I quickly recognized Aunt Maxine's precise penmanship:

I arrived in Crossville at about 6 p.m. on Sunday, May 16th, for a visit with my mother, Mary Ellen Davis, and my grandparents, Mr. and Mrs. Alvin Stein. I had called my grandmother ahead of time to tell her I was coming. I called my grandmother because my mother had been in the hospital, and this is why I called her instead of my mother. This infuriated my mother, so by the time I arrived she was in a bad mood. I did eat supper with her that night.

The following day, May 17th, I spent little time with her, as I was in Carmi most of the day. Tuesday, I made no less than a dozen attempts to talk to her at her trailer. Each visit was short, as she made little sense. We were quarreling mainly because I was concerned over the care of my half sister, Kandi Davis. I felt she should be sent temporarily to live with my Aunt Helen and her family in Wyoming. During one visit to the trailer, my mother got out some alcohol and said that she guessed she would just get drunk. I knew that she had already taken Valium and was thick-tongued from that. I was so disgusted that I took a bottle of pills from her purse and flushed them down the toilet. This infuriated her so much

9

that she tried to squirt me with mace. I took the mace away from her, and she ripped the buttons off my shirt.

After this incident, she spent the rest of the day in bed. Later, I went back and heard her making a phone call. She was saying, "I don't know if you remember me or not, but you treated me a couple of months ago. I have to hang up now." I then checked the number on the notepad and discovered she was calling Dr. Mullenkamp in Evansville. The last time I went to the trailer, trying to talk reasonably with her, it was to no avail.

The last thing she said to me was, "Get out of here and never come back."

I then went to my grandmother's house to tell her I was leaving. I departed for Chicago at approximately 6:30 p.m. on May 18th.

This note is signed by Doug Meyers and notarized by Maxine Randall, the victim's aunt.

I laid the document down on the table and inhaled deeply. What a regrettable last moment Mom had had with her son. Of course, with a suicide, family members were interviewed. I recalled my own conversation with policeman, Glen Murray, Crossville's own version of Andy Griffith, Glen modestly asking my six-year-old self what Mom and I had done on our last night together.

Then, I picked up the envelope labeled "Death Certificate."

I approached it with absolute ignorance.

At the top, it read, "State of Illinois CORONER'S CERTIFI-CATE OF DEATH." The document was divided into three sections, and my eyes were instantly drawn to the center and a black tab labeled "CAUSE."

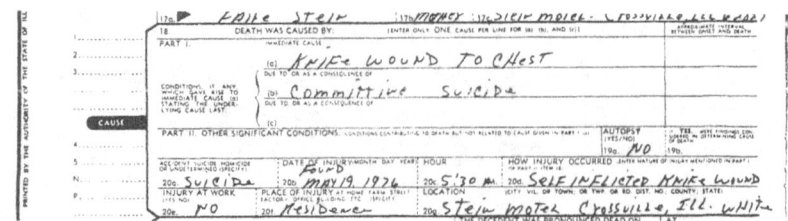

I'd imagined something more poetic. Visualized Mom collapsing on her bed, pills in hand, clad in a heavenly bathrobe, and passing sleepily from dim light into darkness.

This was not that story. I now envisioned a crimson mattress, sirens, chaos. A still life was snapped.

How strange it was that Aunt Maxine had notarized Doug's statement to the police, but that was normal Crossville six degrees.

Alone, I didn't know whether to sit or stand, cry or even laugh at the absurdity of the moment. I missed my mother then. Tender and kind, unpredictable yet affectionate. Mom cried when appropriate, showed sympathy and empathy. I was in utter disbelief that I wasn't warned about the startling contents of the box. No one offered an explanation, shared tears, or hugged me. There were no words to me before or after from anyone, not even Gram. Just nothing.

My first suspicion that Mom didn't die of natural causes came at about the age of eight when a boy at Sunday school crept toward me and said quietly in my ear, "Haha, your mom killed herself!" I cried on the way home, and when I told Gram about what Charlie said, she marched down the sidewalk of our property toward the boy's home. It looked like Gram was crying, and I knew then that Charlie was right. Couple that with an awareness of Mom's problem with pills, and I'd theorized how she died. A non-violent, run-of-the-mill, all-too-common overdose by a woman in pain. That was sad enough. I had considered that story and lived with it until uncovering the death certificates.

This other story was inconceivable. I didn't blame Gram for shadowing the facts. Putting words to a horrific scene while simultaneously reliving it? Meanwhile, wanting to communicate that gently and clearly to a child? The gory details of Mom's passing became impossible to verbalize. Gram's life had been crammed with difficult circumstances. I guessed she was just out of words.

In that 1987 crushing blow of a moment, after years of living with my parents' sordid legacy, I could easily imagine leaving Crossville forever.

Within a week, I was off to college. I never spoke to Gram or Doug about the box, and by now, they had both been dead for many years.

Homicide had never entered my mind until I found the inquest article in the basement boxes in 2015.

* * *

"COULD she really have done that? Stabbed herself to death?" I wondered to a friend.

It was 2015, shortly after I had discovered the article.

"If she was drugged up, maybe. Hard to believe, though."

People can do horrific things to themselves. I knew this.

When I ran the physicians' dining room at a St. Louis hospital, a patient came into the ER after he tried to cut his own head off with a chainsaw. He was schizophrenic. He said he wanted to get rid of his brain.

My friend, from a small town herself, theorized, "There must be someone who knows. It had to have gotten out."

I wasn't sure. I could imagine Gram keeping the details completely to herself.

And what of the death announcement I had seen, stating there would NOT be an inquest?

"Doug died in '97, but he was married for a while. I haven't talked to her in years, but maybe she's on Facebook."

* * *

DECEMBER 28, 2015, 2:57 p.m., I wrote to Doug's wife:

Dear Celia,
It's so good to be in touch with you again. Thanks for sharing your email address.

I can't believe it has been twenty years since Doug's death. I've worked very hard to establish a stable and peaceful life for myself, and now that all is well on the home front, I guess I feel like I have the strength to look back.

These are very difficult questions to ask, and I hope that my asking doesn't cause you angst, but how couldn't it cause angst? I don't know of any way to deliver this gently. It's just heartbreaking.

I began researching my mother's death. I saw the coroner's report years ago, so I knew it involved a knife, but recently while going through some of Gram's things, I discovered an article indicating a coroner's inquest had been held due to "questions about the case." I was shocked.

Only recently have I begun to wonder about Doug's potential involvement. Their argument was detailed in a statement he gave to the police. This statement is in Aunt Maxine's handwriting, which is odd to me.

I have asked Aunt Helen and Rita their thoughts on this. They say (and I believe they're being truthful) that they wondered about whether Doug could've done it, but that they don't know and that Gram had never discussed it with them.

Doug suffered so much as a result of Mom's illness and surely felt resentment toward her. Maybe it was enough to lead him to violence. Regardless, he lived with a terrible burden having been the last to see her.

I just can't believe Mom could end her life that

way. I've asked my friends who work in mental health, and they've never heard of suicide by that manner. Doug is gone, and there would be no harm in knowing the truth. If you have any information, it would be so helpful to me, and I can handle it. I need to know what happened.

I hope life is treating you well and that you're enjoying retirement.

Thank you,
Kandi

JANUARY 3, 2016, 3:07 p.m., Celia wrote back:

My Dear Kandi,

I have chosen not to read your email because I just may not be able to think about it over and over again. A few months ago, I was diagnosed with a brain tumor . . . about the size of a golf ball . . . basically, I am pretty good except a few quirks here and there . . . I try not to think about extra stress . . .Kandi, I am happy for you and your endeavors with your book.

God bless you,
Celia

Celia. The woman who mothered me, who told me when I was ten that it was time for me to start using deodorant. The woman who wrote to me after she divorced Doug, saying she still loved him, dreamt about him, but knew she could never go back to living with an alcoholic. The woman who introduced me to that luscious delicacy called crab. Crab dip! I loved it.

Now she was seemingly pulling back from the leadership role she'd assumed when I was a child. The email left me with more questions than I'd had when I wrote it. It was mysterious and cryptic. How did she know the email was stressful if she didn't read it?

Chapter 2

All Dressed Up

June 2018: St. Louis, Missouri

There was an Anderson window installer working outside my office in our rustic stone and cedar ranch home. He had the new casement windows open, bringing in a gentle June breeze. My furry friend, Moose, our bargain purchase from a central Illinois puppy mill, was supervising the installer. At five pounds, Moose's qualifications were questionable. The uniformed man who had Moose's attention would be wide-eyed that the tick tick of the keyboard he heard was tamping out this shocking tale about my family.

I was thinking about Ethel Serra and what had happened to her to make her so desensitized, compassionless. It's curious how one sentence can stick with you for so many years.

It had been an average Sunday morning at church, other than the fact that our church building had been destroyed by an arsonist torching Southern Illinois houses of worship. Services were subsequently held in the high school while the new church was being built. I was with the choir waiting in the mid-century home ec room

17

for services to begin when Ethel headed my way. All chummy like, Ethel practically galloped across the room, and I prepared for the usual pleasantries. She neared the long banquet table where I waited with the choir and stopped just a few inches away from my seat. Ethel smiled exuberantly, put her hand on the back of my chair, and then began to squawk.

"Joe and I were talking last night. We were trying to remember. Did your mother shoot herself, or was it pills?"

I was eighteen and surrounded by people I had known since birth. Mom's good friend Marian sat next to me. Marian closed her eyes and bowed her head. I watched her, hoping she would respond on my behalf. But Marian sat with her head down and eyes closed for what seemed like minutes. Was she thinking through her next move? She had opened her eyes, raised her head, and shook it from left to right, then looked at me with watery eyes.

"I'm not sure," I responded to Ethel. I wasn't about to tell her the real story, although I'm now positive she knew it.

I think I must have started to quietly cry. Almost immediately, the service began, and the choir walked down the hallway flanked with lockers and radiator heating.

Countless times, I had scurried down that hall with the carefree silliness of a teenager trying to beat the bell, but this was a long, slow walk. I could've, should've maybe even, fallen apart, but the choir kept marching. We turned right into the typing room where Mrs. Sharon Rogier led us through "F-F-F-F, E-E-E-E."

I thought of nothing else for that hour other than what I should have said to Ethel in response. Standing an inch from her witchy face, I should have belted, "What does Jesus think of you right now?"

Gram handled the aftermath, again, much like a lioness with her cub.

She opened the tiny Crossville phone book and furiously dialed. As Gram listened, I waited and wondered if Ethel would deny it.

"I was just curious. I would've thought you'd be over that by now!" Ethel responded defensively.

Gram delivered her parting sentence in a firm tone, voice cracking, "You never get over it. You just survive it."

Slamming the plastic receiver back into place, Gram turned her head to look out the window.

I held Gram's hand, and she whimpered softly.

Gram worked hard to protect me while also keeping Mom's memory alive. My relatives gently preserved every picture and important belonging of Mom's so that I was able to have them as memories. Even before the inquest article came to light, I believed that the story of my mother and grandmother should be told. Still, I didn't want it to cause conflict with the few living members of our family. I had no idea how my mother's sisters would feel about my pursuit of this information.

Throughout my life, Aunt Helen and Aunt Rita had focused on the good parts of Mom. *She was brilliant. She was so naturally gifted at music.* And occasionally a mention of what they seemed to believe was a fatal flaw. *She had to have a man. Any man. Even the worst man. And she picked some bad ones,* they told me.

What a torturous time 1976 must have been for them.

Mental illness and addiction seem to leave entire families feeling so completely helpless, and when the illness is terminal, the devastation is massive.

The notion that Gram wouldn't want me to be asking these questions, even years later, stuck with me. It was hard to think about flat-out defying her wishes that this ugliness should be held in confidence.

But there had to be something about the greater good in there. My own greater good was at risk. My list of health problems was growing—endometriosis, spinal fusions, and breast cancer. I knew my anxiety about the past was likely a factor. I truly didn't think I could survive chemo again.

Gram suffered quietly and privately for her own valiant reasons. Keeping the details hidden had been the only strategy available in Crossville. In the seventies and eighties, there was only one physician in Crossville, and he wasn't offering the kind of intense counseling Mom—and those affected by her illness—needed.

I'd given up the research at least twice, thinking to myself at times that maybe I just didn't want to know. But then, I came back. In P. I. mode, it was intriguing. In daughter mode, it was crushing. I'd learned about parts of my mom's life I had never even thought about. I winced at the image of her being in such agony that she would stab herself. What could've precipitated such despair? An undiagnosed condition causing physical pain? A line from one of Gram's 1959 letters to Aunt Helen stated, "Called to check on M.E. [Mary Ellen]. She sounded more alive, so I'm hoping she's coming out of her depressed state. Sometimes she does have honest to good-ness pain, I know. But this time, it was the result of a good case of nerves."

I needed more information.

As I entered the second half of my life, I had less professional ambition and more drive to seek truth and resolution. My remaining relatives were in their twilight years, and soon I'd be left with only my own memories.

IN THE WINTER OF 2016, I visited the White County Courthouse to look for a coroner's report or any other documents related to Mom's death. The papers I had seen in the safe deposit box in 1987 were nowhere to be found. I assumed someone in our family had closed Gram's bank accounts after her death and filed the documents away for safekeeping. I asked. No one had seen them.

Months before the trip to the courthouse, I reconnected with a long-lost friend, Carol. Our classrooms had adjoined on the third floor of Marquette High where I taught drama and English in the nineties. When I felt compelled to tell this story, Carol came to mind. Carol was a spectacular creative writing teacher and was vastly more English-y than me. I needed a confidante. To whom could I tell all of this? At forty-seven, I was still figuring out how to explain what happened to my parents.

Carol and I met at an upscale sports bar in a ritzy area of St. Louis. It seemed a good place to have a drink and whisper. We found a booth by the open kitchen and with watery drinks, over several hours, we sipped as I nervously laid out the story. I showed Carol pictures of Mom at various ages (e.g., 5, 18, 25, 40). I showed her the tender letter from Doug to our mom asking if she'd be cured this time. I told her about the safe deposit box. I told her about Gram with her tenacity and wit. Finally, I told her how Mom died.

Carol was instantly passionate. When it came time to head to the courthouse, she gladly accompanied me for the two-hour trip from St. Louis to Carmi. We headed south, down Interstate 64 through Belleville, Illinois, then Mt. Vernon, and finally Crossville. The trek felt menacing: frozen fields with cut cornstalks piercing upward from the rock-like, brown dirt. In the summertime, I loved this familiar drive. Gorgeous waving strands of wheat blowing in the wind and then, with the next turn, miles of bright green corn. But it was winter, and in winter, I hated it.

"We'll see someone I know," I warned Carol. "I don't know. Maybe not. I forget I haven't lived here in thirty years."

I folded the napkin I'd gotten with my Americano into a V-shape and moved it nervously across my lips. Was I being disrespectful to my family? I reminded myself that the facts of Mom's death felt too ominous to overlook.

Whatever paperwork Carol and I discovered wasn't going to change how I felt about Gram, who was neither a liar nor a vigilante. Gram had witnessed the years of trauma Doug endured as a result of Mom's problems. If she covered something up, she was acting on her bone-deep instinct to protect Doug and avert one more catastrophe.

At five thousand citizens, Carmi was substantially bigger than Crossville and housed the county seat where we were headed. When the Walmart opened in the eighties, Gram and I suddenly found reason to be in Carmi daily. I knew a lot of Carmians.

Carol and I made our way down Main Street Carmi, over the marshy Little Wabash River, past a few car dealerships and the old Dog-n-Suds, where I was afraid to order root *beer*, surely a sin. Then the Steak House, which wasn't exactly a steakhouse but had the most delicious crispy-edged cheeseburgers with hot-off-the-griddle toasty buns. I nostalgically pointed out my old haunts.

"We took gymnastics in that old gas station! Shoot! You missed it."

Carol gazed left and right. "This definitely isn't how most of the world grows up."

I told her of the vicious rivalry in sports between Carmi and Crossville and that when the state threatened to consolidate our schools, the Crossville Tigers went nuts. We planned to fight to the death to keep our little school open. I gave Carol the *pièce de résistance* when I explained Crossvillians believed that Carmians were snobs because they were from the city.

If I encountered someone I knew, I could lie and say I was just working on a family tree. As we walked in, that's what I thought I would do. We found the circuit clerk's office. Perched on the laminate counter of a simple 10 x 15-foot office was a white business card printed, *Megan Allenton Nash, Circuit Clerk*.

As teenagers, Megan and I played summer softball together. So on this day, with Carol listening, we spent a few minutes catching up before I explained, in a much euphemized way, why I was there. She sent me to the records room, where I could look for legal documents containing Mom's name, and meanwhile, she printed out a copy of the death certificate.

Carol and I found a record of a motion filed after one of Mom's suicide attempts, to commit her to the Anna State Hospital, originally known as The Illinois Southern Hospital for the Insane. The court records noted our family physician had been called to testify. The physician stated in the transcript that he suspected schizophrenia. Was schizophrenia genetic? I'd always wondered when the darkness was going to hit me. It seemed unavoidable.

Carol and I returned to the clerk's counter, and Megan passed the certificate to me, seeming to notice the cause of death. She looked up at me, carefully considering her words. With a benevolent smile, she quietly told me, "You know, Sheriff Abbott is still around. He lives right down the street. I am sure he'd be happy to talk to you about your mom." I was thankful the person who'd recognized me was Megan and not Ethel Serra.

Bill Abbott was in his nineties. I didn't imagine an unexpected visit regarding an old case was on his agenda that day. I pictured Bill sitting on his sun porch watching reruns of *Matlock* and me showing up to ask, "Do you remember my mom's sanguineous death in 1976?" I opted for a phone call.

Me: "Hi, Mr. Abbott?"

I told him I was Mary Ellen Stein's daughter. He spoke in a jolly tone, and I regretted that I might be curbing his enthusiasm. But he was a cop. Maybe he loved this stuff.

Bill: "I took your mom to the state hospital in Anna a few times."

Me: "Yes. I'm doing some research on her illness. She died in May of '76. You came to our home the day she was found."

Bill: "Yes. I don't know how much you'd like to hear. I remember it well."

I was startled by his prompt candor. Without any further encouragement, Bill laid out exactly what he recalled. He communicated with the fact-based accounting style of a lawman viewing a crime scene.

Bill told me that when he entered our trailer, he found Mom adorned in a beautiful red nightgown. He used the words "dressed up." Mom was lying on her bed, face up. He remembered the wound being close to her heart. Sheriff Abbott stated unequivocally that it appeared she had planned it. I was now completely baffled. However, I felt my spirit lift a bit at the thought that I could be safely back to the suicide theory, which at that precise moment was more acceptable to me than murder. I can't say why. Bill and I said a cordial goodbye. I planned to write him a thank you note but never did.

Megan and I exchanged follow-up emails, and she referred me to the county coroner who might help me find other records. I was disappointed to learn the 1976 files were destroyed when the basement storage area flooded. It was a massive setback.

Following Megan's suggestion, I looked for copies of records at the state level. They could find no coroner's report for Mary Ellen Davis.

How was it that I was forty-seven years old and researching what happened to Mom? How did Mom end up circling the drain? It reminded me of the old Dow Scrubbing Bubbles ad. "Aaah, help me!" Little white bubbles with faces went spinning toward the drain. Then, gone, down the hole, nothing to be done. Plenty of onlookers took in the sight, and though they tried so hard, no one could help her. Mom plummeted down the hole.

In 1964, Kitty Genovese was supposedly murdered in New York City with thirty-eight onlookers doing nothing as they watched. Later, evidence showed this wasn't actually true. Several people did call the police. One woman ran outside to do something. Onlookers don't always see the real picture but only parts of the whole, and most people do want to help.

I knew more than the average person about depression and addiction. I *knew* my parents didn't plan to desert their kids, but it still felt like desertion. Like a swing thought in golf, I'd carefully plotted out how to live with my abandonment.

My survival theory: I was better off without *them* as parents. The new possibility that Mom may not have died by her own hand changed my feelings. What if she had been murdered? Maybe she actually wanted to live and get better.

Say it wasn't suicide. Could I have saved her? I couldn't have. I know. The facts told me she was profoundly ill. Our entire family, our entire town, had tried to save her. Pulling back, looking at the whole story, I was trying to truly comprehend how a bright, fun-loving girl turned into a woman who essentially went mad. I shouldn't have needed permission to ask questions about my own mother, but it seemed I wanted permission when it came to this sacred topic. I was terrified of hurting our family with my questions, but I needed to talk about it. Had Mom died of leukemia, we would've talked about it.

> Dear Mom and Gram,
>
> You always hoped I'd become a letter writer, so here it is. Heaven Post. My only way to reach you.
>
> You've both been gone so long. I hope you've found peace, wherever you are. Hope you have talked and said all the things you weren't able to say to each other in life. I hope you've been able to speak from the heart and shed the scars of the past.
>
> It's so hard for me to tell you about this. Don't know that you're going to like what I say here, and you've every right to disapprove. If you're in the midst of a good Scrabble game and the angels have whipped up a big batch of our favorite homemade Party Mix, ask them to give you a few minutes for a private family moment. I have so many questions about what we call Heaven, but that's another conversation.
>
> I'm writing a book. I have entertained every possible feeling you may have about it. I have begun and then stopped writing multiple times, each time strug-

gling to proceed without upsetting anyone. I tried writing it as fiction. It was impossible. I needed to tell the truth.

I have so much respect for you, Gram, and everything I say on these pages is intended only to honor your memory and share your remarkable life story.

Mom, I don't know how you would feel. I wonder if you would even mind. Having your story told might be a victory for you. Everything I say on these pages about you is for the purpose of learning why and how you died. Maybe I'm afraid what happened to you could happen to me. I look at your picture every single day, and I just hope that I can somehow make the slightest bit of difference in the world on your behalf. I know that you tried as hard as you could to take care of me. I know that you loved me. You just couldn't be here anymore.

I can't live the rest of my life with this giant weight on me every day. I've got a pretty good life going, but I need to file away the past.

Send me a sign you're okay with this. That would sure make this a lot easier. Before I go, it is very important for me to know who is winning at Scrabble. Do you just play one never-ending game? But that wouldn't result in a winner, and that's not how we do things, now is it? Who has the Q? It'll make you or break you. I love you.

~K

Chapter 3

Mother and Daddy

1944: Diary of Mary Ellen Stein, Age 13

The following are authentic excerpts of letters, journals, and other documents belonging to my mother, Mary Ellen.

Dear Diary,

It's my first entry, so I'd better tell you all about Crossville and its goings on!

It's finally Saturday! Edna Ruth and I get to go to the premier of *Hollywood Canteen*. I'm so happy Mother gave me permission. She's been in the hospital all week with a terrible rash. Dr. C said it was nerves and kept her all week in order for her to rest. She's coming home tomorrow, and we have the house all straightened, weeds pulled, and the sidewalk swept. I hope that keeps her nerves down.

"Hollywood Canteen" debuted last year and was nominated for THREE Academy Awards! It's just now coming to our theater.

We never get to see the good movies when the rest of the world does. It feels like no one even knows Crossville exists. All the big stars are in it—sixty-two to be exact! Some of my favorites are: Jack Benny, Kitty Carlisle, Jane Wyman, and the Andrew Sisters.

I wish Lois Ann and Bernice could come to the show, so we could sing along with the Andrew Sisters. We practice our music after school every day that I don't have track or marching band.

Mother loved it when we did "Don't Sit Under the Apple Tree" at the Fall Festival. Mother's mother, Grandmother DeLain, sewed us matching dresses and then made us promise we would never sing "Rum and Coca-Cola." She doesn't like us singing about liquor.

Grandmother DeLain hates it when the three of us giggle during church. Once we performed at Revival and giggled through the entire song. The preacher finally told us to just go sit down.

I looked back at Mother once and even she was giggling. She was sitting in the last pew with Grandmother and Aunt Maxine, Mother's sister. They always sit there, so Mother can sneak out as soon as the message is finished. She has to get home to start frying the chicken for lunch.

My little sisters are so cute and funny, but they drive me crazy! Sometimes I am downright mean to them. It's just too much fun to tell them stories about monsters.

Helen is ten now and too old to tease, but Rita is only seven and believes anything I tell her. She is the cutest little thing and follows Mother around all day. Before she was in school, we had to make her a lunchbox too. She would go outside with Mother to hang sheets on the line, and when our school lunch bell rang from across town, she would sit down and eat her sandwich just like the big kids were doing.

Now, for more about Crossville. Last year, I wrote a theme on the importance of hometown pride. I went down to the White County Chamber of Commerce, and Mother helped me find some books. The town charter was filed on October 12, 1895, at 11:05

a.m. The original plot of Crossville was one-half square mile (isn't that a gas!).

Thomas Cross donated land for a railroad project, and that area became Crossville. Around 1900, there were four passenger trains running through Crossville every day. Special trains were even added to the schedule during times of popular ball games, and these trains would be full to the brim with excited fans heading to St. Louis or Chicago to watch their boys play. Mother used to take the train to see the Cardinals. She loves baseball.

We always have to repeat Mother's first and middle name when we get outside of Crossville, "Faire DeLain Stein," and then spell the whole thing out several times. Everyone in town knows how to spell it, other than the country people, and there are quite a few of those.

The original Oliver Pierre DeLain came to America to fight with Lafayette during the war of 1812. Grandfather was the fourth Oliver Pierre DeLain. Townspeople ended up just calling him "Bud." He died before I was born.

Mother and Daddy own a motel, and that makes things exciting. Mother has a notebook of "people," where she writes down true stories about our weird roomers. There are the people on their way to here or there or nowhere if they're staying around Crossville for long. Then there are people who check in and out the same afternoon. Mom tells Rita and Helen that those people are having a "party." My little sisters don't understand why the people leave so soon. They always want to go to the party, and Mother has to tell them we are not invited. They always ask us, "Why are the lights out if they're having a party?" It makes Mother and me crack up.

Besides the motel, we own a farm, a filling station with an apartment above it, our own house which Dad built and paid for in cash. Then we have rental houses next door. This keeps my mother very busy while Alvino, the nickname I gave Daddy, is out gallivanting around. At least the motel being full puts Dad in a better mood.

The oil boom is why Mother is so busy. All kinds of engineers, drillers, and derrickmen are sent by the big companies to live in Crossville for months or years. When our wells run dry, they will be moved to a new place and start all over.

Dad won't let Mother hire anyone to help, so Mother is stuck with everything. She cleans all the rooms and washes and irons all the sheets every day. Mother also mows the lawn and takes care of the rental houses next door. Then, she does the laundry for us girls and Daddy. And she has to cook. Grandmother says it's too much.

When the motel was full last year, Dad decided to rent out a bedroom in our house! The front entrance of our house that faces the highway takes you straight to the upstairs. Mother said Dad must've had this plan in mind when he built the house, but he sure didn't tell her. I thought he should rent out one of the downstairs bedrooms, but that would mean he and Mother sleeping in the same bed and Mother sure didn't want that. We even have to share a bathroom with the renters.

I have always liked talking to older boys. My teacher, Mr. Prince, calls me "precocious." I had to look it up. None of the guys are from around here which makes them more interesting to me. We sometimes have singing practice when we don't really need to, and we end up just talking to the oil guys. It's just polite, I think, to learn about anyone who lives right across the hall from you. I just don't let my mother and dad know that I talk to the men. Daddy would go ape. He would have me sent away and locked up!

1947: Diary of Mary Ellen Stein, Age 17

Dear Diary,

I've been keeping a secret, afraid Daddy would find this diary and read it, but I don't even care anymore if he does! Johnny Meyers is his name. You won't believe how we met. He lives across the hall from me! He just turned twenty-two and has already been to college!

By the time Mother invited Johnny down to eat dinner with us, she had already figured it out.

Mother REALLY warmed up to Johnny when he helped with dishes after dinner. He took to my sisters immediately, too.

Johnny and I started spending each evening together, just talking on the front porch or taking walks along the road by the motel. I heard Mother and Dad talking about it constantly. Dad thinks I'm a little kid.

Mother is on my side when it comes to Johnny. Dad can't stand that we're happy and in love, so he just goes outside in a huff and "stews" around, as Mother calls it. Really, most people in Crossville are afraid of Dad.

Johnny, Mom, Aunt Helen, Aunt Rita, and Gram

Mother said I was getting too big for my britches and should make sure I enjoy my senior year. I'm still the drum majorette and am in the orchestra. I play French horn, flute, or percussion in the concert band, depending on what is needed. I'm a cheerleader. I'm on student council. I had the lead in the senior play, and our principal, Mr. Sommer, nominated me for the National Honor Society. I don't think Mom should be worried about me losing my school spirit.

Johnny and Mom

Mother allows me to go on rides with Johnny in his car. We drive up to the Dairy Maid or to the Pig Oven in the evenings. We make out sometimes, but we also have long talks. He tells me about growing up in Kansas, being in the Navy, about how hard he had to study to become an engineer. We never run out of things to talk about.

I've recently gotten the gumption to start talking to Johnny about how things will be when we're married.

And that's my secret, Diary. Dad, if you're reading this, too bad!

We plan to wait until after my graduation. I don't want anyone to think it's a shotgun wedding like Floyd and Mary Anne had. Johnny gave me a ring on my birthday this past October. I accidentally left it on during dinner, and Dad noticed. Johnny excused himself to go upstairs and read. While I was helping Mother with the dishes, Dad proceeded upstairs with his shotgun. I didn't even know what was happening. Johnny told me about it afterward. Johnny thought it was so ridiculous that he laughed.

I've never been so embarrassed. Dad is just like his own father. Mother says that every time he blows up. I'm not Daddy's little girl. I am upset with him most of the time. Mother says I shouldn't lose my cool because it just provokes him.

Dad hit me in the face last year when I smarted off to him. If Johnny had been here, Alvino would've been sorry. If Mom would put Daddy in his place, I wouldn't have to do it. She just makes fun of him behind his back, but never says it to his face. Sometimes it's just not funny. I can't believe she laughs about it.

Last year before band contest, I needed a new dress. I have scored a First or First Superior every year. You'd think Dad would be proud and want me to look presentable. I couldn't understand why he wouldn't allow Mother to buy me a dress, but any money that is collected at the motel or the filling station or for rent goes straight to Dad and then he gives Mother what he thinks she needs. What he thinks she needs isn't enough to even pay the bills, let alone buy groceries or clothes! Once Mother even had to get a loan at the bank for food. That was when I went crazy and told Dad he was the meanest person I had ever met. Mother knows it.

I may punch Dad back one of these days. The next time he makes Mother cry or touches her, I don't know what I'll do. It's good when Johnny is around. He can reason with Dad, but once we are married and gone, I'll be worried sick about Mother.

Mother is very eager for me to marry Johnny. I guess she just wants two less mouths to cook for. She doesn't even seem the marrying type. She is different from my friends' mothers. They don't mow the grass or learn to repair things with the *Feminine Fix-It Handbook*. That's an embarrassing book that Mother leaves on the desk in the kitchen. Other mothers just ask their husbands to do it, but Dad is gone a lot.

Mother has been helping me plan a small ceremony. And on June 4, 1949, I will become Mrs. Johnny Meyers.

Johnny's mother gave me a book on marriage. I've been reading it. It's a scream!

The Secret of the Home

THE SUBJECT we shall discuss in this chapter is that of the private relationship which should have its God-given place in the married life. "In the beginning, God made them male and female" (Matt. 19:4). The male was to be vigorous, strong and fit for battle. The female was to be tender, gentle and sweet for the nurture and care of her babies. Through that contact between the two which God has ordained, it has become possible for love to be consummated and for little ones to enter into the home that God has prepared. In the quiet of the bedroom, alone with each other, two hearts are welded together and this special joy, which has been ordained of God, becomes the normal and natural relationship between the bride and the bridegroom.

The acts of the first night that you are together may be the means of permanently injuring your hearts or of beautifully melting them together. Many factors enter into this new experience. There is danger of injury through carelessness. There is danger of disturbing the sensibilities through failure to properly consider the feelings of each other, both mental and physical. There is danger of so acting that dislike is created instead of gracious tenderness and attractiveness. Let each respect the wishes of the other and seek to make this new experience one that shall be remembered with joy and not with sorrow.

It must be remembered that the husband is probably much better acquainted with these matters than the wife. She may feel great hesitation about being perfectly free in this new relationship. She may have delicate feelings and great sensitiveness concerning her body. These conditions must be recognized and honored by the husband. Do not demand of her that which she hesitates at the moment to give. Show kindness with patience. She may not know what is about to transpire and may be

unhappily surprised by what is suggested. Do not
lower yourself in her estimation by acting unwisely.
Treat her with the utmost deference and respect
while you explain carefully and fully that which you
are expecting to do. Her heart will respond and she
will be attracted to you as you show her the loving
affection and the tender expressions which she de-
sires.

Miss Stein Bride
Of John Meyers

MRS. JOHN MEYERS

Chapter 4

Crime Doesn't Pay

April 2017

"**W**ait, wait! Read this part!" I said.

I was laughing like I hadn't laughed in a long time. Carol and I were sitting at a hip restaurant on a chilly spring day. There was nary enough room on the table for all the artifacts related to Mom's life plus our deviled eggs with pork cracklings. I placed the documents, all still emitting the smell of Gram's trunk, in chronological order and pulled out one of the most notable pieces.

I flipped the yellowing 5 x 7 pages of *Happiness in the Home*, the manual Mom had received from Johnny's mother. I read aloud to Carol.

As a rule the husband will be better informed on the things of the world than the wife. He is out in the world. He knows about buildings and plumbing. He understands what taxes must be paid and the rules relating to street paving in front of the home. He is not supposed to know about the kitchen

We roared, making a bit of a commotion in the restaurant, which was now very quiet following the noon rush.

"You can still buy books on marriage from this guy."

"The topics are so random," Carol added.

> first love. No matter what goes wrong with the food, in your judgment, do not complain or criticize. Give your sweetheart a loving embrace and suggest that it would be so much better if the coffee were poured after you sat down instead of before, so that it may be hot when you are ready to drink it.

We were speechless. The world was in the middle of its love/hate relationship with Trump, and gender roles were a topic coloring everything.

"Your mom didn't go to college, right?"

"No. Women just got married back then. I know they all loved Johnny and thought she'd be happy being a wife and mother."

"When did she start to change? Can't we ask someone?"

"After Johnny died. I think."

I thought back to Gram's use of the term "nervousness" in a letter. Anxiety and mania weren't terms laypeople knew in 1948.

"I'm going to see my aunts in June. I'll try to work my questions into a conversation. No idea who knows what."

June 2017: Billings, Montana

My cousin Jack and I sat at the granite kitchen island in his beautiful rustic modern retreat at the base of the Rocky Mountains in western Montana.

I had flown west to meet up with Aunt Rita before heading on to Montana to see Aunt Helen.

Mom's younger sisters were eighty and eighty-two, respectively.

"You know, I want to talk to you about something tonight."

"Hmm. That's ominous," Jack responded.

I couldn't tell him not to be scared. I was totally perplexed about what the rest of the family knew about Mom's death.

"We have those ribeyes. We can talk over dinner?" he suggested.

"That's good."

Except I thought what I always thought. Mom's death wasn't really dinner conversation.

Jack was gathering his lunch and stuffing various items into an Osprey daypack. He kept a headlamp in his backpack because he wanted to be prepared to help a stranded motorist change a tire. It happened once when it was very dark out. He didn't want to be so remiss next time.

Through the window behind Jack were the majestic Rocky Mountains, reminding me how much I didn't really matter. I wondered whether I should be focused on enjoying this awe-inspiring part of the world rather than rehashing the past, then reminded myself rehashing wasn't my intention. It wasn't about garnering sympathy. It was about knowing what happened to my mom. Maybe, if I was lucky? Understanding *why and how* it happened.

"If you'd like a project," Jack mentioned, "I've got a bunch of stuff in the garage you might want. There are *a lot* of family letters. They could be fun to look through."

Jack brought in several large bundles, pristinely preserved and obviously opened with care. I couldn't believe the size of the stacks. There were nearly fifty letters from 1958 alone, a critical year for Mom. The letters looked as if they had been under the care of an archivist.

I filled my coffee cup and said hello to Bandit, the Karelian Bear dog who wouldn't hurt a fly, but who was still carefully monitoring the perimeter of the yard. I plopped myself on the leather couch and began reading. Gram's clever storytelling had me cackling all morning. I belly laughed. The letters read like a diary, Gram trumpeting the goings on back in Crossville. She never wanted her girls to forget what was happening at home. Letters were an outlet for Gram's constant fretting which she masked with humor. They were a shining example of her abiding affection for her children—a letter a week for years.

Later that night, I briefed Jack about the research I'd done over the past year, showing first the startling inquest article and then explaining Mom's cause of death. He slumped down in his chair and stared back at me with heartbroken eyes.

"I thought it was an overdose."

I hated upsetting him, but I knew I had to explain the motivation for my investigation. Jack's sadness was evidence of the first unintended consequence; on some level, my aunts, cousins, and Doug's son and ex-wife were going to be brought in, and I'd have to come to terms with it.

* * *

RETURNING TO ST. Louis a week later, crammed into a window seat, I picked out all the letters from the years Mom and Johnny were married, 1948-1958. It was a difficult task on the small fold-down tray. The letters were mostly from Gram to Aunt Helen but also several from Gram to Mom and Johnny.

Once they were organized by week, month, and year, I handed the good ones to Lisa, my partner of many years, who read them and passed them on to Aunt Rita across the aisle. The flight went by in a flash as we quietly giggled at Gram's vivid storytelling

The precious letters were invaluable heirlooms of a simpler time when the world was so small; news came through the mail and the newspaper.

At last, the wheels of discovery were really turning. Whatever was happening with Mom in those years was sure to be in those envelopes.

On a blistering hot day that July of 2017, I sat on the floor at my home and searched for any nuggets, any events that might tell me where it began to go wrong. I started with the earliest letters.

In 1948, Mom and Johnny were married in a simple ceremony in Henderson, Kentucky. Baker Tool and Die Company had transferred Johnny to Henderson, about an hour from Crossville. Gram was putting out a fire between Mom and Grandad, who refused to attend the wedding.

Johnny & Mary Ellen on their wedding day

The next writings are from actual family letters which have been pieced together to more efficiently tell my family's story. When necessary, content has been added to provide context to our story.

1948, Faire (Gram) in Crossville, Illinois, to Johnny and Mary Ellen (Mom) in Henderson, Kentucky

Dear Mary Ellen and Johnny,

Well kids, I'm a mother-in-law, and I planned things pretty well if I do say so. The weather was almost perfect for your ceremony.

You mustn't let Dad get the better of you. Can't believe he couldn't or wouldn't close the filling station. Typical. I hope it didn't ruin your day. Johnny is the right man to deal with your dad. Not many sons-in-law could tolerate him.

While cleaning yesterday, I found several old signs in Alvin's junk drawer that would've been perfect for him to use had he come to the wedding (a little fibbing, though): "Gone to the barber shop." "Gone to the farm." "Be back at 4 p.m." "Closed for a few days."

Hope Baker will leave you two in Henderson for longer than a minute. If I'm lucky, you'll be back to White County with the next transfer.

I've been busy, busy this week. Cleaned the boiler room, and I've washed twenty motel rugs and five bedspreads yesterday and today. Then I hauled away three truckloads of junk from the apartment above the station. So I'm in the clear if I can keep Alvin in the dark. Last time he helped me purge, he threw away exactly ten nails, two bolts, and three screws. Of course, they were rusty, so don't worry. A man moves into the apartment tomorrow (he hopes) if I get it cleaned.

When shall we expect a baby? Been considering names: Kate, Isabel, Emily, Julie, Douglas, Hugh, Bret, Alan, Rebecca. Write!

Johnny & Mary Ellen in Henderson, Kentucky

The truth: Alvin (Grandad) didn't support the marriage. He just couldn't get past his shotgun mentality. Maybe Grandad was jealous of the attention Johnny received from the women in the house.

When Grandad's father died in 1949, he and Gram inherited a second farm, including livestock, on the outskirts of Crossville. Gram was ill-equipped to deal with the mud and muck livestock farming would bring into her house, and she had no time for the additional work. Grandad was often off fishing when things at the farm went awry. Word around town was that his Airstream at Kentucky Lake was more than just a place to stay while fishing.

Gram worked her fingers to the bone, and in the late evening, she used her pen to stay connected to her children. Her first grandchild was now on the way.

Faire in Crossville to Mary Ellen in Henderson

Dear M.E. and Johnny,

I'm sure glad you've completed your "assignment". Your letter telling the good news came today, and believe it or not, I haven't even told one person—not even hinted. I'll try not to gush, but I am happy, and if you don't mind my interfering, I'm hoping for a girl. There's no doubt the news will get sounded around. Really, I've told only Grandmother, Maxine, Aunt Sara, Uncle Joe, and Miss Sadie.

Just for a change, I'm not gonna tell you what I've done this week, except that I've done plenty. I'm "done in" and I'm "done for"—I can do no more, with the exception of a few odds and ends that I may bump into before midnight.

Dad's been off fishing at Kentucky Lake, and it hasn't been my day. I mowed all day yesterday and today and broke the power mower. Then I let his two sick pigs die at the farm. Henry and Gene are taking care of "arrangements" for them, for which I gave their wives some dish towels. Grandmother is the only one I know who feels sorry for me, except me. She has been staying with me at night. She thinks I need the company.

I know you're busy, so you're under no obligation to write again unless you feel like it. I won't ask when you'll visit. I'll just guess and see how close I get. Be careful.

Love,
Mother

Faire in Crossville to Mary Ellen in Henderson

Dear Mary Ellen and Johnny,

It's been two days since your visit, and I'm already thinking about when you'll be back. It's too quiet around here.

Did John's headache subside by the time you got to Henderson? I wonder what is causing them. I'm thankful you don't have headaches with your pregnancy. I did all three times.

How are you feeling this week? Any more ideas on names? I'll try and stay out of it and let you live your life. But, I do have more thoughts if you want them. I'll have my bag packed by the middle of March in case you decide to hurry things up a bit. I imagine you'll feel like you're ready by then.

Faire and Alvin

Please tell John again how much I appreciated his help with the apple tree. I've a
notion to pour kerosene on the thing and
kill it. That would eliminate a lot of
applesauce work for me. Anyhow, only John
can tolerate your dad long enough to help
him with any job.

The boiler has gone out in the motel.
Alvin has been supervising the workers all
morning. I expect them to walk off and leave
him with it, which would suit me fine. Let
him struggle with that boiler to no end.

Sending a picture your sister took of us.
Don't we look happy? You be careful and
write!

Grandmother DeLain (Faire's mother) in Crossville to Mary Ellen and Johnny in Henderson

JOHN AND ELLEN,

GREAT-GRANDMOTHER IS A SPECIAL TITLE THAT I'LL WARM TO. CAN'T BELIEVE I'M THAT OLD.

THANK YOU FOR THE PHOTO. I CAN'T WAIT TO SEE JOHN DOUGLAS'S LITTLE FACE FOR MYSELF. JUST GET HERE WHEN YOU CAN.

GUESS YOUR MOTHER IS WILLING TO ACCEPT A "HIM" AFTER ALL. SPEAKING OF YOUR MOTHER, SHE HAS BEEN WORKING NONSTOP SINCE RETURNING FROM HER VISIT WITH YOU — TOO MUCH. THERE'S NO STOPPING HER, YOU KNOW. SHE SURE NEEDS TO GET AWAY FROM THAT MOTEL MORE OFTEN. MARY ELLEN, IF ANYONE EVER TRIES TO WILL YOU A MOTEL, DON'T BE INTER-ESTED! IT'S A REAL WORRY AND A WOMAN KILLER!

YOUR MOTHER TELLS ME JOHNNY IS GETTING UP WITH THE BABY IN THE MIDDLE OF THE NIGHT AND THAT HE LOOKS TIRED TO HER. IT'LL BE A BIG HELP WHEN BAKER SENDS YOU BACK HERE. WE CAN ALL PITCH IN, AND WE WILL.

JUST WANTED YOU TO KNOW WE ARE ALL THINKING OF YOU. GIVE JOHNNY MY LOVE.

LOVE,
GRANDMOTHER

Johnny, Mary Ellen, and my half-brother, Doug

Still no real sign of Mom stumbling, but there were obvious under-tones in those letters. I knew I was getting close. Johnny was "tired" and having headaches. On days when I often dreaded what I might read next, lyrical pictorials of 1950s Crossville renewed me, Gram's soulful renditions of the mundane tempering how much I missed her.

Following in Mom's footsteps, in 1958, Aunt Helen married her own oil man, and she and Uncle Frank set out immediately for his job in Wyoming, 1,310 miles from Crossville.

Aunt Rita was next in line. She married Uncle Sam, and they were catapulted as mere nomads, lugging their home, an Airstream, between oil sites in the plains of Kansas. Nowheresville of all nowheresvilles. Letters were the only way for Gram to find Aunt Rita who was expecting her first baby.

This next letter was the first indication of Mom's "moods." She and Johnny were back in Illinois before being sent to Kansas for his next assignment with Baker Tool and Die.

Faire in Crossville to Sam & Rita (her son-in-law and daughter) in Liberal, Kansas

Dearest Sam and Rita,

Where are you? I'm sending this letter to your old P.O. Box figuring that it'll get forwarded to you. I wish you would write. Baroid Oil needs to do a better job of letting in-laws know where its men are taking their daughters!

Connie is not one of my favorite names but if you like it, then it suits me. You did ask me what I thought and I told you, but it's not always that people think I'm right.

John and M.E. made it from Henderson with everything in tow Sunday night. They didn't have much. That big house must've been practically empty. The piano which John bought for her for Christmas (you probably knew that), the somewhat new couch, a bed, and kitchen table. For your information, Mary Ellen has decided to go on living even though her sisters have moved away. Sincerely, though, she has been quite cheerful.

Douglas is a ball of fire! Last night, Mary Ellen left him here while she went to sit with Nancy, the neighbor girl who's been in the hospital with a broken leg. Anyway, I was practically flat on my back by the time Mary Ellen returned to pick up Douglas. We played "men" and every other sort of game. He is never ready for bed! Never! Douglas follows Johnny everywhere. He is wearing us ALL out. Would be helpful if he had some boy cousins around to play with!

Guess I'd better hurry. The Highway Post Office is due shortly. Also must pay my respects at The Drug Store. Then when I've finished loafing, I must decide what to do with some green beans the "provider" brought in from the farm yesterday. They're so bug-eaten I'd like to give them to those awful chickens we inherited, but guess I'll freeze them instead. Write!

PS: We miss you. Write (but, I know you won't)!

Faire in Crossville to Helen & Frank (daughter & son-in-law) in Rock Springs, Wyoming

Dear Helen and Frank,

I feel like the Queen of Sheba, and finally, I've learned that crime doesn't pay.

It's like this. Last Saturday afternoon, Dad was at the farm as usual, I had time on my hands, so I decided to dispose of some of the junk around here. We have another new renter moving into the apartment above the station. I loaded the car and went to the junkyard. It had changed. All over the place were signs, "NO DUMPING! OFFENDERS WILL BE PROSECUTED!" Everyone still uses it apparently, so I felt justified. Anyhow, after I threw everything out and was making a safe get-away, I saw on one of the boxes ``Stein Station." It was a muddy mess, but I waded in after it and then I walked into something. I'm not sure what it was because I was in a hurry to get away from the scene of the crime. So, I got a nasty cut on my leg (three of them really). Not three legs, three cuts, I mean.

I used all the home remedies I know on them, but Grandmother and your Aunt Maxine thought I should go to the doctor, so that's what I did Monday afternoon. He gave me a tetanus shot and told me to stay on the couch. Monday night, I got stiff all over and ached like I have never ached before. I didn't sleep and was scared to death. I thought I'd waited too long to get the shot. Tuesday, I was really sick, so Maxine took me back to the doctor Tuesday night. He gave me another shot and a bunch of antibiotics, and I'm now OK (only I have to stay off my feet). He told me I must, but he needn't have, cause I couldn't be up if I wanted to. So I'm starting the third day on the couch.

Alvin must be a little worried, or either he's afraid the neighbors will have him

```
arrested   for   cruelty   to   dumb   animals,
because  he  told  me  I  don't  have  to  mow  the
lawn  this  week.  And  that's  why  I  feel  like
the   Queen   of   Sheba.   Incidentally,   Alvin
doesn't  know  where  the  accident  happened  or
that   I   was   disposing   of   some   of   his
"antiques,"  so  don't  you  tell  him.  Like  I
said,  "CRIME  DOESN'T  PAY!"
   Be  careful.  Tell  me  about  your  inter-
esting  week.  I've  plenty  of  time  to  read!


                                            Love,
                                           Mother
```

I read the "Crime Doesn't Pay" letter to my friends, and we all decided it was the best of her stories. While we were aghast remembering that dumping was actually legal and commonplace, we agreed tetanus was a rough punishment. Gram was just trying to keep the wheels on the cart. "Cruelty to dumb animals." It was as sad as the dump story was comical. Alvin didn't offer to mow the yard himself, instead allowing her to skip a week. Then she got to mow the grass herself, twice as high, with a manual push mower, the next week. Some of Gram's letters enraged me.

* * *

It was the summer of '58. The average yearly wage was $5,010, and Bobby Darin hit the billboards with "Splish Splash." Letters showed Johnny and Mom were leaving Illinois, headed for a new posting in Hays, Kansas, a town of 20,000. It seemed fate never offered our family one dull moment. In September of 1958, Aunt Helen's husband, Frank, was nearly killed in an accident on a dimly lit country road when a truck in front of him had no flag marking the iron post protruding from the bed of his truck. The post crashed through the windshield of his truck straight into Uncle Frank's skull. He was flown to a hospital in Salt Lake City. Gram immediately left on the train for Wyoming to care for their newborn son. Miraculously, he made a full recovery following six weeks of treatment. After a long return train trip, Gram sent a letter to Aunt Helen confirming she'd arrived safely back in Crossville. Fall was coming. They didn't know Providence was about to deliver yet another slap.

September 1958, Faire in Crossville to Frank & Helen in Rock Springs

Dear Frank and Helen,

How are you two getting along without your night nurse/nanny/housekeeper/cook? After all those weird dreams I had about Crossville while I was out there, last night, of all things, I washed diapers in my dream. No kidding. I turned all night long. I was cleaning a closet while washing the diapers, but the baby kept crying and the doorbell was ringing, and I couldn't find anything I needed.

Mary Ellen hasn't sold the house yet, but she has prospects. We heard of one today that seemed promising—a Halliburton family moving here from Benton. They're coming tomorrow to look at it. Doug is not very enthusiastic about moving.

On the trip to look at houses, M.E. and Johnny took a boat ride with Johnny's work friend (pic enclosed) and then the friend hosted a party. They had a big time! Mary Ellen's mood seemed to be better when she and Douglas returned. My fingers are crossed.

There is one bright spot in this moving—my kids will be close together—closer anyhow, and we can go in one direction and see everybody. When Dad begins to talk of closing up for two months, buying a trailer and going places, he'll have my whole-hearted cooperation. Your dad is occasionally reasonable, but sometimes we "discuss" things that don't happen. Anyhow, I'm pinching pennies. I'm not even gonna buy a new hat for a while.

It's nearly nine o'clock. I've had too many interruptions. Write!

Love,
Mother

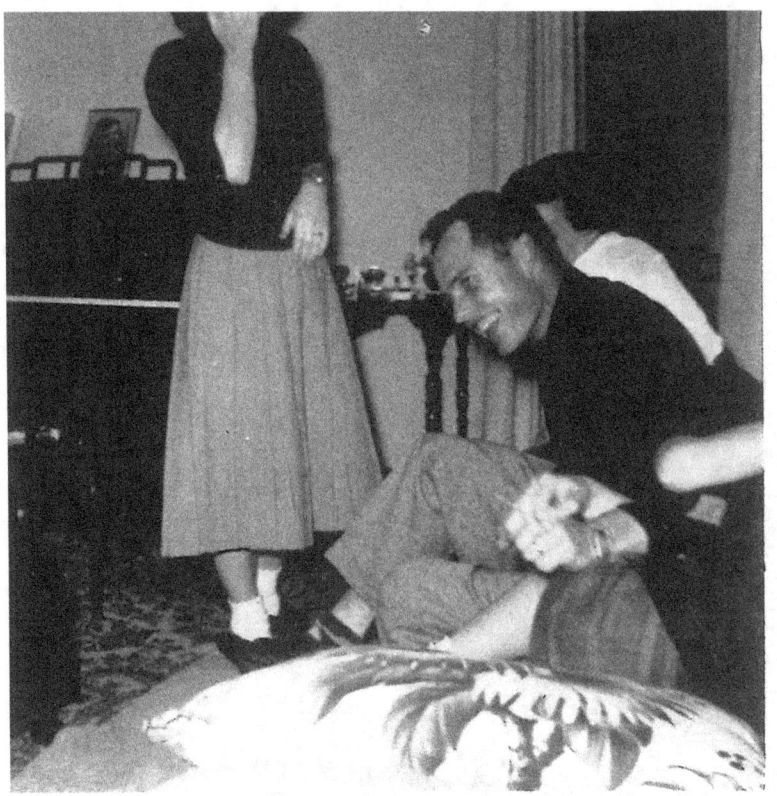

Johnny

Johnny, Mary Ellen, and Doug

Chapter 5

To Be Thankful in All Circumstances

This chapter's dramatization is based on information that my family shared with me.

I n the fall of 1958, *American Bandstand* with Dick Clark was preparing to go national. Though the free-loving sixties loomed on the West Coast, in the Crossville heartland, young couples were still meeting in church.

Harry Caray and Jack Buck captivated listeners with the St. Louis Cardinals play-by-play on KMOX radio. America was strong and proud, and oil was still booming in Southern Illinois. Though down from the previous year, the Stein Motel operated at full capacity most nights. At $9.00 per night, all nine rooms were spoken for through September.

Heading southwest on the two-lane highway toward Carmi, there was a great bend in the road giving motorists a sudden visual of the busy Stein's Corner. The soaring mid-century neon sign trimmed in cobalt blue told passersby the Stein Motel was open. The anchor of the property was the Stein Station, a Texaco franchise. From the station, a sidewalk proceeded five hundred yards past the four-bay garage on the left, followed by the motel, a typical single story motor lodge of the day. The driveway then turned sharply away from the motel over to the two-story wood framed house with a small backlit OFFICE sign hanging at the front door.

Each motel room was 150 square feet, give or take, with radiator heating, black and white television, and a bathroom, housing a small shower and commode. Aluminum red rockers sat perched outside the rooms on the concrete walkway, and a gray water fountain with a porcelain basin provided ice cold water after a long day in the field.

At the north end of the motel, nearest the filling station, was room Number One. Number One stored neatly organized cartons of Ajax and bleach and stacks of crisply ironed sheets. Past Number Nine was the boiler room full of wrenches, spare parts of all shapes and sizes, and grease guns.

Gram sat at the motel office desk finishing her paperwork. Her desk was pushed against a wall of gleaming, varnished oak paneling. It was smartly organized with a stack of 3 x 5 pre-printed registration cards, skeleton keys, a maroon ledger for transactions, a drawer for cash, and an Apsco pencil sharpener. Leaded glass windows enclosed the porch turned office on all three sides. This allowed Faire to keep an eye on guests and see who might be ringing the bell, come the pitch black of midnight.

A pale September afternoon sunlight came in through the grids of the leaded porch windows, and Faire noticed a new smudge on one of the panes. She'd think about the smudge all day. She yanked a desk drawer open, using its cylindrical red marble pull, stored her maroon ledger back in its usual place, and rose to find the Windex. A black rotary phone hung on the wall and below it, a tawny, flowered loveseat where guests could be seated to make complimentary calls. The phone rang, and Faire hopped up to answer, "Stein Motel."

"Hi, Mother. I finished our letter to Mamie. I want you to read it before I write the final. I'll stop on my way to choir; then I can mail it tomorrow."

"All right. Doug coming with you?"

"He'll go next door and play with Carol Ann. He's nine. He doesn't need to be supervised every minute."

"Talk to Johnny last night?"

"No. I was out. Doug wants to call him this evening."

"Where were you?" Faire asked.

"Just next door. OK. Bye, Mom. I'll see you in a little bit."

Pausing after the call, Faire chewed on her bottom lip, hoping that Mary Ellen was paying enough attention to Douglas on these evenings Johnny was in Kansas. Hoping Mary Ellen wasn't losing herself in too many daiquiris.

On the patio near the office door, a red lawn rocker confiscated from the motel walkway sat under the carport attached to the side of the house. Mornings and evenings were Faire's time and mostly the only time she sat down. That day's batch of "bounty," as Faire wryly referred to it, she picked before the sun rose—two bushels of green beans. The garden drudgery kept Faire's mind from cogitating on things she couldn't change.

At 4:00 p.m., bushel basket between her legs, Faire started on the vegetables. She'd try to be finished in time to leave for United Methodist Women (UMW) at 5:15, if Alvin returned from the farm on time. She rarely felt like attending UMW. Her mother thought she should, so she did. She dreaded church and had little in common with the other Godly women who with great pride baked and knitted the days away. Meanwhile, *their* chivalrous husbands brought home the bacon and once a week, after dinner, mowed their sensibly sized yards.

Each little, green shelly bean made a tink into the metal stock pot wedged between Faire's legs. The Shelly Beans, a trade name of Bush's beans who had by then gotten into the seed business, had to be shelled and canned. Each spring, Alvin planted one of the largest gardens in town. At least, he managed to get the seeds into the ground all by himself. Now that their daughters were all out of the nest, Gram and Alvin wouldn't need such surplus in the wintertime, but he planted the same nonetheless. The remainder of the garden work was up to Faire. Alvin wouldn't pay for city water. A perfectly good well provided it for free. Faire lowered the aluminum bucket by rope, struggled to get it angled correctly for the dip, and then raised it no less than twenty-five times each evening. She would lug the bucket, unbalanced and stumbling, through the dried and clumpy dirt, dumping water onto rows of corn, beans, potatoes, and melons. It was a dogged task for Faire's 4'11" frame.

By 4:30, the calm of dusk approached. Though the season was fading, the sights and sounds of summer still rejoiced. A five-acre corn plot with a sweet green roll of hills dazzled behind the Stein property, and the silhouette of the giant oak planted near the field would hold her gaze. "The provider" was often away in the evening, and she was her own boss. It was a renewal of spirit — the share of Faire's day which brought more customers but also baseball on the radio. She continued snapping off the ends of the beans, making each piece symmetrical to the last. A game for the brain.

While snapping, she considered the following work day and organized a plan in her mind for getting everything accomplished. It was all labor. No creativity, no freedom, nothing requiring the use of one's smarts or education. Faire simply felt herself a workhorse pulling a cart through a never-ending field. As for tomorrow, as long as all of the guys left for the fields by seven, she'd have the rooms cleaned in time to hear her soap at noon on CBS Radio. Set in the small town of Oakdale, Illinois, she found the program particularly silly but with a simple plot she could follow while she pressed the sheets.

At 4:45, the beans were finished. Faire used a piping hot washcloth to scrub her underarms and legs, did a swift full-body dusting of perfumed talc and pulled a knee-length orange zip-up summer dress over her head. She applied powder to her face from a Maybelline compact, gave a quick application of a modestly colored lipstick, and felt she could pass muster.

Faire zipped out of the bathroom, over to the writer's desk in the kitchen and added something to one of her lists. A sectioned walnut organizer sat on the desk and stored envelopes and lined paper for the newsy letters she'd had been writing every week since her girls moved away ten years earlier. Between Faire, Grandmother DeLain, and Maxine, they covered it all. Pictures were exchanged with most letters, allowing Faire to see what was really happening with her ducklings and their new little ducklings. She kept each letter in its envelope in order to know what day each was mailed and received. Her daughters did the same.

The emancipation of their three girls had lightened Faire's load. The phone calls, giggling, singing, and sundry noises made Alvin unbearable. She longed for her kids to be closer, but she had three sons-in-law, each from good homes and each with excellent career paths. In Faire's book, Johnny Meyers was Man of the Year, every year, since taking on Mary Ellen in 1948.

AT 5:00, Faire spotted Mary Ellen pulling off the two-lane Route 1 Highway which connected Crossville and Carmi, seven miles to the southwest. Faire had been disappointed when Ellen and Johnny rented the house in Carmi, but it was such a nice place. It was a brand-new house, and she could understand why that would be very enticing to a young couple. So she decided not to complain about the short distance between them. The miles also might keep Mary Ellen from fussing with her father.

Mary Ellen darted through the front screen door of the porch office, up the single step into the kitchen, and plopped down into a chair at the newer kitchen table Faire had ordered from Sears and Roebuck. She had paid cash to hide it from Alvin. It was the same table Faire served every blasted meal to him on. With Mary Ellen back in Illinois, Faire was grateful she'd have a place to escape when she needed it. Otherwise, it was her mother's house, and that was more complicated.

* * *

Around Crossville, Faire was known for her interest in fashion and love of fine hats, which developed following her summer of working in millinery at Sonnenfeld's Department Store in St. Louis. Enter Mamie Eisenhower. The First Lady had been donning a litany of lovely high-end hats from her first appearance with Ike Eisenhower. When Faire suggested that Mary Ellen write letters as a way to pass an occasional sleepless night while Johnny was away, Mary Ellen knew exactly what she would write — a letter to First Lady Mamie Eisenhower. Mary Ellen could only imagine how happy her mother would be if, by some great stroke of luck, Mamie sent Faire one of her hand-me-downs. Faire scurried into the kitchen, squeezed Mary Ellen's shoulder affectionately as she passed by, and poured a repurposed glass jelly jar half full of Coke. She scooted the five-pound adding machine out of the way, and Mary Ellen passed the letter to her mother.

Dear Mamie,

This is not just another fan letter. We are ARDENT fans, so please resist the temptation to let your secretary take care of it.

Having always been a fan of presidential elections, and having just turned twenty-one before the 1952 election, Ike was my champion. I doubt that Mr. President's campaign manager worked any harder on his behalf than I. From the time your pictures began to appear in newspapers, I swooned over your husband and my mother swooned over YOUR hats!

Being a great lover of hats and not infamous in our small town for her collection of them, Mother has long yearned for a fabulous piece of millinery direct from the head of our First Lady. It is upon her request, Mrs. Eisenhower, that this letter is being written.

It would create great excitement if Crossville's "Mamie" appeared in the Easter Parade donning a creation direct from the White House. Of course, to accentuate it, I shall cut Mother a new set of "Mamie" bangs and insist that she buy a new dress solely for the purpose of "coming out". Should you choose to comply with this humble request, I can assure you the hat would be worn with great care and pride.

May I say thank you, in advance, and add that I remain a devoted fan. Packages can be received at the following address:

Faire DeLain Stein
Stein Motel
Crossville, Illinois 62827

With Warmest Regards,
Mary Ellen Stein Meyers

* * *

"Is it too wordy? Can you imagine how many letters she gets?"

"She might just read yours. It's clever," Faire said.

"Maybe you should place some lined paper below your stationery so that your writing isn't sloping downward. She'd notice that."

"Yes, Mother." Mary Ellen could barely contain her excitement. "Mom, I will DIE if she sends you a hat!"

Faire nodded. "Well, honey, it gives us something fun to think about anyway!"

The smells of early autumn were blowing in from the field behind. The massive garden glimmered bright green in the fading light.

"Is Dad at the farm or on one of his other 'field trips'?"

Mary Ellen had promised her mother she would try to keep her big mouth shut around her dad, especially about his extracurriculars.

On those lonely nights since Johnny left three weeks ago, Mary Ellen spent a lot of time investigating options for her own future. Mary Ellen's fondness for Johnny made life, at times, quite nice. But what of her own wishes? What about flying planes or designing the world's most beautiful and functional buildings? She'd read a book on architecture and gone out to the small local airport to inquire about flying lessons.

Mary Ellen checked her look in the bathroom mirror, grabbed the letter, and exited through the screen door off the porch, letting it slam as usual.

* * *

FAIRE FLEW OUT of the gravel driveway, leaving a cloud of dust in her wake. "Lead foot," people called her. In fifteen seconds flat, she made it past The Pig Oven and the rival filling station to the four-way stop. Rolling through the stop and turning left, Faire made her way down Main Street past Sturm Funeral Home, Rister Hardware, the drug store, and the Crossville Post Office, where she liked to give a quick wave to Postmaster Jim Westfall. She liked to say he was the smartest student she ever taught. Jim always greeted Faire with utmost respect when she came to the counter—Miss Faire.

Looming over Main was the signature viaduct that lifted the once busy railroad tracks over the road. The slope of the land down either side of the tracks was just perfect for winter sledding.

The full commute to church, taking less than a minute, put her in the parking lot by six. The Crossville United Methodist Church started out as a one-room chapel in 1900, but as of 1950, an addition, identical to the original building, had doubled its size. The two buildings connected by a hallway stood like siblings, gleaming white and looking appropriately churchy with their wooden frame and black trim.

Rushing down the aisle of the main building, the old wooden floors creaked. Faire heard the familiar dallianced style of Mary Ellen on the piano. The dumbed down hymnal music came to life with Mary Ellen adding the grace notes and inflections that the composer had originally written, but that the hymnal publishers had thought unnecessary for the common pianist.

Mary Ellen used the piano as a way to settle herself down. She began learning piano from Faire at three. By six, she was learning from Martha Denbo and was playing full pieces on Sunday mornings. Faire hurried past Mary Ellen into the newer addition and down the stairs, humming, "Holy, Holy, Holy, Lord, God Almighty" as Mary Ellen's dynamics reflected the rise and fall of the piece.

Faire arrived at the bottom of the steps and found a seat in the circle of ladies. UMW meetings usually consisted of scripture reading, announcements, and assignments related to upcoming events, then followed by coffee and pie. The big finale of the evening—clucking, chatter, scuttlebutt.

Tonight, Pearl Stanley was at the helm. Faire knew exactly how Pearl would deliver the scripture because they'd been classmates for twelve years. First Thessalonians 5:16-17 was Pearl's choice. Pearl lowered her tone and thoughtfully shared the verse: *Rejoice always, pray without ceasing, give thanks in all circumstances; for this is the will of God in Christ Jesus for you.* To be thankful in all circumstances — the Crossville way.

By 6:45, both gossip and dessert had commenced. Faire immediately began to plot her escape. The preacher's wife, Mrs. David, had been tipped off that the Steins might be counted on to help pay for some of the new hymnals she had on order from Church Supply of Chicago. Faire's sister, Maxine, the church treasurer, had warned Faire it was coming.

Faire knew she couldn't sneak any more money to the church without Alvin noticing. The oil would slow down sooner or later, and so would business. Let the preacher approach Alvin himself. He'd be sorry.

Above the whistling of twenty female voices, the black 1942 rotary phone rang once, then twice, and the room quieted quickly so as to hear the operator, Gladys. Pearl answered, listened a moment, then glanced around, clearly looking for someone. "Call for Mary Ellen!" Pearl announced. "It's someone from Kansas."

Gladys transferred the call, having already explained to the voice on the other end, "They won't answer at home. Faire's at church tonight. So is Mary Ellen. I'll put you through to the church basement." It was a number Gladys knew by heart.

Faire grabbed the phone, and Pearl went to find Mary Ellen.

"Is this Mary Ellen Stein Meyers?" he began.

"This is her mother. They're getting Mary Ellen."

"It's good that I'm able to speak with you first, ma'am. I'm calling from Hays, Kansas. My name is Sergeant Earl Cross. I'm with the Kansas State Police. Your daughter is the wife of John William Meyers of Carmi?"

"Yes." Faire's voice dropped.

"John works for Baker Tool and Die and has been working in Hays?"

"Yes," Faire said again, softly.

"John has been in a car accident. An elderly man hit him broadside at an intersection. He's here at St. Anthony's in Hays. I'm sorry to tell you, but they don't expect he will live through the night."

That dear boy. Faire lowered herself down onto the folding chair beside the phone. She took several seconds to catch her breath. Her tears were visible to the room.

"Here is Mary Ellen. Can *you* tell her what happened, please?" Faire implored him.

"Uh . . . yes ma'am. I guess I can," said the officer.

Mary Ellen listened to his story, and her tiny frame collapsed at the knees as she held her fist to her chest. Faire helped her hang up the phone and then pulled her upright.

"We've got to leave right now, Mary Ellen. We need to get there as soon as we can. I'll get Maxine to pick up Doug. Is there an atlas in your car?"

To the church ladies still watching, Faire appeared overcome with feelings they'd never observed in her. Absolute defeat and decimation.

Was Hurt Saturday In Kansas

JOHN W. MEYERS, 31, a resident of Carmi until about two weeks ago when he was transferred to Kansas with the Baker Oil Tool Company, died Tuesday afternoon of injuries sustained in a wreck near Hays, Kansas, last Saturday.

Death came to John William Meyers, 31, of the Mann addition in Carmi, at 4:30 Tuesday afternoon in St. Anthony Hospital at Hays, Kansas, after sustaining head injuries in an auto collision at 2:20 Saturday afternoon.

Mr. Meyers, who was employed by the Baker Oil Tool Company, had been transferred to Hill City, Kansas, two weeks ago; however, his wife and son remained in Carmi until adequate living quarters could be obtained.

The accident occurred on a gravel road five miles east of Hays, Kansas. An auto driven by a 71-year old farmer of that locality struck the Meyers car in the side at an intersection. Both men were alone in their cars and the driver of the other auto was killed instantly. Nobody saw the accident.

The deceased was born in Paradise, Kansas, on February 12, 1927 and had been employed by Baker Oil Tool Company after receiving his engineering degree. He held the position of service engineer with that company, and had been a resident of Carmi for a number of years. He was the son of Mr. and Mrs. Leonard Meyers and was a graduate of Farina, Illinois, high school. The family has resided in Illinois for the past 15 years.

He was a man who had the respect of everybody, and his indus-

Article continued on next page…

in his industry and was well-loved by his many friends and family. He will be buried on Friday at Coles Cemetery in Grayville.

Chapter 6

Swiss Steak and Valium

Mom was a widow at 27.

The aching, the utter chestful of loneliness. The impact of a sudden and accidental death is barely survivable for even the sturdiest of individuals.

Here it began, for my grandmother, great-grandmother, and aunts; they became watchmen. Our family lost more than a beloved man in Johnny. They lost Mom's anchor.

Gram wasn't naïve enough to think that Johnny would've completely tamed Mom, but he tethered her to something good. He *was* good. Who else would love her enough to endure her ups and downs?

I hoped to be able to blame tragedy for Mom's bad turn. Any woman left alone with a child at such a young age would be put off-balance.

Perhaps because Mom had been prescribed sedatives to cope, this led her to years of self-medication. It was a way for me to romanticize her illness.

Grandmother DeLain, Gram's mother, was a proper and wiry woman of no more than 110 pounds with bony, arthritic hands. She never complained and spent her time reading, particularly about John Adams, praying, and being thankful in every circumstance.

Great-Grandmother DeLain and Aunt Maxine lived together only five blocks from our house. As a kid, I could get there on my bike in three minutes or less. I would dart across the southbound two-lane highway, being very careful of cars making the curve at Stein's Corner and ride one block past Flora and Jimmy Layton's tiny house. As I approached Main Street, I could see the back of the singular brick structure that housed most of Crossville's businesses. I made a left at Rister Hardware and rode one block down Main Street, under the viaduct, then right at the Crossville Telephone Company. I'd arrive at Gram DeLain and Aunt Maxine's house having barely broken a sweat.

An aging Great-Grandmother DeLain would sit in a rocker in front of the gas stove and read or write notes. She mailed this letter to Aunt Helen's husband, Frank, days after Johnny's burial.

These additional letters from 1958 revealed the undeniable facts about Mom. In an indication of the gender roles of the time, Great-Grandmother DeLain thanked Frank for allowing Aunt Helen to come home to be with Mom.

September 1958, Grandmother DeLain in Crossville to Frank in Rock Springs

DEAR FRANK,

IT WAS SWEET OF YOU TO BE BOTH MOTHER AND FATHER TO THE BABY SO THAT HELEN COULD COME TO ILLINOIS. YOU'LL NEVER KNOW WHAT A RELIEF IT WAS TO ALL OF US AND THE PEOPLE OF CROSSVILLE WHEN WE KNEW THAT HELEN WAS COMING TO BE WITH MARY ELLEN.

THIS IS A TRAGIC THING—SUCH SADNESS. WE ARE ALL SO BROKEN UP OVER LOSING JOHN AND FEAR WHAT IT WILL DO TO MARY ELLEN. SHE GOT THROUGH THE FUNERAL FINE, PLANNED

*EVERYTHING HERSELF, AND IT WAS A NICE SERVICE. EVERYONE WAS
SO KIND AND HELPFUL AND SO MANY, MANY FLOWERS . . . TOO
MANY.*

*FAIRE LOOKS AS BAD AS MARY ELLEN. THEY BOTH HAVE
WORRIED AT TIMES WHEN THERE WASN'T TOO MUCH TO WORRY
ABOUT, BUT NOW THEY HAVE A REAL WORRY. JUST HOW MARY
ELLEN WILL REACT REMAINS TO BE SEEN.*

*HELEN IS THE MOST OPTIMISTIC ONE AND HOW GLAD WE ALL
ARE THAT SHE IS HERE. I HAVE HARDLY SEEN HER SINCE THE
FUNERAL. SHE'S IN CARMI WITH MARY ELLEN MOST OF THE
TIME.*

*JUST WANTED YOU TO KNOW WE'RE THINKING OF YOU. DO BE
CAREFUL. WE DON'T NEED ANY MORE WIDOWS IN THE FAMILY.*

*LOVE,
GRANDMOTHER DELAIN*

The entire village was grateful. The words, "the people of
Crossville," were immediately injected into my heart. Without even
knowing it, Crossville's citizens were offering support services and
community resources. Friends and townspeople were right there. No
need to download some "we need to help out" type shared calendar
through which each person could choose an ever-so-convenient time
to help.

Also prominent were the things left unmentioned in Great-
grandmother DeLain's letter to Frank. Everything but grief faded
into the background.

Each and every other autumn was awash with anticipation. The
Fall Festival was the big event of the year. Held each October on
Main Street, the two-day celebration was complete with an egg toss
on the grass between Schalk Appliance and the Sturm Funeral
Home. For the greased pole climb, townsfolk shimmied up the
painted metal post that supported the specially-erected bandstand.
From there, Rotary Club members called the cakewalk numbers as

villagers stepped around the painted white circle in front of the post office.

Our family didn't even notice.

Mellow, and only giving the World Series three sentences, Gram sent the first letter to Aunt Helen that she could muster on October 2, two weeks after Johnny's death.

It was also Mom's birthday.

Gram's pensive mood about my mom caused her to reflect on the birth of her first child.

1958, Faire in Crossville to Helen in Rock Springs

Dear Helen,

Twenty-seven years ago, today, I took my last dose of castor oil. Come to think of it, it was October 1st (given just to hurry things along on the second). Don't let any doctor ever do that to you (give you castor oil, I mean).

I'm watching the World Series. Casey Stengel is on a tear. I'm for the Braves.

Mary Ellen is still getting cards and letters. Mary Lou, and the Baker girls, dropped in this morning and brought coffee and donuts. This afternoon, although Ellen doesn't know it, Jane, Farris, and Keith are taking a birthday cake. I've invited her and Doug for a birthday supper, but I'm not sure they're coming. They're very busy and still doing exceptionally well.

Helen, the night you left, Mary Ellen had hives but is otherwise well and has seemingly been doing fine in the evenings.

The remainder of Johnny's effects came this week. With them was a small, white New Testament, the one Betty Cross gave you when you were in her Sunday school class. You must've given it to Doug who must've given it to Johnny. It was very dirty. Apparently, John had been carrying it in his car.

Grandmother DeLain got good news today—no malignancy. I think she'll perk up now. She's been quite down. Doctor's fee was $10 only. That was a pleasant surprise, too.

It's so cool here. We've had light frost a few times. I dread the winter. Be careful!

Love,
Mother

I felt Gram's sorrow when she mentioned dreading the winter. Then, I felt my own regret. The women of Crossville who gave so much of their time comforting Mom were the essence of community. I had no idea the extent of their kindness after Johnny's death. I wanted a do-over for all those Sunday mornings I sat next to those very same women at church, oblivious to what they'd done for our family. I wanted to go back and say thank you.

Gram had no time for her grief. She had complicated problems. She was physically spent, too weary to go on, but having to work like a dog just to meet her basic human needs. No massage, afternoon coffee, or acupuncture. No book club, no weekend at the lake, no romantic dinner, and never a hug from an adoring spouse. Gram relied on a few simple things for support. She had a handful of good friends, Coca-Cola for liveliness, and chocolate and baseball for comfort.

My grandparents had enough money by Crossville standards, but Alvin dolled it out when he was in the mood. Gram had *no* money of her own, save what cash she could sneak from the tills at the motel and station.

That fall, with the last of the garden's bounty coming to an end, Gram would've felt pressure to preserve it all. Alvin would've snarked if apples, potatoes, or beans had dropped to the ground to rot. No wonder she loathed kitchen work.

For years to come, in the quiet moments, the unhealed wounds of her life were written on her face. She stared at the sidewalks and rows of trees, where she watched Johnny lovingly walk side-by-side with Mom, his hand placed gently in the small of her back.

Meanwhile, far away, life was moving on for two other daughters who were young and needed Gram's attention and domestic advice. Within the paragraphs of this next letter, I found a story that would begin to answer my questions about Mom.

October 1958, Faire in Crossville to Frank and Helen in Rock Springs

Dear Frank and Helen,

I've so many things to talk about tonight that I hardly know where to start. Guess I'll just dispense with formalities and proceed.

Steak. Helen, a Swiss steak is not a certain cut of steak but rather a method of preparing it. I call this Swiss steak, but it isn't in the truest sense.

Buy a piece of round or sirloin, 1½ to 2 inches thick, pound the daylights out of it, and add flour and seasonings while pounding. I doubt that you have a meat hammer, but a regular nail hammer will do the work. Use as much flour as you can pound into it which is probably one-fourth cup. Brown it well on both sides, add water, and simmer two to three hours. You're probably thinking you've never seen me pound steak. I buy minute or cubed steaks which have been put through the tenderizer, and they require no pounding.

German chocolate cake—recipe enclosed.

Ellen? This is a long story. Last Wednesday she went to Mr. Lowe's to have her hair cut. While he was cutting her hair, she went to sleep. Twice he woke her, but the third time he was unable to rouse her. They called me, and I told them to call Doctor A., which they did. He sent her to the hospital by ambulance where she finally regained consciousness. They gave her glucose and kept her overnight. The doctor found two packs of pills in her purse. Of course, he took them. She's had nothing except an occasional Bufferin since then. She's not been alone, and we don't intend that she will be for a time. She hadn't slept for forty-eight hours, had eaten very little— just living on pills and nervous energy. I suspected that she was "drunk" on pills several times, but I had no way of knowing. She admitted nothing. Now, she admits that it was just easier to take a pill than face facts. She also knows that she's in danger of losing custody of Doug. In fact, she will, if she can't do better and fast. She's been at Lou's and then here until today. Grandmother went home with her and will stay a few days. Since this happened, she sleeps ten to twelve hours every night and eats all the time. She looks like a different person and talks distinctly and not with that thick tongue. You know what I mean, Helen. She says she's learned her lesson, and I believe she thinks she has. We can only hope. But, we do know she has nothing to take. We looked the place over.

I don't know how you'll like this, but here it is. Friday when she finally came to her senses, she realized that what had happened could happen again. She called David Stanley at his office and made a will and provisions for Doug's custody in case she'd die or became incompetent. She has always said that if she couldn't raise Doug, she wanted you to have him. So, that is the way she did it. If anything should happen, you will have complete personal custody of Doug and of his inheritance. You two talk this over. Let us know what you think. It's a big responsibility, and of course, it's your decision. This was all done without my knowledge, but I know she made the right decision from the standpoint of Doug's welfare. I hope you can accept it. She's better now than she's been in two years. But, you know her . . .

If you want to say anything you'd rather Ellen doesn't see, regarding Doug, just put

```
a  separate  note  in  your  next  letter.  She
reads  my  letters  from  you,  usually.
```

```
                                  Love  to  you  both,
                                               Mother
```

```
P.S.  Uncle  Joe  is  helping  Ellen  decide  how
she  will  take  care  of  the  investments—how
much  income  and  how  much  cash.
     Here  is  what  it  amounted  to:
```

- Social Security $167/monthly for 10, maybe 14 years
- Workman's Comp $34 weekly for approximately 7 years
- $20,500 John's retirement (she got this today)

And right there it was, right in the middle of a letter about Swiss steak. I was awash with compassion for Mom. Johnny's death was the ideal situation for Mom to begin to numb herself.

Gram was praying like hell and stealthily, almost morbidly, planning for the worst, in case Mom didn't make it. Gram sounded at times disconnected to the story. With careful anticipation, she subtly directed the whole family to batten down the hatches. She could control nothing; but she could be prepared.

I'm burdened by what Mom was doing to warrant losing Doug. Did it indicate Gram may have been making threats herself—threats intended to snap her out of it? "You know her..." and "...do better" show Gram's lack of the knowledge we have today that Mom's problems weren't behavioral but the result of illness.

Was Mom neglecting Doug? Not able to get him to school? Mom wasn't abusive. Gram would've fully intervened had that been the case. But neglect lies in a gray area. Harder to measure than a bruise.

While other children were enjoying Indian summer and mastering the spin of a hula hoop, the days after Johnny's death were monochromatic for Doug. While other little boys created time machines and chased fireflies, my brother did not. He was suffering. Johnny was his safety net and now his lost companion.

Mom followed Gram's letter to Aunt Helen with her own letter a few days later, indicating Johnny's sister, Ginger, was getting involved in planning for Doug's care. Mom wasn't having it.

October 1958, Mary Ellen in Carmi to Helen in Rock Springs

Dear Helen,

Three cheers for me! It's way past bedtime, but I'm finally writing. I'm not going to pat myself on the back yet, though. If I'd finished all the letters I'd started to you two, you'd have a good-sized autobiography.

I suppose you've been informed by Faire D. that you, Helen, are now Doug's official guardian in case anything should happen to me —guardian of his person and estate. If this is not to your liking, please let me know, although I intend to do absolutely nothing about it. Made a will a couple of weeks ago when I was staying at Lou's. David called in a couple of neighbors to witness and sign it. Lou said if she had known such a royal occasion was coming, she'd have served champagne! Got that little detail taken care of in a hurry after Ginger remarked she would like to have Doug, not in case I wasn't here, but now. Made me mad enough to spit nails, but as is my custom, I kept myself under control and remained my sweet, normal (?) self. Ha! Really, though, the Meyers have all been very nice. Doug and I spent last Saturday night and Sunday with them— went out for pizza Saturday night.

Guess you heard about my extra ten pounds in two weeks. My appetite suddenly became uncontrollable when I woke up to the fact that I couldn't survive without sleep and food. You know, it's amazing what three meals a day and eight hours sleep will do for you. I may not stop when I reach one hundred pounds—ninety-five now. I had forgotten, but it's awfully nice to feel good again. I wake up every morning at 6:10 on the dot and am ready to get up. Sort of disgusting on non-school days, though.

Grandmother is fretting and is afraid I'll go to sleep writing this letter. Faire D. brought her down to babysit me.

Did you know the old man who hit Johnny had no insurance but was well-to-do? David is working with the family to try and get a settlement. I have to file a forty-page estate tax form. Ugh.

My Cub Scout is doing much better. Douglas had me baffled for a while but is acting normal again—noisy. He doesn't want his momma out of his sight for very long. He seems to fear something will happen to me. He also keeps me in line on driving. He watches the speedometer like a hawk.

Gotta get this in the mail and get back to work. This is Election Day, so guess I'll go cast my vote and probably take Grandmother to Crossville to cast hers.

FYI, Doug struts like a proud peacock in his Cub Scout uniform —cute! Did you ask Mom what he wanted for Christmas? Just guess. More Cub Scout equipment! He has the knife (ugh) but wants the emergency kit, toothbrush, comb and Cub Scout fun book. Don't blow yourself. He'll get more than he needs, as always.

Johnny's mums he planted last summer are lovely—white, pink, and purple. I took a basket of them to the cemetery last week. I intend to take some more before they freeze. I also ordered his monument last month, and it should be erected before Christmas.

Going to school is out, I guess. Uprooting Doug right now might be bad, so will sit tight until I get a definite feeling one way or the other.

Love you,
Ellen and Doug

Mom acknowledged her issues but also seemed strong and positive, looking toward the future and thinking about school. She wanted more. Mom wanted to be able to provide for her Cub Scout.

Nonetheless, the surfacey nature of Mom's letters portrayed a threatened woman, shadow-boxing around the big topics—the overdose itself and the reasons why Johnny's sister, Ginger, wanted Doug.

Mom wanted it to seem she handled things with aplomb, but in reality, was wobbling.

She was perilously thin and broke out in hives when Aunt Helen went back to Wyoming. She was bursting with pain, but she didn't even mention the grief.

In 2014 at a retirement home in a Chicago suburb, Aunt Helen, Aunt Rita, and I visited Johnny's sister Ginger, then in her eighties. Ginger spoke to me tenderly about her memories of Mom, but she didn't sugarcoat things. She didn't talk to me as if I couldn't handle her honesty.

Ginger told me that Johnny's chronic headaches turned to migraines and that near the time of his death, he had confessed to his family, "I don't know what I'm going to do about Mary Ellen."

Johnny, the masculine oil worker of the 1950s who planted mums and carried a Bible. I pictured him reading it over a sandwich of thick-sliced Emge bologna and a vacuum thermos of coffee. He would've been such a nice man for me to call my dad. I stared at his picture mournfully and thought of what might've been.

I needed to understand the days following Johnny's death. It seemed September of 1958 was the beginning of Mom's epic illness and the year of her first institutionalizations at the Anna State Hospital—the spot formerly known as The Illinois Southern Hospital for the Insane.

Chapter 7

Happy Birthday

September 2018

People behaving strangely or badly isn't considered medical in nature. No one thinks to bring a casserole when you come home from a psychiatric hospital. People are just afraid of you—afraid to say too much or too little. I was completely frightened by my mom's tears. The first of my mind's portraits: she would sit on the red shag carpet in the narrow hallway outside our bathroom, face in her hands, and cry. The pressure to attend to a young child, clearly overwhelming for her.

I spent my first birthday, August 4, 1970, at the Anna State Hospital, exactly one hundred miles southwest of Crossville. As I sat perched on Mom's hip while she smiled sadly, an onlooker must've offered to capture the moment. And Doug spent his day driving me to Anna. He was nineteen and squinted indignantly at the camera, unable to fake a smile. The picture sickened me, remembering that I was the subject of Mom and Doug's vicious confrontation on the night she died.

Doug, Mom and me at Anna State Hospital

Mom and me at Anna State Hospital

Anna was the closest option for treatment for Mom. In 1958, in rural America, there were no options beyond institutionalization. Conditions treated ran the gamut from alcoholism to homosexuality, the developmentally disabled to the criminally insane. Even patients with mild depression could be institutionalized for months.

Anna State Hospital

Originally known as the Illinois Southern Hospital for the Insane, the Anna facility stood juxtaposed to the small town of Anna, renowned for its racist acrostic, "Ain't No N****** Allowed". The village was platted in 1854 with the hospital opening later that century. Along with many other towns in the lower part of the state, Anna was known for being a Sundown Town where people of color were expected to leave by dark. Thank you for plowing our fields, but we have no place for you to lay your head.

Closely tied to its neighbor Jonesboro, locals call it "Anna-Jo." In 2010, there were 4,442 citizens in the combined city with a median income of $39,602. The incomes of 20.2 percent of the population were below the poverty level.

The establishment of state mental hospitals in the U.S. was partly taken on by reformer Dorothea Dix, who testified to the New

Jersey Legislature in 1844, vividly describing the State's treatment of people with mental illness; they were being housed in county jails, private homes, and in the basements of public buildings. Dix's effort led to the construction of The New Jersey State Lunatic Asylum, a cringe-worthy name.

Later in the century, a psychiatrist from Philadelphia, Thomas Kirkbride, developed an asylum design based on a philosophy of a moral treatment of patients. The idea of institutionalization was central to Kirkbride's plan for effectively treating individuals with mental illnesses. Anna State Hospital was constructed under the Kirkbride plan. The location of the hospital was presumably chosen because of the abundance of open space and the low-cost of the land. Lush farmlands abounding and plenty of quietude added to the appeal.

Thomas Kirkbride

"THERE IS NO REASON WHY AN INDIVIDUAL WHO HAS THE MISFORTUNE TO BECOME INSANE, SHOULD, ON THAT ACCOUNT, BE DEPRIVED OF ANY COMFORT OR EVEN LUXURY ..."

THOMAS KIRKBRIDE

Kirkbride's asylums were large, imposing, Victorian-era institutional buildings, with the defining feature being wings extending outward like spokes on a wheel.

Kirkbride's idea was to allow individual corridors open to sunlight and air ventilation through both ends, which he believed aided in healing the mentally ill. Each wing would contain its own "comfortably furnished" parlor, bathroom, clothes room, and infirmary, as well as a speaking tube and dumbwaiter to allow open communication and movement of materials between floors. The furthest wings from the center of the building were reserved for the "most excitable", or most physically dangerous patients.

ANNEX MALE WARD No. 2. ILLINOIS SOUTHERN HOSPITAL. Anna, Ill.

Annex Male Ward, Number Two

Patient rooms were suggested to be spacious, with ceilings "at least twelve feet high," but only large enough to house a single person.

In addition to the intricate building design, Dr. Kirkbride advocated the importance of "fertile" and spacious landscapes on which the hospitals would be built with views that "if possible, should exhibit life in its active forms."

Kirkbride suggested the hospital grounds be a minimum of 100 acres in size. The foliage and farmlands on the hospital grounds were sometimes maintained by patients as part of physical exercise and therapy.

Over the course of the nineteenth and twentieth centuries, the campuses of these hospitals often evolved into sprawling, expansive grounds with numerous buildings. At the time Mom was first admitted, Anna State Hospital consisted of a shocking number of buildings, all connected by underground tunnels. At times it housed up to two thousand patients, more than twice the size of Crossville's population.

* * *

SITTING on my own patio in the fall of 2018 helped me experience the sights and sounds of the season just as Mom would've sensed them in the pivotal fall of '58 when Johnny died. Everyday moments were intertwined with my intense journey. From our high-top dining table, I heard Lisa cleaning up the patio near the pool. She'd often belt out a girly shriek. The residents of a nearby nature preserve often found their way into our pool. After nearly twenty years of living in the city of St. Louis, we were still getting used to this new suburban Wild Kingdom.

"I just came out here, and there was a mouse floating on top of the solar light thing!" Lisa said. "He saw me and jumped in! I was trying to save him. Now he's drowning."

Hurricane Florence was obliterating South Carolina, Paul Manafort had agreed to cooperate with the Mueller investigation, and it seemed everyone we knew was getting married.

The National League pennant race was coming down to the wire with the Dodgers battling our Cards for the second wildcard spot. They were dead even at 88 wins and 62 losses each.

Nervous energy was buzzing in our world and beyond. I was rehearsing Handel's *Water Music* like mad in the mornings, preparing to do the prelude at my friends' bucolic Vermont wedding. I was at once bleaching my teeth and scanning sites like Asylumprojects.org, a "wiki" of 2,100 articles on asylums and sanatoriums worldwide. I read the postings on Asylum Projects, looking for the words "Anna" or "Choate." Most of the postings got no responses. They were largely from family members on a wild goose chase, hoping to find lost relatives who had disappeared into the bowels of this or that state institution.

Claude ████ *September 15,* ████ *5:42 pm*
My great-grandmother died there on ████████ Any information concerning the reason for her being admitted and the circumstances of her death would be greatly appreaciated.

Ruth ████ *November 10,* ████ *11:24 pm*
I am trying to find information on my grandfather Ben ████████ who died in ████ at Anna State Hospital

Lucy ████ *March 2,* ████ *9:22 pm*
My great grandmother, Nora Ann ████ died on 3/28/████ at the Anna State Hospital, she was ████ years old. The family never talked about her, but I know she was buried in ████████ and I know her parents were Henry ████████ and Harriott Elizabeth ████████ She had 10 siblings. I would appreciate any information on her. Thank you! I can be reached at 1733 ████████.

Asylum Projects postings

I needed to verify that 1958, following Johnny's death, was the year of Mom's first admission. I had learned about the Freedom of Information Act. According to Illinois Public Act 097-0623, as the surviving next of kin, I could request a deceased patient's records "including but not limited to those relating to the diagnosis, treatment, prognosis, history, charts, pictures, and plates, kept in connection with such treatment of patient." The hospital must provide records within sixty days of receiving the request.

Seemed doable.

There was little about Choate online other than a link to the Illinois Department of Human Services site, and there was no records request form. I found a Facebook page. Like The Asylum Projects, The Choate Facebook page contained more posts from families seeking information. The page struck me as officially unofficial. A Choate employee had set it up with good intentions and hadn't looked at it since.

Choate didn't respond to any of the Facebook postings asking for help. It would've been easy for them to direct people to their records department. It could've created goodwill with former patients and their families. Was the Facebook page set up to get reviews? I found it outlandish that a state-run facility, housing forensic patients deemed unfit for trial, would publicly gun for five-star reviews.

Meanwhile, the administration couldn't find the time to respond to posters so desperate for information that they were pleading repeatedly on the same Facebook page. Strangers interacted with each other on the page but no response from Choate Hospital. Many of the posts started with "I'm looking for..."

I tried getting someone on the phone at Choate. I called the main hospital number and was transferred to the records department.

I'd no idea what to expect and was uneasy as I dialed.

"Hi. I'm wondering what the process is to retrieve medical records on my deceased mother who was a patient there, starting in 1958, I think. It could've been earlier."

"Well, you have to have a court order. That's if we have anything. Many records burned in a fire. I can see what exists and let you know."

I didn't hear back and called again several weeks later.

"Choate records."

"Is this Nancy?"

"Yep."

"You may remember me. I called inquiring about any records on my mother, Mary Ellen Stein."

"Oh shoot. It has been crazy here. I still have your note. I'll check today and call you back."

Later that day . . .

"I found some things on your mother. Can't give you details, but there are some admission and discharge notes. May be more on microfiche but takes a while to retrieve that stuff."

"Can I come down and get copies of them?"

"You still need a court order. I don't know that anyone has ever actually done it."

I paused to consider how impossible that sounded.

"They never want to pay the fees for copying records. I guess the state's attorney at the courthouse or the circuit clerk would be your best bet for finding out how to do it."

I thought for a long time about what our conversation meant to me and all the other families looking for records. It meant a process more dreadful and prolonged than, say, colonoscopy prep.

Four days later . . .

"State's attorney."

"I was referred to you by the records department at Choate. They told me I needed a court order to get my deceased mother's records?"

Silence. She finally said, with a crawling delivery like you'd hear deep within Appalachia, "I've never hurd anything like that ba-four. You need a court order they say-ed? You'll have to talk to the sur-cut clurk."

"Choate said that I needed to petition the court and that the state's attorney's office would..."

"I don't think that's ri-ot. Just a minute."

Before I could protest further, she transferred me to the circuit clerk. I retold my story from the beginning, and she seemed puzzled and irritated by my questions. There was a protracted silence.

"So, how do I go about petitioning the court?"
"Write to me, and I'll get it to the judge."
"Which judge should I address the letter to?"
"There's only one. I'll get it to him."

* * *

I EMAILED the circuit clerk and copied both the county Freedom of Information office and the state's attorney's office.

Exactly a week later, I received the following response via email from the Office of the Chief Information Officer in Jonesboro, Illinois, dated September 11, 2018:

Dear Ms. Davis:

Please consider this our response to your attached Freedom of Information Act request, received via email on September 4, 2018, and summarized below:

I am researching my mother's specific health history for my own information and as information I will use in a book on mental health and its effects on the family. Please find the attached declaration and death certificate. If a certified death certificate is required, I can get that from White County. Her pertinent patient information is below. She had multiple hospitalizations, and I am looking for any records which may exist.

We have neither custody nor possession of records responsive to your request. We consider your request completed. If I may be of further assistance, please let me know.

Sincerely,
Rollie Hawk, Chief Information Officer

I followed up again, explaining that I realized Union County didn't possess the medical records. I obviously realized they were held at Choate. He responded:

ROLLIE HAWK 9/12/18

I'm afraid I wouldn't know anything about that. Freedom of Information Act requests are what I handle and from the County's perspective we don't have those records. Sorry I can't be more helpful. Rollie

I wasn't prepared to be the first person to be asking these questions. I couldn't fathom that *NO ONE* had *EVER* made a similar request. If Anna had once housed over 2,000 people, how is it that not one family member had gone through this process?

After Rollie's message, I also received a response from the circuit clerk, Tiffany Busby:

Dear Ms. Davis,

I am in receipt of your request for information pursuant to the Illinois Freedom of Information Act dated August 28, 2018. Please be advised that your request for information is **denied.**

Both the Illinois Courts and the Illinois Attorney General have determined that the Freedom of Information Act is not applicable to the judicial system. The Clerk of the Circuit Court is a "non-judicial officer of the judiciary" and as such is a member of the Judicial Branch of the State Government, and therefore, exempt from the requirements of the Act.

However, all court files are public records, and unless impounded or sealed under state law or by your order, such files are available for public inspection. Therefore, you are welcome to view all our files not sealed or impounded. Files may be viewed any time during my office hours which are from 8:00 a.m. to 12:00 p.m. and 1:00 p.m. to 4:00 p.m. Monday through Friday. Copies are $2.00 for the first page, $0.50 per page for the next 19 pages, and $0.25 per page for each thereafter.

They seemed to get the impression I was looking for some type of courthouse records on commitment or the like.

An attorney herself, my wife Lisa advised me. While I constructed a new plan for getting the records, I spent much time wondering what Anna was like for Mom when she first arrived there for treatment.

That fall continued to be chock full of activity for me personally. Lisa and I hosted a Halloween party to celebrate my five-year remission from breast cancer. While I swept pink glitter and feathers into small piles, I wondered about October '58. Was Mom relieved to get the help she needed? Did the staff at Anna know what they were doing?

THE FOLLOWING SCENE, *while fictional, is based on diaries and letters written by my mother while at Anna State Hospital. The intake notes were gleaned verbatim from my mother's medical records.*

October 1958

"Good morning, Mary Ellen. I'm James, one of the nurses here. I've got some papers we need to fill out."

A tall man of about thirty sat down at a stainless-steel table across from her and between his gloved hands held a set of forms labeled "intake". Mary Ellen looked down, noticing that the posts of the table were secured to the floor with bolts.

"Is this your first time here?"

"Yes." Mary Ellen sat across the shiny, narrow table and stared down at the composite tile floor.

"Is this the first time you've been hospitalized for an overdose?"

"It's the first time I've been here."

"What personal effects do you have?"

"Cosmetics and clothes."

"Medications, scissors, pens?"

"Yes."

James continued, "I have to take those from you. We want to make sure you're safe."

"I have some notes I need to finish, so I'd like to keep the pen."

"They have crayons in the activity room."

Mary Ellen looked at him. "If I wanted to end it, I bet I could find something besides a pen."

"Address?"

"Permanent address? I live in Carmi, but you better put down Stein Motel, Crossville."

"You live at a motel?"

"My parents own it. Our house is right there."

"So no street address?" James asked.

"No. Just put Stein Motel. It'll get there."

"Did your mother bring you here from Carmi? I didn't see anyone with you when you walked in."

"The sheriff brought me. He was probably afraid to come inside. My mother called an ambulance last night when she couldn't get a hold of me. They took me to the ER in Carmi. They must've called Mom, and she decided I needed to come down here."

"You had another ER visit in September."

"My husband was killed in September. I took too many sedatives and fell asleep at the beauty shop. How about that one! Not on purpose . . . I lost track of what I'd taken. I guess I must've done it last night again."

The intake nurse made notes as Mary Ellen answered his questions:

REASON FOR ADMISSION: Acute brain syndrome related to drug intoxication and hysterical personality. Patient was admitted to Carmi Hospital last night. Patient states: "I was taking, at one time, up to twelve dextroamphetamine tablets daily and not able to sleep for three or four days."

IDENTIFYING DATA: Mary Ellen is an attractive, white, twenty-seven-year-old widowed female with some history of depression. Patient has a nine-year-old son.

FAMILY BACKGROUND: The patient's parents, Faire and Alvin Stein, apparently had a rather turbulent marriage. They fought constantly, and the mother, Faire, discussed her marital problems with the patient, including her husband's extramarital affairs.

INFORMANTS: Mrs. Stein, the patient's mother, reported that when raising their children, she and her husband fought frequently about discipline. She felt he was too strict. The informant stated that her daughter was never satisfied for very long and that she'd been overly interested in boys since she was a young girl.

PHYSICAL EXAMINATION: The patient is in good general physical condition and is conversing intelligently.

"Your mother called and asked to speak to the doctor who would be treating you. He'll call her later after he meets with you."

"Of course she called. She hardly lets me out of her sight."

"Most mothers want to control everything," the tech insisted.

Mary Ellen jockeyed the conversation. "How does your wife handle that?"

"I'm not married."

"You? Single? Well, let's have coffee while I'm here!"

He paused to consider her proposal. "I'm not allowed on the locked floors."

"You're always down here in the bowels?"

"There are some excitable patients, so only highly trained nurses are allowed on those wings."

The nurse moved to Mary Ellen's side of the table and gently placed her doll-like arm on the cold table.

"I need to draw some blood."

"They did that in Carmi."

"We need to check it again. A lot can happen during transport."

"Ha. Really . . . well, the sheriff did not share his pills with me."

Retreating from the thought of impending imprisonment, she modified the topic again. "Do you watch *Hitchcock?*"

"I work mostly nights."

Mary Ellen went on. "It was good this week. Douglas loves it. A man lies in bed for hours because he believes a snake is on his stomach. He's paralyzed by his fear. His friend doesn't believe him. Thinks he's making it up. The friend finally says he'll call a doctor. The doctor helps the guy stand up, and there is no snake! His friend laughs at him. When the doctor leaves, and everyone is asleep, the *friend* gets bitten by the snake and dies. It reminded me of myself. No one believes me when I tell them I'm sick."

She lowered her head, and a tear streamed down the side of her face. "Mom tells me to play Solitaire at night. I just can't concentrate. Once the sun goes down, I get so sad. They gave me Valium for sleep. The script is for a half or one pill at bedtime. I take more than that. Can I get Valium here?"

The nurse didn't respond.

"I have a son. Did I say that? He is just now starting to act like himself. He worshiped his father. Everyone worshiped Johnny."

Eventually looking up at her, the nurse said, "We find that patients with children get better quicker than others."

"Mom thinks I'm a lazy mother. I overslept once, and Doug missed school. She now drives by to see when I leave to take him to school. I don't even know how she has the energy."

"This is the last section of the form. Would you say that you've been depressed?"

She folded her arms across her chest and crossed her legs. "Wouldn't you be?" She looked away. "I don't know. Not really."

"It's important to answer honestly."

"What kind of other crazy people are here?"

"Patients have various problems. We treat alcoholism, sexual perversion, the criminally insane, mental retardation, manic depression, schizophrenia. There are people like you, and there are people who behave like animals and are medicated twenty-four hours a day."

"How do you know I'm not schizo?"

"I don't."

"All right. You're ready to go upstairs, " the nurse concluded.

Mary Ellen gathered up her things, including the notes on Douglas she'd brought from home. From the time he was born, she had kept a notebook of the many stories about Doug and his big personality. Johnny included some of his own anecdotes and just a few months ago had returned from Kansas with a poem he thought should be pasted in the thick pages of their family scrapbook: "What is a Boy?" The poem's theme—how to survive an inexhaustible son.

Doug began saying words at about ten months. At eighteen months, he could carry on a conversation. From eighteen months on, he loved for someone to read to him and would listen for hours.

Now four years old, every night at supper, we are given a playback of the day's TV commercials. I must use Simon Wax because the "Shine lasts five weeks!" And, "Fall City Beer is the beer for me!" (Loud slurp, then "Mmm! Good!"). He becomes indignant if we fail to use one of his recommended products.

He enjoys watching "Dragnet" with his "Da-da". He prepares by dressing up in Johnny's sport coat and hat and begins to talk like Sgt. Friday using phrases like, "Sorry, ma'am."

Forever portraying a role, our little outlaw is sometimes a soldier returning from war or Superman. When his daddy opens the door to tell him good night, he can expect to be met by The Lone Ranger on a flying mare.

He is never ready for bed, never ready to get up, and always too tired to pick up his toys. When he falls asleep, we look at that innocent little face and wonder how he could be such a downright demon.

On one of my nightmarish Christmas shopping trips to town, trying to curtail him, a saleslady asked where he got so much energy, and his prompt reply was, "I ate a slice of energy-packed Sunbeam bread for dinner!" That happened to be true.

New words and phrases are constantly appearing in his vocabulary. "Are you nervous, Mama?" is one of his favorites.

In her room, Mary Ellen stared at the heavy, wooden door with the small, leaded glass window and thought about home. Her mom wouldn't have slept last night. Between her own worries and now, having to help with Douglas, she would be a nervous wreck herself. How did her mother end up in such a fix with Dad? It was something she had brooded about so often.

Chapter 8

Armored Wings

2019

"Success of your marriage depends greatly upon realization of a woman's sexual duties."

In 1944, *Mother and Daughter, A Reliable Guide to Sexual Happiness* was compiled by The National Social Hygiene League based in Washington D.C. I found a copy buried in more family memorabilia. The organization was formed during the age of the push for STD awareness and anti-prostitution sentiment. It offended me on so many levels.

I had no idea where we received the booklet. I couldn't imagine Mom received it from Crossville schools, as it contained an open explanation of personal and public sexual health.

"It is not alone in the arms of the prostitute that venereal disease is contracted. Many a supposedly 'pure' high school girl have been known to be the cause of widespread venereal infection. Facing America, at this time, is the need to stamp out the terrible scourge of social diseases. The women of the nation, it appears, must provide the will to do it."

"What? WHAAAT?"
I was shell-shocked.

Gram and Grandad were married in 1930, a full fourteen years before the handbook was published. If what was explained in the handbook was the expectation of women in '44, what could the thinking have been in '30 when Gram was married? Matrimony wasn't about love. Marriage was about what each could offer in terms of service to the other. Women needed a provider. Men needed a place to sow their seed and someone to cook and clean. Gram enjoyed some aspects of domestic life, but a Betty Crocker image would never have been what she wanted for her legacy.

If Gram had reviewed the booklet with her kids, it would've been riddled with cheeky commentary. Though she was highly principled, Gram wouldn't have taken the book seriously. It would've sounded incredibly old-fashioned to her.

I want to be clear that this is *my* feeling. I don't represent other family opinions when I say that Gram managed to choose a spouse who no one could say a single good word about. Hard to believe. Don't we all have one decent quality? It's possible he was softer in his younger years. He must've felt affection for us, but it was buried in anger. All Gram could do was lament her decision to marry him. If your mother and father and respected relatives are pushing you to be a forgiving Christian woman, tolerant and sympathetic, how can you make a drastic decision for divorce? Had Gram left him in the 1930s, how would she have provided for three children on the salary of a teacher? Adjusted for inflation, a yearly teacher's salary of $1,300 in the 1930s would be roughly $20,000 today. She probably ciphered the numbers and realized it was infeasible.

Our family did do the work of life so well. We pounded it out every day from dawn to dusk. We were pragmatic but enterprising — took business risks that paid off. We paid our bills early. Went to church, made straight As. Faire and Alvin had three beautiful daughters, glowing in Technicolor pizazz, and from a distance, it was admirable.

Gram was so vast in spirit but not big enough to cancel out Alvin. When Alvin was home, he did more damage than Gram could deflect. The wide expanse of Gram's armored wings wasn't enough to shade his influence. He had a stormy temperament, but it wasn't that Alvin was only swinging fists. He was controlling and selfish. His meltdowns were usually related to his preoccupation with money. If the refrigerator was held open too long, Alvin would yell; if too many lights were on, he would stomp around and get in Gram's face; if someone was using the phone longer than he liked, he would simply pull the phone from their hand, mid-conversation, and slam it down.

Gram and Grandad's daughters: Aunt Rita, Mom, & Aunt Helen with their firstborn children, which includes Doug

Gram found herself in a co-parenting situation with a man who was unable to love. Alvin made nothing easy. His brutality towards our family saddened me almost more than Mom's death.

It augurs well that there was a connection between my mother's lifelong vicissitudes with men and the lack of love she received from her father. Gram had no resources to pull from when Mom began abusing pills. Rural bootstrap attitudes tell us not to blame others for our poor choices, and Gram didn't. I'm not even sure Gram realized the generational fallout of her choice of spouse. Her marriage was just another circumstance she must've been pondering during her contemplative stares out the bedroom window.

Gram's own sympathetic heart was another barrier to divorce. She was a fan of the underdog. She rooted for the Cubs until her last breath.

In our home hung this framed advice: "I shall pass through this world but once. Any good therefore that I can do or any kindness that I can show to any human being, let me do it now. Let me not defer or neglect it, for I shall not pass this way again."

Encouraged to behave like a woman of strong character, Gram looked compassionately upon Alvin and the abuse he suffered at the hands of his own father.

Mary Ellen, Doug, Alvin, & George Stein (Alvin's father)

I supposed it was possible, sometime in their early marriage, that Alvin may have shed some tears to her, confided in her about his pain. The face of Alvin's father, George Stein, was hair-raising—his physical presence as imposing as his sharp German surname. George Stein's enormous appendages dangled awkwardly from a Bigfoot-sized specimen. The boy on whom George practiced his haymaker became a man who did the same to his family. Like women the world over, in all levels of society, all Gram could conjure up was hope. Her hope never evolved into action. She *hoped,* with the help of God or by fate, that Alvin just might pass away sooner than later. Gram aged and became more fed up, and she wished for his disappearance with startling frankness.

Despite the emotional drain caused by her noxious relationship, Gram remained lionhearted. She jotted down this quote in one of her notebooks: "The key to boxing isn't how hard you can hit but how hard you can be hit."

Near the end of her life, she told me about a poem she'd studied in college. It was one of many pieces of literature Gram turned to for strength.

Invictus

Out of the night that covers me,
Black as the Pit from pole to pole,
I thank whatever gods may be
For my unconquerable soul.

In the fell clutch of circumstances
I have not winced nor cried aloud.
Under the bludgeonings of chance
My head is bloody, but unbowed.

Beyond this place of wrath and tears
Looms but the horror of the shade,
And yet the menace of the years
Finds, and shall find me, unafraid.

It matters not how strait the gate,
How charged with punishments the scroll,
I am the master of my fate:
I am the captain of my soul.

"Invictus" is translated from Latin into "unconquerable". The word itself has become familiar. It was the namesake of Britain's wounded veterans' games and the title of a modern movie starring Morgan Freeman about a South African rugby team.The poem delivers its message with a powerful wallop. When Gram introduced me to it, we read together from *The Home Book of Verse,* which she stored in her beautiful glass-fronted bookcase.

William Ernest Henley wrote "Invictus" in 1888. Henley suffered from tuberculosis and consequently, at age sixteen, his left leg had to be amputated. His right leg was barely saved after multiple foot surgeries. As he recovered in the infirmary, he became emboldened and was moved to write the poem, "Invictus," which became a canon of strength in the face of adversity.

The mighty stanzas conveyed such pain. It was Gram's canticle.

No matter Gram's lot, she made it work. Was she truly happy? I don't believe she was happy in the way we all would've wanted her to be happy. The word is too strong. I think she *almost* was though. She made the best of it, kept things on the rails. And no matter what, she was always still loads of fun, full of laughter.

A famous standoff with Alvin over money forced her to go to the First National Bank of Crossville where the bank president was a friend and loaned Gram $500 to buy groceries and pay bills.

After that embarrassment, Gram developed her own revenue streams, shrewdly ensconced from Alvin.

In the 1940s, Gram began collecting coupons. She enjoyed trimming them from the paper with surgical precision. George Neighbor and his father operated the only department and grocery store in Crossville, and when Gram shopped at Neighbor's, she'd turn in all the coupons she'd clipped that week.

She hadn't bought the products, of course. George would simply cash in the coupons for Gram. What she netted could have only been in the hundreds of dollars—harmlessly beguiling, but I'm sure it saved her from debt many times. I assumed Gram cooked up the idea, and like everyone else in town, George felt sorry for her and went along. I learned later of his universal generosity. He had done financial favors for countless families in town.

Faire, aka Gram

You could ask anyone who knew Gram, and they would agree, she was the hardest working person they'd ever come across. Her hands were constantly busy.

She spent half of her life cleaning. A story on *CBS Sunday Morning* about the benefits of keeping the hands busy caught my attention. Gram was onto something.

All chores have one thing in common which is that they keep our hands occupied. The story presented research that showed working with your hands can alter brain chemistry.

Dr. Kelly Lambert, a neuroscientist at the University of Richmond, made up a term called "behaviorceuticals." Like pharmaceutical influence, when we move and engage in activity, the neurochemistry of our brain can change in the same way a drug changes it.

She went on to say that in the nineteenth century, doctors used to prescribe knitting to women who were overwrought with anxiety "because they sensed that it calmed them down some." The researchers used rodents to study the hand-brain connection. Rats made to dig for a reward seemed to be happier when compared to what she called her trust fund rats "who got a pass on doing any physical work. So, when [they] took an animal that was really in tune with the environment and [they] just gave them their rewards, without having to work for them, their stress hormones went high."

As of 2015, jobs requiring analytical skills—desk jobs—had increased 94 percent from 1980, while jobs requiring physical skills went up only 12 percent. Many modern workers sit all day and press buttons. Bushwhacking through the day filled Gram with a rapturous high at day's end, her own brand of "behaviorceuticals."

Gram never touted herself as being a highbrow intellect, but she *was* well-read and curious. She'd have been a resourceful Della Street to some Perry Mason-like lawyer, a place where she could really be in the thick of it, having folks around who could match her clever wit. Instead of Perry, she got "Mister" in *The Color Purple*—a husband with a basic education who used his wife to serve his every need and, what is more, humiliated her by being unfaithful.

In December 1959, Gram first mentioned Alvin's wandering eye. She seemed offended, saying he'd been eating lunch "downtown" every day and is getting "thick with Effie." The reference was subtle because, of course, she would never have come straight out and complained.

Gram mitigated the "yes, sir" home life by being a different person in public. She broke out of that mold at high school basketball games. She was a bombastic fan at Crossville basketball games and was known to give an aggressive dressing down to every ref who went against her team. She was not the model of femininity expected of women of the era.

As a girl, she aspired to attend Lockyear Business College in Evansville, Indiana. She believed she'd be a masterful accountant. There was no arguing that. I was only eight when she taught me how to balance my checkbook using her hand-cranked antique adding machine. More interested in the adding machine's cool buttons and sleek black finish, Gram fumed when I pulled the lever and smashed my hand inside the bowels of the machine which she apparently needed right that minute. It took at least thirty minutes to free my hand.

I know she was thinking, *I'm too old for this crap!*

AFTER THE DEATH of my father, Gram never let my paternal grandfather, L.E. Davis, forget he had an obligation to help in my rearing. L.E. wasn't much of a parent or grandparent. Gram knew he would need a lot of reminding. She insisted I send letters to my grandfather at the Holiday Inn he owned in Benton, Illinois.

A remarkable coincidence that both my maternal and paternal grandparents owned hotels.

I hated writing those letters. I barely knew him and had no idea how to bring up the topic of Christmas or my upcoming birthday. I began the letters with niceties and then Gram fed me the rest. *Tell him you're on the honor roll!*

If my grandfather didn't respond, we wrote again.

AS MOM SURELY PONDERED, how did Gram even end up with Alvin?

I went on a journey back through the archives of Gram's earliest years looking for evidence of how she met Alvin.

Chapter 9

I Shall Always Remember You

Gram was among the elfin percentage of women, estimates say 5 percent or less, who had any post-secondary education in the Roaring Twenties.

In 1926, Gram's parents paid only $15 per term for her to experience college. They sent her off to school in Carbondale, Illinois, with the gift of a beautiful jade fountain pen embossed with "Faire DeLain."

The Roaring Twenties resonated in southern Illinois as much as any other part of the country. Across the states, people of all ages were defying prohibition; buying colorful, expressive clothing; and rejecting some of the traditional moral standards followed at the turn of the century.

The year 1926 must have been the only time in Gram's life she experienced anything close to a "roar." Her stories sparkled, and she held a girlish grin as she reminisced of shenanigans in class, escapades with friends.

I loved reading the memorials expressed in the margins of the yellowed pages of her college yearbook, *The Obelisk*. A doe-eyed

Faire DeLain was in the first row of freshmen on page 122. Her bestie, Gertie Harris, is a page ahead.

Faire DeLain   Gertie Harris

Within its 264 pages are heartfelt handwritten notes to Gram, in exquisite penmanship, worthy of the front of a wedding invitation—something you'd pay an Etsy artist to recreate.

> Dear Faire:
> Glad to have met you in school. Funny we hail from the same county but have to come to SINU to get acquainted. I shall always know you now. Your father was our mail carrier.
>
> Love,
> Beulah
> Grayville, Illinois

In 1926, affection was communicated with utmost care by twining sentences or a careful, meaningful signature. Hallmark printed its first Christmas card in 1926. It was a time when sentiment was tantamount to technology, when distractions were minimal, when apps didn't exist, when your posse was everything. Your whole world lay right in front of you. Romance, courtship, and really knowing someone happened through simply listening and speaking.

In December of 2018, I dug Gram's yearbook out once again. I wasn't getting anywhere with the Anna State Hospital records. I still woke up every morning with a fifty-fifty, flip-a-coin feeling about Mom's true cause of death. I was in a lull for a couple of reasons.

My writing coach was peppering me with the same question: "How is this book going to end?"

I had no idea.

My mother-in-law had recently passed away. Dot had been my pal for seventeen years, and her death legitimately sent me into an unexpected tailspin, which I decided was largely due to my own mom issues. I wasn't feeling well—physically or emotionally, and I was mad that I was feeling sorry for myself.

Lisa and I had little to give each other. She was tapped out after her mother's long illness and holding down a big, new job. Who could blame her for being emotionally empty after her mother's death? And I felt guilty having needs of my own that I couldn't control.

It hadn't been a storybook ending for Lisa's mom. The hospice team was exceptional, but the morphine didn't totally do the trick. She was miserable right up until her last breaths—this after years of painful decline. She passed away on a cold November night, ill-at-ease, curled into a fetal position, at a weight of fifty-nine pounds. A brutal ending.

No amount of breathing exercises or flute music could soothe us. It was the first time I wasn't coming right back after the death of a loved one.

"Are you okay? You've had so much loss," people asked me through the years. It was the first time I didn't know how to cope. The first time I wanted to give up. The first time I wasn't a grief superhero.

Lisa said to me, "You never smile anymore."

I was writing a book, working to purge all of this sadness and loss. Was it working?

I was out of the gratitude that had helped me survive for forty-eight years.

It took me weeks to get a grip, but I saw a therapist and got back on the writing wagon. I dug out Gram's yearbook in December 2018, on a day perfectly representative of the gloom and doom of a Midwestern winter. I thought the yearbook might bring back my mojo. Holding it gave me such a feeling of warmth for a time and place I hadn't experienced but was so grateful Gram had.

The cover of the yearbook was black with a simple 3x4-inch embossed gold Southern Illinois Normal University logo.

I had only known the school as Southern Illinois University. I'd never noticed the "N" which was very obvious that day. Inside the front cover, the first page was half missing. I reminded myself of the character Mayella Ewell in her dramatic scene with Atticus Finch.

"Who dun it?" Mayella shouted.

That's what I wondered! Who had damaged this valuable memento? Then I noticed my name scribbled in crayon just above the tear mark on the page. Gram should've spanked me, but it's unlikely she did.

I read the pages in more detail than I had before, noting the elegance of the book. This yearbook had class. It was a striking symbol of a cherished time in history. Even the freshman motto made me want to stand up straight, pump my fists, and feel my power.

These freshmen, that large, alert, body of young men and women who have freshened our school with their presence. They come from the high schools of Southern Illinois, eager to become a part of our college, willing to fight for their honors, and able to hold them.

So dramatic.

* * *

IN CONTEXT, THE "NORMAL" in Southern Illinois Normal University referred to the idea of instilling normal model standards in every student. The goal of the colleges was to produce a uniformly educated workforce of teachers who could train their students to eventually power a newly industrialized America.

On the campus of normal universities were lab schools. The children being taught, their teachers, and the teachers of the teachers were often together in the same building. By the late 1800s, normal universities were opening across Illinois.

Carbondale was one of the many towns, the impetus of whose growth was furnished by the completion of the Illinois Central Railroad in 1864, giving the town easy access from the north. The railroad provided a navigable route to the school from densely populated northern Illinois cities.

In 1864, Carbondale, Illinois, was a small town with a population of fifteen hundred. East Main Street was occupied by cotton ginning factories and woolen mills, and the space in front of the depot was a marketplace for the exchange and shipment of cotton, tobacco, fruits, cereals, and all the other products which came out of the region.

By 1920, Carbondale sported fine, modern, brick schools replacing the wooden structures of earlier days. Fifteen churches were erected in Carbondale as well as an Elks Club, Lions and Rotary Clubs, two banks, two building and loan associations, four hotels, and a library. Paved and gravel roads radiated like wheel spokes in almost every direction, and additional railroad lines led from Carbondale in six directions.

Recalling the stories Gram shared, thinking of her shenanigans, all got me into a better emotional place. I was pulled into the "roar" of the twenties and then, a series of vignettes came into view. This led me to find what took Gram back to Crossville and a life with Alvin.

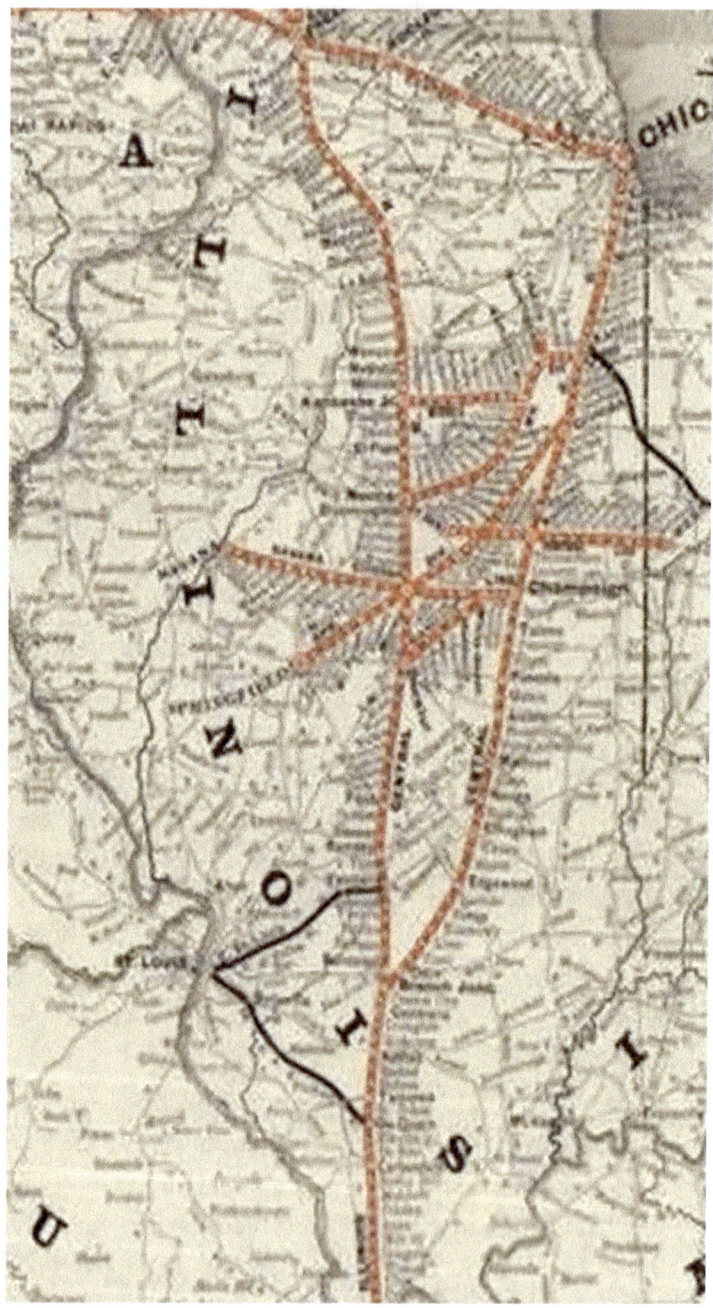

Illinois Central Railroad, c. 1864

The following dramatization, written from my grandmother's point of view, is based on stories she directly shared with me.

September 1926: Faire

I left for college on a Thursday afternoon in September. My mother's parting words were, "No gambling. No dancing." I had already decided to do both.

Dad's words were, "Meet lots of people and learn as much as you can about everything." I had already decided to do both of those, too.

Gertie Harris had been my classmate since kindergarten at Bell School. Gertie and I spoke our minds to each other and thought we'd be suited as roommates. Gertie was as small as I was and wore perfectly round, black wire spectacles on her tiny button nose. The morning we departed, she was wearing a sophisticated black dress with a flattering lace neckline and looked like she was headed to Paris rather than Carbondale, Illinois. Pure "bon vivant."

We sat across from each other in the wooden pew-like benches of the stark rail car. I hated winter. It was the worst part of living in Illinois and the only reason I ever thought of leaving; otherwise, it was good by me. We had Lincoln.

"Let's look at our schedules! Gertie, are you sleeping already?"

"I'm just thinking with my eyes closed. What time do you think we'll need to get up tomorrow?"

"More importantly, what will we do at night for fun? Think Miss Shanklin stays home every single night to babysit us? Probably," I pontificated.

"Possibly we will be doing homework at night?" Gertie quipped back at me.

"We're out of school at 3:00. And we won't need to study every night. I want to go to the basketball games. Did you know there's a boxing team? I wonder if they get all bloody."

I thought about all the options placed before Gertie and I in Carbondale, a town of 7,500, plus a campus of 1,500. Everything that buoyed my interest was about to be a touch away. I expected Gertie wouldn't be much interested in sports, but I hoped she'd get the school spirit. My thoughts transitioned to the Saluki cheers Maxine and I had been making up. Sisk! Bam! Haw! Saluki's Hoo-Rah!

Dad and I had read about how the ancient dog, the Saluki, came to be the mascot for Southern Illinois Normal University. It was sure a weird looking dog. At least the school had chosen good colors. They weren't as good as Crossville—orange and black for tigers—but maroon and white pleased me almost as much.

"There's a football game Saturday against Charleston," I exclaimed.

"I don't know if I have something to wear." Gertie was always worried about the practicalities and her wardrobe.

"Our house is one-fourth mile from the campus entrance. Shanklin had that in her advertisement. We can walk anywhere. Should be close for what she's charging!"

Gertie thought I was too young to be worried about money. She smirked at me and continued reminding me of what she thought was most important.

"We have to go first thing tomorrow to pay our fees and get books."

Gertie squinted at the tiny print on the paper listing her course schedule. "Which language course are you in?"

"Latin. Fretted all summer about that. I was out of my head when I picked."

"Why not French?"

"I'll pick that Winter Term."

"Me too, then!" she agreed.

"What are your other classes?"

"Modern Europe, Rhetoric, English Poetry, Trig, Latin, Physical Education, Music. When do you have P.E.?"

"Section 160 at 2:00."

"Me too."

"We are going to see plenty of each other," Gertie proclaimed.

I didn't know how small our room would be or how many other girls might be on our floor, but I knew the school required landlords to meet certain standards. Dad had checked it out thoroughly. I read the requirements to Gertie from the handbook:

NORMAL BULLETIN

Southern Illinois
State Normal
Bulletin

1874

1926

July, 1926
Catalogue Number

Published Quarterly in
January, April, July, October

Vol. XX   CARBONDALE
ILLINOIS   No. 1

OTHER STUDENT HOMES IN CARBONDALE.

Much of a student's success depends upon the conditions at his boarding and rooming place. He must have not only fresh air, pure water, wholesome food, even temperature and good light in his study room but also favorable conditions for study and for sleep. The following conditions as applied to rooming places meet the approval of the faculty:

On the part of the householder—

1. Men and women not to room in the same house.
2. Premises hygienically clean and supplied with good, sanitary water.
3. Good light in study rooms and rooms heated to not less than 68 degrees.
4. Telephone accessible.
5. Parlor furnished at reasonable times.

Mom and Dad's house was never warmer than sixty-two degrees in the winter, so I was very enthused by such a luxuriously warm temperature requirement! I'd stopped messing with the bed warmer long ago, and my sheets were always frigid.

Plus, curfew was 10:30! Gertie and I had already noted that weeks earlier. *So liberal!* I was over the moon.

The conductor heralded our location. "Next stop, West Frankfort. West Frankfort, ladies and gentlemen, followed by Herrin and Carbondale."

* * *

Tillie Horsfield was searching the train platform with extreme focus when our train pulled up. She looked down and checked the note in her hand. "Faire DeLain and Gertie Harris, I bet." Gertie and I were easy to spot; both of us under five feet with black hair and full faces. Tillie grabbed my hand with such gusto, she propelled me backward and I stumbled on my bag.

The conductor began handing belongings out of the luggage car. Most students came with a large steamer trunk and a laundry box. The brown fiber parcel would hold just a few garments and was secured by a canvas strap. It was ready for postal trips back and forth to Crossville. Sending it home to be laundered was cheaper than having my clothes professionally cleaned, Mother said.

"Hello." Gertie stuck her hand right out and grabbed Tillie's with similar spirit. It was like Tillie was about to get the last bill from a stack of cash.

"I'm Tillie. I'm Miss Shanklin's helper or secretary, kind of. She lets me borrow her car when I need it, and I do errands and things. The car is out front."

"Thank goodness. I can't lug this thing very far," I quipped.

I couldn't imagine how Tillie and I, with Gertie in her fancies, would get all of this to Miss Shanklin's car.

Tillie waved for help from one of the Negro pursers.

The purser was a lean man of average height with beautiful skin and an encouraging smile. I estimated he was nearly thirty. I was mesmerized by his complexion and the reserved, careful way he spoke. Almost all of the pursers were Negro.

As our group walked around to the front of the depot, I felt uneasy that the purser was carrying all of our luggage with no help from us, so I started a conversation. "Are you enrolled in the school?" I asked the purser. "We're freshmen. I'm Faire, and this is Gertie. We're from the sticks!"

He nodded in the friendliest of ways, as much as he could with the weight of our suitcases pulling at his arms. The purser sat our luggage down at our automobile, and I put my hand out to him.

He grabbed my hand, fingers only, and squeezed them a bit. "Wilbert Sable. Not in school. Wish I was. Only went to the first grade. But my boy is in the fifth grade here at the Negro school. We intend for him to go all the way through high school. College if we are able."

Gertie and I exchanged glances, both knowing this was the actual first Negro we had ever met. I made a mental note to find Wilbert when we came through the depot at Thanksgiving.

No fewer than fifteen black Model Ts waited in front of the lime-stone depot. Most of them seemed to be picking up women our age. As far as I could see, there were girls walking to their boarding houses. I could pick out the young men, some of them dandy and some thick and lumbering.

Tillie herded us into the vehicle. "Squeeze in the front! It's only a quarter mile."

Tillie looked like the Buster Brown boy on the box that my little sister's new shoes had come in. She wore a jacket like Amelia Earhart. Tillie knew the ropes and had a helpful personality. I liked her immediately. How nice to have a *big* sister for a change. I was happy at once to be getting away from my little sister Maxine's fits. She ran away from home at least once a week, me fetching her from here or there.

The Ford Model T Depot Hack, whose seats were crafted from walnut, fit three in the front with an entirely open cab. The grainy wooden seat was warped from humidity. It was a balmy eighty degrees that day—about right for September in Illinois. And it was almost supper time; I was hungry.

I had never seen a completely paved road like the one that took us down East Main, and I'd only heard of grand houses like the ones we were seeing along the road. Dad said Lindell Boulevard in St. Louis was lined with them—the ones the rich Europeans built for themselves to stay in when they arrived for the 1904 World's Fair.

"What time is supper?" Gertie inquired.

"Five o'clock. Did you sign up for board? If not, there's a small gas cooking stove in your room. Not sure how well yours will work."

Gertie gave a belly laugh at the thought of cooking a meal, let alone lighting a stove.

I didn't know how to cook, didn't want to cook. "We can just eat the pie Mom sent."

WITHIN THE HOUR, eight other seventeen- and eighteen-year-old young women introduced themselves to us in the second floor hallway of 106 Mill Street. There were three rooms on the second floor and two on the third. We were on the third, next to Virginia Parrot and Emma Baker from East St. Louis, Illinois.

I killed the time before dinner by reading through the handbook, double checking the wheres and whens of the next day. I was nervous, for sure.

"Oh, here's the school song! You know, they sure talk a lot about the character of SINU students. How do they know about our character? They've never laid eyes on us. You could be a bank robber, Gerts."

We powdered our faces and walked down for the welcome dinner at five o'clock. It was the first time we saw Miss Genevieve Shanklin. She looked about thirty with crimped brown hair parted on the side. Miss Shanklin wore utilitarian glasses, a scooped neck brown dress, loafers, and exuded an air of no-nonsense. She did give us enough of a smile that I decided she was likable. The disposition of a teacher. While we took our seats, Tillie busied herself sweeping the porch and front steps.

"It's so good to meet you girls. You've all gotten acquainted, I hope. Arlina will be bringing out dinner soon. Have you met our lady, Arlina?"

A tiny Negro woman in a black uniform dress and black loafers, no less than eighty, waddled out in a great hurry. She was the smiliest woman I'd ever seen. Her teeth took up most of her face, and her hair had been pressed into a straight bob.

"Hello, Misses. Welcome, and we wish you luck. Now, you girls just let me know if you'll be missing supper on particular nights. We don't want to waste food." Arlina rushed off. She seemed terribly busy.

I couldn't imagine cooking for twelve people every night. Torturous. Mom had never been able to get me interested in cooking.

I'd noticed a large garden in the back and, therefore, couldn't wait to see what was coming from the kitchen.

What a feast: new potatoes in butter, baked ham, fried okra, and carrot salad.

I had never seen such delicious-looking food in all my life. I was just hoping that Dad had actually signed me up for board. I'd never been quite so excited about eating.

Gertie grinned at me across the table, her eyes huge with expectation. We were gluttons. I would have to tell Mother and Dad in my first letter. While we feasted, Ms. Shanklin asked us questions about our backgrounds, as if to verify we weren't imposters just trying to get a nice meal.

"Two of you are from Johnsonville, two from Crossville, and two from Golconda?"

The other four were from Elizabethtown, Shawneetown, Herrin, and Carmi. The rest of the girls were interested in teaching elementary. I was the only one considering a secondary school certificate.

The subjects I was interested in weren't for little ones. When I mentioned accounting and literature, they all squealed and thought I was nuts. Tillie announced she was enrolled in the Business for Secondary School program, and she'd be happy to talk to me about it. Mother wasn't enthused about my aspirations of a high school teaching certificate which required extra schooling and an extra year away from home.

During our dessert of apple pie made with apples from the two trees out back, Ms. Shanklin reviewed the rules.

"Everyone have your handbook? Turn to page eighteen, and look at the bottom of the page. Tillie, will you read numbers one through six?"

There was a small paragraph and then a list of rules:

Student Homes: Responsibilities of Students

1. Quiet and order in the house at all times.
2. Proper care of furniture and premises.
3. Repair of damages beyond ordinary wear.
4. Householder to be notified when students expect to be out later than 10:30 p.m.
5. Absence from town to be reported to householder and address left.
6. Vigorous cooperation on the part of both student and householder, in case of contagious diseases within the house, to prevent the spread of additional illness.

Shanklin followed the reading of the rules with her own solicitations. "By September 20, you will need to let me know what services you choose for the rest of the term."

She passed around a slip of paper with the following options, telling us that some of our parents had already decided on our behalf:

```
Board and room - $6 per week
Room with light housekeeping by Arlina - $4
per week
Rooms without light housekeeping and no board -
$3 per week
```

All the girls arose from the table and walked out front to enjoy the evening air underneath the covered porch, but straightaway, I followed Miss Shanklin.

"Excuse me, Ms. Shanklin. I'm Faire from Crossville."

"Faire, good to meet you." She leaned in and squeezed both of my upper arms with genuine warmth. "What nice parents you have."

"Thank you. They have a nice life in Crossville. It's quiet. Dad is the postmaster *and* county coroner." We laughed, and I could tell she could picture the scene.

"Did Dad already sign me up for board? He's the berries if he did. The food was delicious."

"Arlina has the book. Let me check."

Miss Shanklin walked through the swinging wooden door into the kitchen at the back of the house. The 1880 Victorian Era home may have lost its glamor but hadn't lost its charm.

Miss Shanklin swiftly returned, acting like she just had to get outside to supervise the others.

"Arlina has you on her list for meals. Gertie, too."

"That's such good news." I leaned over and quietly told her that Gertie's father was the bank president and that I already figured Gertie had been signed up.

On the porch, Miss Shanklin droned on about this and that. "You girls know that if you are feeling homesick, we can always drum up some kind of entertainment. We had a book club last year that everyone enjoyed."

"Yes, ma'am. I'll consider that."

I didn't mind reading, but discussing a book for hours sounded worse than a little homesickness.

At 6:30 a.m. the following morning, I was already enjoying a very grown-up morning by having coffee in what once would've been a grand parlor. It now adjoined the dining room and was a warm but utilitarian 20×30-foot space meant for socializing and study. There were two fireplaces for winter months, three settees, a coffee table, and a couple of mismatched dining chairs. I loved it. The room had one seat for each roomer.

Gertie was still in our room primping, so I picked up *The Daily Press* for the score of yesterday's baseball game and noticed the massive headline, "Yanks Win Over St. Louis Cardinals." Not a pleasant way to start the day. I cheered myself up by reading the article, "My Friend Babe Ruth," written by the player's confidante who wanted to tell the world that despite his gruff manner, The Babe actually had feelings that were sometimes hurt when he let the fans down. I found it hard to believe. After Sports, I skimmed three paragraphs describing Helen Keller's stint on Broadway.

Tillie sat near the coffee table, counting and recounting her funds for book fees, then left for the kitchen. I'd already counted mine in my room.

Arlina rang the breakfast bell, and at 6:45, Tillie was bringing out food. In the middle of the dining table were sliced fresh peaches and biscuits with sausage gravy or apple butter. It was an inspiring start.

All the girls were dressed in their freshest outfits and were in high spirits. At 7:30, we ten walked together toward Wheeler Hall for registration. We engulfed the sidewalk. As far as I could see in front and behind me, the walkways and streets were packed. There were hundreds of students, and another 1,200 or so being housed on campus and they'd already be in line for books.

Dad sent me to school with $20, a good deal of money, but I wasn't to spend it unless I had to. Whatever I had left before Thanksgiving break, I planned to spend on a Saluki souvenir for Dad.

Gertie and I waited in line for an hour. After we were registered, we bought our books. My stack was massive. We balanced the textbooks like firewood on our arms while we plodded to the cafeteria.

Gertie and I were given bologna sandwiches and sat at long, wooden tables as we ate them. We could see hundreds of students still in line at the bookshop. We decided to find our classrooms. At 3:00 p.m., Gertie and I were finally finished and walked five blocks back to the house. The campus buildings looked ancient to us, as many were built in the 1860s when the university opened. Behind campus was vast farmland, still a bright green with corn. There were festivities for upperclassmen being held in the fields. A manicured rectangle of grass was ready for the football game Saturday. My eyes couldn't believe the size of it. *So far for a touchdown*, I thought. Those fellows must be awfully fit, and I couldn't wait to see them.

As soon as we hit the front door, we could smell Arlina preparing our dinner. I suggested to Gertie that we go help her, and she scoffed.

"We don't know what we're doing! No way am I going to embarrass myself."

Gertie and I took longer than usual to get up the steps, having stopped twice along the way to steady ourselves. My books felt twice as heavy as I remembered my little sister being as a baby – maybe even twenty pounds. Our room was at the back of the house, and our door was the nearest to the fire escape making it hot in September, and it'd sure be cold in the winter. It was wonderful on that day. Our three windows opened to reveal the two massive oaks in the backyard.

Gertie and I each had a dressing table on either side of the double bed; there was a 2 x 3-foot pine table with drop leaves at the foot of the bed, and an antique gas heating stove which Tillie had warned us about.

I sat down at the table and opened *Modern Europe*, the largest of my stack of books.

"Look at chapter six, 'The Dutch Republic?'"

"This is awful! Will I have to read this whole book? Too late now. It's $1.00 to change a class, so I'm stuck."

Gertie had been staring at the pages of our Latin textbook for fifteen minutes without uttering a peep. "Here's what I have to say to you about *Modern Europe* . . . Ad Mortem . . . To Death! Bored to death!"

Gertie flopped on the bed, and we cackled our heads off.

* * *

"Good morning, girls. I'm Vivian Land, your gym teacher. Please sit in a circle on the floor while I call roll."

We carefully lowered ourselves in our dresses to the wooden floor, stretched our legs out straight and waited for instruction. Three Negro girls sat opposite me. I counted a total of twenty-one students, twice the size of CHS class of '26.

"This term, we will work on our own physical health, and we will learn the methods of applying these principles to children. Some of the habits we will establish are hygiene, sportsmanship, and leadership. Our units of study will be group contests and games and folk dancing."

"We will start off today with hygiene. Do each of you have a toothbrush?"

Gertie and I both raised our hands and exclaimed in unison, "We both got a new one for Christmas!"

I felt certain I had a lot to learn. Mrs. Land discussed diseases and how to prevent them. I hoped we would hear about diphtheria. My baby cousin, Alan Reed Sanders, hadn't made it to six months. I'd always wondered why he got diphtheria, and the rest of us didn't. He was the sweetest little boy, and I loved to sit on the porch and rock him to sleep in the evening. Aunt Sarah cried for months after he passed.

After class, Gertie was up to something when she walked over to Miss Land.

"Thank you, ma'am. I really enjoyed the lesson."

Gertie nervously felt her long, shiny necklace. "I was wondering, when we get to the folk dancing curriculum." She paused to check the teacher's receptiveness. "Do you think we could try the Charleston? We've been dying to learn it! Do you know it?"

Miss Land grinned like it was a predictable question.

"I do. We might have to do it on the sly. I don't want your parents blaming me if you go to the dark side." She chuckled.

"Yes, ma'am. A Saturday would be so fine. Thank you, ma'am. See you on Wednesday."

* * *

By the second week of classes, we knew Miss Land was going to be our favorite of the teachers. She was young and fair. She followed all the sports teams at school like I did, and we liked her cornball jokes.

"Do you have a boyfriend?" Gertie inquired in front of the whole class.

"I do."

"Does he work here? Who is it?"

Gertie persisted. "What's he look like?"

"He looks like Albert Einstein," she said with a grin.

"All right. Let's try and learn something today. Each of you, find a partner."

Friends grabbed hands with friends. I matched up with Rhea, and we all sighed heavily when we realized the Negro girls were oddly numbered. There was a standoff. Hildred, our least favorite classmate, stared at the remaining Negro girl. The moment hung for seconds, which seemed like a very long time. Miss Land waited for it to unfold. She took steps toward Sara, and my heart became inflamed with compassion. I couldn't believe it. *How cruel*, I thought. Who are you bumpkins to be scoffing at Sara?

I intercepted Sara from Miss Land.

"Thank you, Faire. Take your partner's hand. Let's learn the Virginia Reel."

Our dance lesson began. Hence forward, Sara and I were dance partners.

127

Around the beginning of October, we talked Miss Land into the Charleston lesson. We met on Saturday at the reservoir, which adjoined the football field. There was a small grove of trees in the back corner, and we decided it would be the best place for us. No one would see exactly what we were doing.

"I wasn't about to carry that big phonograph out here, so we'll just have to hum it."

All righty.

"The Charleston is a swing, so it's in two. It goes fast, but we will start slowly."

I reminded Gertie to never mention this to her parents who would tell my mother.

The whole class belted it out. "Bah-bah-baah-bah-bah-da-da-da-daah-dah-dah-daaah!"

I remember that Saturday being one of the best days of the year. After our lesson, it was time for the school's football match with Bloomington-Normal University. My classmates and I ran to the field and bounded up the bleachers. I watched Sara go to her section with the other Negro students. I was vexed every day at the difference in how Sara experienced life at school. It wasn't that the teachers were overtly mean, but Sara was treated as if she was flat out less — less intelligent, less worthy.

Sara's last name was Le Roux. Her mother and father were second generation African slaves whose parents were brought over in the early eighteenth century by the French inhabitants of Illinois. Before the Civil War, most counties in Illinois had abandoned the practice of slavery, but it remained in almost every southern Illinois County for many more years, and two of those counties were White (Crossville) and Gallatin, where Carbondale was located. At the close of the Civil War, Illinois became the first state to ratify the Thirteenth Amendment to the Constitution of the United States, which abolished slavery nationally. Between touchdowns, I wanted to stand and remind everyone about this and imagined saying, "Attention, hillbillies, slavery has been illegal since 1865! Do you mind if

Sara and I sit together?" I really thought that might do the trick. When I talked to her about my feelings, Sara begged me to pipe down; so for her sake, I put a sock in it.

A few weeks after the Charleston lesson, Sara and I went on an excursion to the north side of Carbondale. It was my idea. I told Gertie I was at the library.

We practically sprinted down the dimly moonlit sidewalk on the north Carbondale street where Tillie had dropped us. Our arms were locked as we ducked down a slope of steep, crumbly concrete steps and knocked on the door.

"Yes?" said a deep baritone voice.

"Peanuts," Sara said back to him. "Just stick with me," Sara told me. "These crazy people in here may all be bamboozled. Hold tight."

"Drunk?"

"Faire! Yes, drunk."

"I've never seen anyone drunk! I want to see!" I charged past Sara into a vibrant and crowded basement club. Groups of people were whooping it up. They were dancing and bopping around to the brassy sounds of the stage band. A Negro woman with a velvet voice was serenading, "Where'd you get those dimples, honey?"

I found a tiny table near the dance floor. All the customers were drinking something clear and strong out of child-sized little jars. A man quickly came to our table and slapped down two glasses.

"No, thank you. We're just here for the dancing."

The waiter checked with Sara, and she smiled but also firmly shook her head no.

"Get out there, Sara."

"No. You do it."

Sara wore a wistful blue dress. Her chin-length hair fell in a naturally wavy style, not like the feigned crimps the other girls pressed into their locks. She looked like she had an ethnicity all her own. I wondered if anyone thought we were sisters. She had a full face like mine, dark brown hair like mine, and wide-set eyes like mine. But, Sara was much prettier than me.

At least two tables of men were plotting their attempt at Sara when I noticed Wilbert from the train station. He was waiting tables in a sharp, white tuxedo shirt, vest, and bowtie.

"I know him! He works at the depot! He helped us with our bags our first day here. He's so nice."

I waved him over, and he smiled. It looked like he intended to come over to us but not straight away.

One of the five or so white men in the club neared our table. I recognized him as one of the blokes who stayed in the house across from us, and I had seen him walking into English Poetry in the class that followed mine.

He stopped to speak. "I've seen you in Allyn Hall. What are you doing here?" He directed his question to me.

"Same as you, Mr. English Poetry?" He threw his head back, mocking the thought.

"Yes. A poet I am . . . 'Wine comes in at the mouth, And love comes in at the eyes.' W.B. Yeats." He smiled modestly as if he was embarrassed by his burst of confidence.

"Clever you! This is Sara, my friend."

"Ah. Very modern pair. How did you two come to be embroiled?"

"We're dance partners in gym," I told him emphatically.

"Well, let's see it."

"No way. We're no good," Sara proclaimed. "Sorry. I'm no good. Faire's got it down. She's good."

"Kent," he said as he gently put forth the hand of a true gentleman. "Faire, eh? How elegant."

"Pfff. Truly not elegant, but my middle name is worse, so I'll stick with Faire."

Kent waved his friends over.

"I'll give it a try if you will, Sara. This song is in two. That would work."

"No ma'am."

"Why come here if we're not going to dance? We could've done this anywhere."

"All right." Sara was regretting her commitment, but we stood together and walked four feet out to the middle of the swiftly moving group.

Sara and I went to town on the floor. Once Sara got over the newness, we swung our legs kicking to the front and bringing them in a wide arc around to the back, left leg, then right. We flapped our arms with vigor and perspired profusely. We were washed-out after the third song and returned to the table.

I rested for several songs and noticed Wilbert sitting down. I went to speak to him and ask about his family. He told me how he had gotten the job here and that it paid well, so it was worth the late hours. When I returned to the table, Sara was quiet.

"Faire, you can't touch that man when you talk to him. If the cops end up here and they saw you with him, he would be skinned alive. And they'd find out who you are, and you'd be sent home. It's illegal for you to be flirting with Negro men, fraternizing with them."

"What are you talking about? I was asking him about his family. I didn't even know I touched him."

"Well, he sure knows. Probably terrified."

"He didn't act terrified!"

"He's married, Faire."

"We're not going to bed together, Sara!"

"It just scares me. Didn't you say he has a son? They'd blame Wilbert for the whole thing."

"What 'whole thing'?"

Sara became teary. "Free black men are captured all the time in Shawneetown and Cairo. They threaten to harm their families, so they just have to go along. They run them south and sell them back into slavery. Southern farmers will pay for a young man they can work to death. What do you think Willie would do? He wouldn't fight back. He would just have to go."

Sara stared at me for a long time, waiting for me to show her I understood. I knew it was true, and I knew I couldn't imagine the fear she lived with.

"I forget what it's like for you."

As we returned to our table, Sara gave me advice I was never able to heed or accept. "We can't just talk people into being different than they are, Faire. We just have to stay out of the way."

* * *

At Christmas, Gertie and I said goodbye to our housemates and headed home for our time off. Arlina made fruitcakes, minus the booze, to take to our parents. On the train, we ate the ham sandwiches Arlina sent.

"Will you tell Myrtle and Pierre about your 'friend' Kent?" Gertie wondered.

"Maybe Dad, but *not* Myrtle. She'll have me back in Crossville and married before I get the sentence out."

"Will you tell your parents about Simon Rosen? Well, the 'Simon' but maybe not the 'Rosen'?"

"You don't think they'd be that way, do you?"

"Who knows?" I rested my head on the window and counted the wiry, barren trees until we made it home. Dad and Maxine were at the station waiting.

"Fairy-Bell," Maxine threw her arms wrapped around my neck.

"You haven't even noticed I've been gone! You've got the whole bed to yourself now."

Dad came to my side and gave me a warm embrace. "Are you smarter by now?"

"I feel like such a Dumbo, Dad. We all think we failed the Trig exam, and maybe we all did! What's been going on here?"

"I'm behind on everything. I've had the flu bug already, but I'm coming back."

"How many citizens corked off since I left?"

"Only four." Dad let out a pitiful laugh. "TB got old Mr. Kuyk-endall. There was a train collision in Carmi last week. The others were stillborns. Never gets easier."

"Is Aunt Jen coming for Christmas Eve?"

"I imagine they'll come that morning."

"Hey Dad, I thought when I'm off in the summer, we could go to a ballgame. Maybe we could see a show at The Municipal Opera, too?"

"Talk to your mother. Fine with me."

* * *

I LOVED to tell the city kids from Chicago that I had a double aunt and double uncle. It took pen and paper for them to get it. Brother and sister married brother and sister. Dad's little sister, Jenny DeLain married Mother's brother, Lloyd McCurdy. They eloped to St. Louis after several years of marital consideration and stayed there. Aunt Jen became a master seamstress at Stix, Baer, and Fuller.

I talked about college without taking a breath. Mother pretended to stir the beans, but I knew she was following. I didn't mention Kent, except to say I had made a friend from a town near St. Louis.

"I was hoping Dad and I might come up this summer for a game." I was dropping hints to Aunt Jen.

"Even better, what about a summer job in the city? You could stay with us. I think your mother might allow it. Gertie would be welcome if she wanted to come."

I was overcome at the possibility.

"I'll write to you about a plan," Aunt Jen whispered to me.

If Mother heard our plan making, she'd start worrying herself sick. Each step I took away from Crossville made her hang on tighter. It took energy to keep us on the straight and narrow which made for a lot of worrying for her. She so wanted me to teach in Crossville like she had. It wasn't that she wanted to keep me from seeing the world but that she wanted me to have the kind of envelopment of love she felt in our town.

* * *

GERTIE and I settled back into our second term. We laughed endlessly, as we muddled our way through English poetry, most of which we decided was way over our heads. But we loved the recitation which sometimes came out in performance late in the evening.

Gertie and I occasionally gathered friends in our room, but with Shanklin's hawk eyes, we had to be careful. We would sneak them in via the fire escape. Kent and his friends held a revolving Pinochle tournament on Thursday nights. I thought I'd never understand the intricacies of such a complicated game, but Kent was as patient as he was smart.

Simon Rosen and Gertie were joined at the hip. They had a similar zest for the finer things, and he could certainly provide them. I never knew what his father did, but since Simon had his own car, we knew it must be something big. For the holiday, he brought Gertie a white, monogrammed sweater from a fancy store in downtown St. Louis.

I still saw Sara in gym class, and we remained kindred spirits, but she had joined the Dunbar Society. This was a group aiming to "give the Negro students a better outlet for any intellectual attainment they may require." It was the only school activity available to minority students. Sports, music, dramatic arts, and other interest-based clubs were for white students only.

Sara had given me perspective. They were special glasses through which I was able to see all the things that many white people never noticed, never cared about, never even knew happened. It was a life-long precious gift.

* * *

Dear Uncle Lloyd and Aunt Jen,
    Hello from SINU. I'm wondering if you've mentioned anything to Mother and Dad about our scheme? It may take awhile for Mother to warm up to the notion. Maybe you've thought

better of having giggly girls in the house all summer?

Gertie has a beau, Simon. Actually, his name is Simon Rosen from St. Louis. He lives on Pershing Avenue if you know where that is. Guess I better fess up that I am also very fond of a boy from Belleville, Kent Tygart. What a coincidence that they both live in your town! How lucky for me!

Simon suggested Gertie and I should apply for work at Sonnenfeld's Department Store on Washington Avenue. He said they hire young women for the summer. From your apartment, he thought that the street car would take us right to Sonnenfeld's. Do you know the store?

I'll say farewell, then. Write to me as soon as you can!

Your loving niece,
Faire (and Gertie)

* * *

I DIDN'T HEAR BACK from Aunt Jen until late in the semester when she told me it had taken some time to win over Dad. He seemed to be hesitant about my being away for the whole summer, but Aunt Jen had worked her charms, and he eventually agreed.

Gertie and I wrote Sonnenfeld's inquiring about employment, and we both received a beautifully printed postcard within a week.

"Thank you for your inquiry about employment at Sonnenfeld's Department Store, Broadway and Washington Avenue, St. Louis, Missouri. Please report for an interview at 9 a.m., Monday, June 2, 1927.

I immediately began wondering if Gertie had something I could wear. I was sure I didn't have anything smart enough. While I'd never been to the store, Simon told me that the finest and most wealthy women in the city shopped there and that they sold suits imported from Paris that cost $150.

We took the Magnolia Star to St. Louis Union Station. Aunt Jen was meeting us at the station. Kent and Simon were joining us for dinner.

They took us on a practice run over to Sonnenfeld's via streetcar, and afterward, we played bridge. Aunt Jen took to Kent quickly. When I asked her the odds of Mother and Dad approving of him, she said, "He seems to cherish you. I think the odds are good."

A life with Kent was gathering plausibility. Mother and Dad would like him, even though by rural standards he was awfully genteel. I knew the real obstacle would be whether Crossville would be the kind of vista Kent needed for his grand teaching plans. He wouldn't be able to change the whole world instructing only ten kids a year in Crossville. If Crossville didn't work out, could I make it in St. Louis? And then there was Mother . . .

* * *

ON THAT RADIANT Monday morning at 7:00, Gertie and I hopped on a red and black jingling, jangling trolley. We hung on as it swayed down Olive Street, sounding entirely like it was about to fall apart. It took us five blocks to Broadway, and we carefully maneuvered the steep stairs to street level, where we spun shyly into the movement of the revolving glass door of Sonnenfeld's. The store was a vibrant display of fanciness like we had never seen. The walls were adorned with aquarelle sketches of the streets of Paris and London. Delicate, formal hats with plumes to the heavens; casual flannel derby hats for men and women; his and hers suits; accessories of all kinds; and a children's department. I knew I was in over my head but was elated by the opportunity. We sat with five other girls on a long, brass trimmed bench next to the front door and waited for our names to be called.

A portly gentleman wearing an expensive suit zipped over, angling for the next interviewee. He called my name and introduced himself as Emile Zeifel.

"You were early. Very good. Most of these girls run late which costs us money."

"Yes, I guess it would."

Business and the making of money, the turning of profit — I hankered to know how it worked.

I barely edged past the closing gold elevator doors onto the plushly-carpeted compartment. Zeifel turned to me as if relieved to be alone and spoke to me with noticeable familiarity. I felt at ease.

His office overlooked the sales floor including the sewing room where the hats were made. I could see twenty or so women with their heads down holding needles and making quick stitches through all sorts of fabrics. He asked me several informal questions, mostly wondering about my interests. He mentioned millenary and asked if I thought I would be able to tolerate the eminence of Sonnenfeld's customers.

"Do you think you'd be able to work with our more demanding customers without any dustups? They can often leave our sales staff in tumult by day's end. Another thing, if you can modulate the twang a bit, you'll stave off some assumptions about your ability."

"I know what you mean, sir. I may be nervous, but I won't show it. I won't ask anyone, 'You-enz ready to pay?'"

There was a crew of young ladies in millenary he thought I'd enjoy working alongside. Mr. Zeifel examined my face and declared it was a proper "hat face."

"Can you start Tuesday morning?"

We passed his secretaries, boarded the elevator and Zeifel pressed #1. He turned to me, smiled, and said loud enough for them to hear, "Yenta, yenta, yenta!" and shook his head. He looked toward me for a response. "Mishegas!"

I was paralyzed. Had they advertised for only Jewish women? At school I had been taken for all sorts of folks – Mexican, Negro, and, frequently, Jewish.

I smiled at him and shrugged.

"I'm sorry, Mr. Zeifel. We are Methodist."

We laughed with gusto, and by the time the doors opened, Zeifel's eyes were watery with glee.

"Oh, I will never forget that one," he said. "See you Tuesday, DeLain. Be at the millenary counter at 8:00 a.m. It was a pleasure."

"Yes, sir!" I exclaimed.

Gertie was already sitting on the bench just inside the revolving glass doors that took us out to a frenzied Olive Boulevard. She looked like an honest-to-goodness patron in a spiffy looking summer blazer and her neatly pressed auburn hair.

"You look happy."

"I got it! When do you start?"

"He suggested I try the Sears and Roebuck store. He didn't think I looked right for the job."

We giggled the whole way home.

* * *

THAT EVENING, we all sat on the balcony at Aunt Jen's apartment listening to "The Dodge Victory Hour" and paging through our yearbooks which we'd received our last week of classes. I was curious to read the sentiments and clever wishes from friends.

"Gertie, look! There's Tillie! She joked about borrowing Morris's stove!"

"Read what Greer said."

Dear Faire:

Glad you don't mind being called the little "French-man." I never could play cards with you cause you are a sure jinx for me. I shall never forget the good times on the front porch and stair steps.

A. Greeroman

"Minnie got a half a page for cheer!"

Dearest Faire:

Really, Faire, I want to come to Crossroads and stay all summer, but I don't have the money for it. I will surely think of you next year when I am sitting all alone preparing my lessons for the next day. Just one more . . . Remember our love affairs (if only in our dreams)!

Gobs of love,
Minnie

MINNIE LAUDER
Miss Lauder from Carterville
surely put us up on our toes and
made us air our tonsils for our
Alma Mater's varsity.

"Kent, what did you write? I hope Mother doesn't see this."

Dearest Faire:

Here is hoping our party tonight turns out OK. With best hopes for the unexpected.

Kent

Kent

Sara

Dear Faire:

If I don't see you next term, it won't be for not trying. I will never forget our adventures. You have

140

shown me the most kindness of anyone here. Best of luck, my dearest.

> Sara Le Roux
> Cairo, Illinois

Gertie found a good position at a shoe store around the corner from Sonenfeld's. It turned out I had something of a gift for selling expensive hats, and Mr. Zeifel would yell down to me in the morning before the doors opened.

"DeLain, you might have a future here if you're not careful. You're about to outsell the veteran ladies."

August 2, 1927

Dear Mother and Dad,

Greetings from the city. I have been thinking of you both every day. The weather has been so humid, but I'll say it's even worse down there!

I have sold two high-ticket hats this week. One was $10.00 (a Newport Maine) and the "cheapie" $7.50. Mrs. Busch bought it for her big steamer trip. She and the mister are sailing the S.S. Dixie from New York City to New Orleans. I bet they'll all be on a toot.

There are so many cars downtown every day, and boy, are they snazzy. It is hustle and bustle from dawn until dusk. I walk to work when it isn't too hot, but mostly am taking the trolley. Aunt Jen is berries and has a hot dinner ready for

Gertie and I every night when we get home at 5:30.

Have you been listening to *Amos and Andy*? We've been listening to the *Palmolive Hour* every night. If I sell two more premium hats this week, I'll stay in the lead for most sales in millenary!

Uncle Lloyd is taking us to Sportsman's next week for the Saturday game. It will be 100 in the shade, but we don't care. It would sure be keen if Hornsby hit one right to me. Will you listen along? I sure wish you could come, Dad. I hope your stomach ache has gone away.

Greet little cousin Kate with a kiss from me. There are silk embroidered baby hats being made at the store for fifty cents, and I might bring one for her. Also give Maxine a little peck, too.

Your loving daughter,
Faire

My vigor was soon stolen. Dad died the very next morning.

Chapter 10

Helicobacter Pylori

August 1927: Faire

Helicobacter pylori killed Dad. He was fifty-one. His death would set the course for the rest of my life. You know, when you're a child, you don't even notice there is a powerful and sensitive center to your body. Your heart is the center of everything — every dip and summit, every daily frustration. I didn't know then what my heart was yet to suffer. It was its first prick.

The flu Dad experienced at Christmas was an infection. He'd been sickly and vomiting most of that summer. When blood began to appear in his stool, Doc Stanley told Mom that he thought the infection might have morphed into cancer. I guess Mom didn't believe it, which is why she told almost no one. Dad became bedridden, was sallow, they said, and had drastic weight loss. There was no possibility of remedy.

With her voice warbling and soft, Mother said to me on the telephone, "I didn't know it would be so fast. I should've called you home last week. I didn't want you to miss the big sale at Sonnenfeld's. You were thinking you'd take the prize for August."

It broke my heart knowing this was on her mind on top of the obvious. "It's OK. I am sorry I wasn't there to help you."

Aunt Jen, Uncle Lloyd, and I left for Crossville within an hour of the news. *Midwesterners are very good at being there, or at least Crossville is.*

Mother was lost, devastated. She looked frail and like she hadn't slept in weeks. She never had any pounds to spare, anyway. Mom told me I had gotten my curves from Dad's mother, from my French heritage. I assumed it was Arlina's pie.

Dad's body lay in his own bed for twenty-four hours after he passed away, right up to the next evening when we had the viewing. I sat with him in between the jobs that needed to be done. I would help Mother with the ham salad and then go stare at Dad. He didn't look at all like himself, but I continued to talk to him as if he were still hearing me. I told him I would be as nice to Maxine as possible, but that I thought the mollycoddling wasn't helping her at all. I told him I'd try not to marry an unschooled drip of a man with no ambition. I told him I would keep cheering for the Cardinals and do my best to make sure that our boys brought home the World Championship again this year. I offered up many promises and hoped I could keep them.

At 5:00 on the night of Dad's viewing, Mother put out the ham salad, tapioca pudding, sliced tomatoes, and pie. Uncle Joe, married to Mom's sister, Aunt Sarah, helped move Dad into a beautiful walnut box. We lined the box with a crocheted throw, and the men carried it into our tiny sitting room. Reverend Willoughby offered a prayer, and one-by-one the people came: the people who had gone to school with him, whose mail he'd delivered, whose dead baby he had come for in the middle of the night. We buried him at Stokes Chapel Cemetery the next morning. It was over too quickly.

Maxine was brooding while I just spit everything out before I even thought. She had outgrown running away but would sit, pretending to listen to the radio with us, but she wasn't really there. She was always for it if I suggested an activity to keep us busy, but she never initiated it. She was protecting herself, I thought, from the outside world, from any possibility of being further scuffed up.

I helped Mom—my way of coping. I watched little Cousin Kate when Aunt Sarah walked to the store or cleaned house. It felt good to be home, for just a while but I realized that my plans were about to be threatened by circumstance; considerably worse, Dad was dead.

There was still a month before the beginning of the term. I wasn't convinced I needed to stay home with Mother. Dad would've wanted me to continue with school, but maybe not just now, given Mother's state. Kent and I had only just brushed the surface of *our future*. I didn't know if he wanted to marry me. I hoped to marry him, but I behaved coyly anytime the topic arose. He had at least one more year of school and since I'd only completed my freshman coursework, I would be limited to an elementary certificate. I was more enthused about literature and accounting than paddling and wiping noses. But I could do it.

When Aunt Jen returned from the funeral, she stopped at Sonnenfeld's where Mr. Zeifel gave her the wages he owed me with an extra $20, saying it was in lieu of flowers—more useful. Mr. Zeifel told her I would always have a job. We'd become quite friendly. My only day off was Saturday when the store was closed for the Sabbath, so I'd seen him most every other day of the summer. He was so kind to me.

"Frenchie, you would have my office in tip-top shape. You'd know where every penny was going! Forget about teaching! I need someone like you up there. I could trust you. You've probably never broken a law in your life, have you? Small town people are different."

Two DAYS after Dad's burial, Mom and I walked down to the bank. It sat adjacent to Neighbor's Department Store, and from Gertie's father's office window, we could see the trains approaching the depot. Mr. Harris showed us what was in Mother and Dad's savings and assured us Dad had done well enough for himself and that like most people in town, we had no debt. We didn't buy things we couldn't pay for in cash.

"You'll be fine, Myrtle," Mr. Harris told us as he looked down at the ledger that covered most of his small desk. "Maxine is twelve?"

"Yes, seventh grade."

"She'll be able to work in a few years if necessary and could help you?" he asked.

"We are so down about Bud. He was a friend to everyone. Has the county found anyone to replace him?"

"I think they have found someone to fill in," I told him. "We thought Dad would be tickled if he knew they couldn't find another coroner to tend to him."

"Oh, he sure would've been."

Mother chuckled. She was only in her forties and had a lot of years of living alone ahead of her. She'd never remarry.

We all sat quietly, each thinking in coeval ways that both tendered our hearts and totally detonated them.

* * *

MOTHER and I sat on the porch swing, and Maxine was on the step twirling her hair when Uncle Joe, Mother's brother-in-law, wandered across the dirt road. He always gave us sound advice. He sat down in the wooden rocking chair and swayed for moments before any of us spoke.

Uncle Joe smiled as we talked. He only touched on piffling things —what had to be done about this and that—but I thought I saw tears pooling when he described how things would be now.

"We don't know what's going to happen with Wall Street. A crash could be coming. We all just better keep our money with Harris up here at the bank."

He looked at me. "We know how you love school, but this might be the time to be home near your family."

Since Dad's funeral, I'd settled on one thing about him. He was my best friend and irreplaceable.

I had one year of fun, I thought. Maybe that was as much as I was entitled to.

* * *

I DIDN'T RETURN to SINU for the Fall '27 term. The primary school that sat on the hill a few blocks from our church needed a woman to teach second grade. A family from Calvin, a tiny village of fifty that sat north of town, had moved into Crossville with their slew of children. Velma Johnson would now teach third grade, and I would take second.

I thought I could finish SINU when Maxine was out of high school, and I guess I was a little flattered that they wanted me up at the school.

Kent and I were too young to even know we were supposed to be making decisions about the future. We planned to see each other once a month. When Dad died, Kent called the house to offer his sympathies. He didn't think his supervisor at the library would grant him two days off, so I told him to forget about coming to the viewing. I knew he was thinking of us. I didn't ask Mother whether it would be all right if I visited Kent at school. I just told her I was going.

On the last weekend before I started my job at Bell School, Uncle Joe took Kent and I to one of the last Cardinals games of the season. We were dying to see The Babe again. I planned to stay for the weekend, but Uncle Joe needed to leave Saturday after the game. He didn't want to leave Aunt Sarah overnight.

The Babe hit his sixtieth home run of the season that Saturday. The Yanks walloped us, but it didn't matter so much—we were still The World Champions of '26. I remembered the article I read in Shanklin's parlor on my first morning in Carbondale—"My Friend, the Babe"—and so I cheered for him. I thought my booing might hurt his feelings.

I told Kent and Uncle Joe all about what I'd read, that the world's most famous baseball player became deeply depressed when he disappointed fans. Kent thought the Yanks were behind the article because they were getting worried his drunken outbursts might start affecting ticket sales.

"I like your beau," Uncle Joe told me after the game and gave me a little wink.

For supper, Saturday evening, we went to a wonderful little soda fountain and drugstore called Katz's. While we sat at the counter, Aunt Jen pointed out a boy working.

"He's from Grayville. Can you believe it?" she said. "His mother was a Sturm and grew up in Crossville."

As the boy passed behind us, hurrying with dirty ice cream dishes and soda glasses, Aunt Jen stopped him and introduced him to our group. We talked for a minute about his job in St. Louis and how frequently he went back to Grayville. He explained he'd be driving back to Illinois the next morning.

He barely made eye contact when he talked to us. I couldn't tell if he was busy, shy, or just unfriendly.

"Do any of you need a ride?" the boy asked. I saw his name tag: Alvin Stein.

"Faire was going on the train, but you could just ride with him, Faire," Aunt Jen suggested enthusiastically. It was as if she'd solved a world problem.

Not wanting to be ungrateful, I agreed, and then I regretted it immediately.

When Alvin walked away, Kent looked at me cross-eyed, and I fell over laughing.

"Why would I pass over someone like you?" I shoved him in the arm of his jacket.

And that's how my married life and motherhood began. Alvin Stein was an accident of my geography.

Chapter 11

I've Never Been Much for Romance

By 2019, I'd accepted I'd never know what happened to Kent when he and Gram parted in 1927. Gram and Grandad were married on June 22, 1930, in a "surprise" wedding.

I ordered a copy of their marriage certificate. It all checked out. The dates on the license matched the announcement sent out by the family.

Gram wasn't pregnant. The dates don't match her children's birthdates. Maybe she feared she was. If Gram actually picked him out . . . actually thought Alvin was a good choice for a partner, I'd have to blame her for some of Mom's trauma, and that was hard for me. Upon their marriage, Gram became unwittingly indentured to a life that would turn out to be a histrionic obstacle course.

Before and after Gram's wedding, everyone in our family had been married at the Crossville United Methodist Church. In all those years, in all those hours of conversation, why in the hell didn't I ever ask Gram the simple question of "Why a wedding announcement, and why in Albion?"

MISS FAIRE DELAIN WAS WED AT ALBION

Popular Crossville Girl Was Wed to Mr. Alvin Stein, of St. Louis, in Quiet Ceremony.

Friends were surprised to learn of the wedding of Miss Faire DeLain to Mr. Alvin Stein, of St. Louis, which took place at Albion Sunday evening at seven o'clock. The couple were accompanied by Miss Nola Puntney and Frank Nicholaus. The ceremony was performed by Rev. Davidson, M. E. minister.

The bride is the popular daughter of Mr. and Mrs. O. P. DeLain and has been employed as teacher in the grade school here for the past three years.

The groom is the son of Mr. and Mrs. Ed Stein, of Grayville and is employed in a drug store in St. Louis where he has been the past three years.

After the wedding Mr. and Mrs. Stein motored to St. Louis where they will make their home.

Their many friends extend their congratulations.

It made no sense.

In Gram's twilight years, I sat by her chair for many hours in conversation about the old days. I didn't think to be more specific in my questioning. We spoke very little about her wedding to my grandfather, and their anniversary was never marked at all. They didn't exchange cards or pleasantries.

Gram wouldn't have wanted a big wedding to-do and probably wouldn't have wanted to walk down the aisle as everyone gawked at her. She certainly wouldn't have wanted some frilly dress. That made sense.

Was Gram attracted to the bad boy image? Alvin was handsome enough, seemed to be ambitious, enterprising, like Gram. Did they have some romantic date, where they talked about opening a motel and a filling station, and Gram found that intriguing? I didn't know how those plans had developed.

Ahead of her time in every way, when *Black Like Me* was published in 1961, Gram read it with fervor. No one I knew, or at least no one my age, had a grandmother who owned a copy. When Alvin was off here or there, she got away with renting motel rooms to Black men and women passing through Crossville. She scoffed at the Sundown Law, knowing she could sweet talk local cops into forgiving her.

Gram expected me to treat all people fairly, regardless of race or status. I hope I have been able to carry that legacy forward.

"Teacher" was a significant aspect of Gram's identity. She pretended to be incensed when a cousin who ran for the Illinois State Superintendent of Schools was "stumping" around the state and made a speech mentioning all the teachers who'd inspired him along the way but failed to mention Gram. She never forgot it and sent Don a five-page poem written in the rural dialect our whole family loved to mock. After two pages of letting him know how excited she was to read his speech, and how she'd rushed through her day to get to it, she hit the punch line:

He reminisced a bit about how it used to be,
When he didn't have his learnin' and wasn't Don Prince, PhD.
Then he talked about school teaching, and he said right off the bat
That he started in White County and how proud he was of that.

He said to all those teachers, "I'll bet you've got a yen
To hear about my kinfolks who were teachers way back when."
I got that excited, 'cause I knew right then and there,
He was gonna tell those teachers about his Cousin Faire.

But Don had no such thing in mind as I was soon to see.
Kinfolks by the score he named, but he didn't mention me.
There's just no word at my command to measure my despair.
I realized Cousin Don now claimed no kin to Cousin Faire.

On and on, Gram's poem went about how Don had broken her heart.

In-between her dressing-down of the refs at Crossville Tiger ballgames and raising three girls, Gram came home one day to find Alvin in the bathroom.

For all the things she kept to her vest over the years, the affliction Alvin came home with that day wasn't one of them. Something about that bathroom itself, that even by the time I came along thirty years later, still reminded her of the humiliation and disgust of that day.

Of course, Alvin was unable to cope with shaving himself and applying the medication for "crabs," so Gram had the "privilege" of helping him. Then she had the privilege of scrubbing the bathroom with bleach–likely scrubbing many more times and probably in the middle of the night when she couldn't sleep.

I don't actually know if he forced her to help him. I can't imagine she would've been bullied into that low of a deed. She honestly laughed at the absurdity of her husband's behavior. She said in a 1949 letter, "I've never been much for romance."

Gram's love life was doomed from the moment she met Grandad, so she adapted and made a life for herself outside of romance. Gram thought progressively on many topics, but for each of her daughters, she set her sights on a potential mate and negotiated the marriage herself.

After Mom, she worried about Alvin's effects on her other two girls and ushered them out of the house ASAP.

Another unanswerable question because I guess I never wondered enough to ask it while she was alive.

Evidence of Gram's total independence and adventurous spirit were the many trips she took by herself, via train and bus, across the country to see her girls and their oil-rigging husbands.

In January of 1959, after Aunt Rita gave Gram her second grand-child, Steven, she set out for Liberal, Kansas, in the southwest part of the state.

America was four years into the Vietnam conflict.

Once in Liberal, she wrote to let everyone know she'd arrived and she described it with her colorful, self-deprecating style.

```
Left Albion on the bus Saturday afternoon at
3:10 p.m. When most everyone left the bus
for a cup of coffee, I grabbed a seat and
made my first mistake—offered to share my
seat with a man.

    I was just being nice, but he apparently
mistook my intentions. I almost got a
boyfriend. Anyhow, it's too long a story to
tell here.

    Arrived in St. Louis at 7:30 p.m. Union
Station was so full of soldiers, I thought
war must've been declared. There were at
least 1200 of them. I ate supper with a
little fourteen-year-old Negro girl and a
college student going back to school at
```

Oklahoma. We killed time together until my train left.

We arrived in KC at 8:00 a.m. Sunday. My train was to leave at 11:35 a.m. At 4:30 p.m., just eight hours late, we boarded our train.

In the car where they put us, the floor was covered with melted snow. No heat. No kidding, it was so cold you could see your breath. I had on two sweaters under my coat, plus galoshes and gloves, and I still shivered.

About 8:30 or 9:00 p.m., they brought box lunches and hot coffee which helped, and then, a water pipe broke, and there was a mad scramble to get bags and feet off the floor.

Eventually, the very handsome brakeman moved me and two or three poor, old, cold women to a place in the very last car. At 3:30 a.m., we reached Liberal. It was fifteen below zero with twelve inches of snow on the ground, but a Good Samaritan was there. A man brought me to Ruthie and Gene's trailer, which I could only identify by the scaffold they told me to look for.

So, now I'm here, and we've just made a flying trip to the hospital, but it was a false alarm. Ruthie is very uncomfortable, but the doctor says it will likely be another twenty-four hours.

That's all from Liberal. I'll let you know when the little one makes his/her appearance.

Chapter 12

A Free Flow of Tears

February 2019

S uicide attempts are significantly higher among adults who have experienced trauma. Events occurring during development can have profound and lasting impact on the brain. A large body of research describes the effect of psychological trauma on children and the severity of the mental and substance abuse disorders that increase suicide risk. Secondly, childhood trauma has emerged as a strong and independent risk factor for suicidal behavior in adolescents and adults.[1]

Simply put, childhood trauma has been shown to have a causal role in depression, PTSD, eating disorders, substance abuse, and dissociative disorders. Not only does childhood trauma lead to increased risk of depression in adulthood, it can affect antidepressant treatment response in adults with major depression.[2]

Yet, every child is different.

Mom's sisters were less affected by Alvin. When I asked Aunt Rita about how Alvin affected her, she said, "I just stayed out of his way. Your mom fought back."

* * *

Life in St. Louis slowed down for me after Christmas 2019, and I talked to my friend Carol who was still assisting me, about making the trip to Anna. I hadn't yet filed the paperwork for the court order I needed to obtain Mom's records.

Documents chronicling Mom's medical history would be a hard pill to swallow. Joke intended. Even if what we received was just a series of index cards with dates of admissions and releases, it could be an indicator of the magnitude of her illness. It could devastate me.

I had to get over my trepidation. Knowing Mom's state of mind in her sickest years would only help me in achieving my goal and answering the real question that was propelling me. How did she die?

Doug was regularly on my mind. I recalled Gram's stories about how difficult his childhood was and how he was once kidnapped by one of mom's loser boyfriends.

* * *

1960: Anna State Hospital Records

MEDICAL HISTORY: Patient is a twenty-nine-year-old, white female from Carmi, Illinois. She was brought to the hospital by the Deputy Sheriff of White County. She was admitted on Certificate of Physician.

She was transferred from Carmi Hospital where she had been unconscious for twenty-four hours following her third suicide attempt. The patient was found in the bathtub by her eleven-year-old son, Douglas Meyers and her mother, Mrs. Stein. The patient had slit her wrists.

In previous hospitalizations, the patient has received electro-shock treatments as well as insulin shock treatments. She has been on heavy medication for several years, sometimes taking as many as fifty aspirin a day. According to her mother, she has been taking Nardil, Valium, and Darvon. The patient quit taking her medication on her own accord two or three weeks ago.

PERSONAL HISTORY (from informant Mrs. Faire Stein, patient's mother): The patient married John Meyers when she was seventeen.

Informant states the patient has a great deal of musical ability, likely a prodigy, playing drums, oboe, flute, and piano, but according to the informant, she has not cultivated this talent.

Mrs. Stein reported the patient threatened to leave her husband, Mr. Meyers, on multiple occasions. Mrs. Stein said the reason for their problems was the patient's unwillingness to accept the responsibility of housekeeping and caring for her child. The patient's husband told her that he would not give her custody of their child and she did not secure a divorce for this reason.

In 1958, the patient's husband was killed in an automobile accident. He had a sizable amount of insurance and the patient was financially secure after his death. She lived off of her stock dividends.

After her husband's death, Mrs. Stein, the informant, reported the patient had several boyfriends. In January of this year, 1960, the patient began dating Mr. Pete Maddon. They fight constantly, but despite this, the child is already calling Mr. Maddon "Dad."

The couple were engaged after only three weeks, but the informant hopes they will not go through with the marriage. The informant, Mrs. Stein, stated that Mr. Maddon is not a good provider and does not treat the patient's son, Douglas, kindly.

Recently during one of the patient's difficult periods, Mr. Maddon took the boy to Oklahoma where he left him with his parents. He had neither the permission of the patient nor of the boy's grandmother, the informant, Mrs. Stein. The informant, Mrs. Stein, says the child is very homesick and has no money to buy his lunch at school. The informant began to cry when she discussed the boy.

MENTAL EXAMINATION: For years, this unhappy and probably self-centered woman has been going from one to another depression. When she was made aware that she may eventually incapacitate herself seriously, she appeared surprised and soon reacted with a free flow of tears. Resentment toward her father was noted and discussed. No paranoid or psychotic ideas were detected during this interview.

1960: Douglas, 10, to Mom in Anna State Hospital

Dear Mom,

Dad called last night and told us what happened. I'm sorry you are sick. I'm getting homesick. I miss you. Grandmother Maddon said we might have to move to another house to get away from Gram Stein. Am I going to stay here?

This school is not as good as my old school. I don't know anyone. I don't know what to say when they ask why I came to this school in the middle of the year. Mikey Stinton asked me why I was in Oklahoma if I was from Illinois, and he said probably nobody wants you. I've had a hard time keeping track of my money.

Aunt Rita came to see me Sunday. They are going to Crossville soon. I thought if you were out in time, I would ride home with them. Please tell Dad to send me my lunch money and weekly allowance. I think you'll be happy if you marry Pete.

Your Loving Son,
Doug Meyers

Chapter 13

Daddy, Daddy

1960: Diary of Mary Ellen, 29, Anna State Hospital

Mother is right. Being away from me is unsettling Doug. She gives me the same advice each time I falter. "Snap out of it!"

Two days after Johnny died, Mom wanted me to send Doug back to school. She was constantly advising me. "You've got to get out of bed and get Doug to school. Laying around all day isn't good for either of you. This is an awful thing. You don't deserve this, but you weren't exactly smitten with Johnny those last few months."

She kept going. "He wasn't coming home on weekends. He told me how you were acting. Staying away was better than coming home to a wife who didn't want him around."

"Johnny treated me like a child. He thought I needed to be supervised. Like you do. The two of you trying to fix me — make me domesticated, trying to settle me down. I'm sorry that house-work isn't what interests me."

"Other men are what interests you. You just couldn't be content. Johnny had his share of opportunities, I'm sure. Any of your girlfriends would've married Johnny in a heartbeat. But you were all he wanted."

And then she stopped before she got in a last good blow. "I really wonder if his accident was intentional."

A long pause followed.

"That farmer admitted he hit him, Mother! Johnny and I were doing fine. We were working it out. You saw the Kansas pictures. Didn't he look happy?"

"Yes. He did. Because you were coming around showing interest. Is Pete ready to take care of a family? He won't treat Doug like he's his own."

"You may be right, Mother, but I can't raise Doug by myself. He needs a father figure, and I get lonely."

The night Douglas found me in the bathtub, Pete had run out on me. I was pressuring him about marriage. Douglas was at Boy Scouts, so I went on one of my binges. It's always bad when I'm alone for long. Johnny's been gone a year, and no one comes by anymore.

COURT HOUSE NEWS
MARRIAGE LICENSES, 1960
E. N. MADDON, JR., CARMI..........28
MARY ELLEN MEYERS, CARMI....28

* * *

COURT HOUSE NEWS
DISSOLUTION OF MARRIAGES, 1963
E.N. MADDON, JR., CARMI...........31
MARY ELLEN MEYERS, CARMI......31

* * *

Mom and Joe Kovacs, 1967

Kovacs, Maddon Wedding

Mr. and Mrs. Alvin Stein announce the marriage of their daughter, Mary Ellen to Joe Kovacs.

The couple was married at the United Methodist Church in Crossville, and a reception was held in the basement following the nuptials.

The bride wore a short, modern dress and a white adornment on her head. The groom wore a tailored black suit.

IN THE CIRCUIT COURT OF THE SECOND JUDICIAL CIRCUIT
WHITE COUNTY, ILLINOIS

FILED

MAY 26 1967

William F. Sharp
CLERK OF THE CIRCUIT COURT

MARY ELLEN KOVACS,

    Plaintiff,

-VS-

                      NO. 67-04-41

JOZSEF P. KOVACS,

    Defendant.

FILED

4. That since the date of the marriage, without justification or cause, Defendant has been guilty of cruelty toward the Plaintiff, in that he has struck, hit and pushed Plaintiff causing her physical pain and injury; That Defendant has frequent fits of anger, degrades, insults and curses Plaintiff and makes outbursts and threats against her, all without any cause whatsoever.

WHEREFORE, Plaintiff Prays:

(1) That the marriage between the plaintiff and defendant may be dissolved, and a decree of divorce from the bonds of matrimony be entered herein, according to the Statutes of the State of Illinois in such case made and provided.

Mom at Christmas

Chapter 14

Hope You Get Out Tomorrow

January 2019

Valium is the most prescribed drug in history. As it reached widespread popularity in the sixties, the FDA encouraged testing. Experiments on animals showed that the sedative, my mom's go-to tranquilizer, caused animals to lose interest in caring for their young.

I HoeP You Get WellSoon
HaWORYOU MUhtYt
IHoePYouGet Outto
Mora.
Dir Doulas

Through time and conversations with family, I started to recognize Mom was likely "nervous" and taking sedatives before Johnny died. One crucial letter of Doug's was on my mind. It showed me that Mom was seemingly hospitalized when Doug was so young that he was barely able to use a pencil. One of the first sentences he could write was "get well soon."

Valium was a benzodiazepine drug that was invented and marketed by Hoffman-La Roche Laboratories beginning in 1963. In a decade that was far from sedate, the government was becoming worried about the widespread use of marijuana and LSD by teenagers and college students. To cope, Mothers around the U.S. were taking Valium to manage their stress, and in 1966, "Mother's Little Helper" by The Rolling Stones, reached number eight on the billboard charts. By 1962, over 2,000 doctors and 20,000 Americans were taking Valium, including President John F. Kennedy.[1]

The push for "bennies" started in the fifties when two thousand drugs in the benzodiazepine family were discovered as a remedy for anxiety. A group of these drugs was first tested on animals at the Boston and San Diego Zoos, and when administered to hostile and aggressive monkeys, another sedative, Librium, caused them to act more docile and tame. Benzodiazepines bind to specific receptors to strengthen the effect of an amino acid called gamma-aminobutyric acid (GABA) in nerve cells. This reduces the turnover of other neurotransmitters, therefore depressing the central nervous system. The dampening of the nervous system reduces anxiety and causes muscles to relax. This leads to sedation, reduced cognition and motor function, and sleep.[2]

I heard a story from a friend who worked in what we now call behavioral health about an elderly patient who was admitted to a local hospital when she wasn't able to take enough Valium to ease her anxiety. She was prescribed Valium as a young woman and had been taking it for decades. The only remedy was to send her home with a Valium pump, which would keep her at a level needed to prevent withdrawal. There was no hope of weaning her off, given her age and fragile condition.

When Valium is discontinued, users can experience severe withdrawal symptoms, such as seizures and psychotic reactions.

* * *

I RELIED on Mom's letters to map out her life throughout the sixties. I knew some about husbands two and three from Gram's chronicles.

Pete Maddon, despite Doug's hoping he would make Mom happy, was "lazy," which Gram no doubt viewed as the worst kind of awful.

Number three, Joe Kovacs, was Hungarian, and everyone suspected he married Mom as a way to gain citizenship. A bright spot was when Joe's father visited from Hungary, and he taught Mom to make *real* goulash, which I recalled being luscious. Gram felt Joe was mean to Mom and probably witnessed the abuse indicated in the divorce decree.

Husband number five was my own father who she met in 1968, at Anna where he was being treated for alcoholism.

When I imagined male and female patients mingling freely, I had a visceral reaction. It made me uneasy, but my friends in mental health enlightened me, asking, "Would you hold cancer patients of different sexes quarantined and away from vital socialization?"

There were many moments that made me realize how ignorant we *all* are about mental illness, even me. Socialization is one thing, but Mom and Dad were doing more than socializing.

In the evenings, Mom wrote letters to Dad. I was thankful for them. It was the only time I felt like she was *real*. She didn't paint herself as healed or fine, as she had in other letters. She was completely vulnerable, laying out her addiction to tranquilizers, and revealing what a deeply loving and fatally insecure woman she was.

If I leave and you stay, I will be scared, yes, and very sad, because I need you so very much. I will probably wish I had a tranquilizer as I do right this minute, but if I were in there in bed with you, I don't think I'd feel this way at all.

Does it frighten you, me saying that I wish I had one pill, or two pills, or three pills? Or whatever it would take to calm me down?

I'D ALWAYS BEEN ready with snarky verbiage about my parents' relationship. It was how I coped with my abandonment.

"They met when they were both in treatment for addiction. Having a kid . . . good idea, right? I mean, they couldn't take care of the kids they already had. My mom had Doug, who was eighteen, and she'd already been married three times. My dad had been married twice, and had Mark and Robin who were teenagers. It wasn't a good match."

I was judgy—really judgy. It was easier to be sarcastic than to suddenly fall into the lugubrious abyss of my past. There was probably a name for my behavior.

I read Mom's love letters to Dad and didn't want to make fun of them anymore. Whether it was healthy or not, she loved him very much.

The letters and poems Mom and Dad exchanged while they were immured illuminated them for me in their raw states. I was getting information first hand and not in the hand-me-down way I'd learned other things from Gram.

"Your dad was very good looking," Gram would tell me, or she would say, "You have Davis hands. Big! And good for the piano. I wish you'd play."

Gram hinted, "Your dad's father didn't treat him very well. They spoiled him with money but didn't pay any attention to him."

She hinted that Dad's arrested development had a lot to do with his drinking, yes, but also being born to an ambitious man with deep pockets didn't help Dad either. My grandfather apparently had no idea what to do with a child.

From Mom and Dad's rooms, in their late-night loneliness, they exchanged lengthy epistles. It was painfully evident how desperately she needed to be loved.

10:30 p.m.

Dear Bob,

It seems I had almost forgotten there is a Man Upstairs until tonight. You've heard me say I doubted the Virgin birth; but the existence of some sort of God I do not doubt, for in the past I have known the peace and tranquility that comes with having faith in Him.

Tonight I feel so small, so inadequate, so helpless because I have let you down. I am praying desperately that He will help you and show me how to help you. And, at the same time, I'm wondering why the heck He should listen to me when I've ignored Him for so long.

Even though I've experienced the same fears and anxieties you feel, it's still difficult for me to realize you're this way, too. You see, to me you aren't an alcoholic who has degraded himself and his family for many years and lost all self-respect. To me, you are a man I've grown to respect, admire, and love.

Also, my dear, you're the someone I've learned to depend on. I really don't know how I'm going to manage when you're gone. Bob, I don't even feel complete when you're not around. You are my whole world, you know.

Now, I asked myself, "How can a man who is all these things to me, when I entered this place wanting to die - how can a man who had made me want to live again feel so inferior and unsure of himself?"

If I were leaving and you were staying, I would be scared, yes, and very upset and sad, because I need you so very much. I would

169

probably wish I had a tranquilizer. Oh, please, honey, let's spend Friday and Saturday in x-ray - all day!

If you would take me in your arms and hold me tight and reassure me that everything was gonna be all right; you know I can do it and that soon we'd be together, and that together, we could and would lick these problems of ours; tell me how much you loved me; this is what I would need from you. On this, I believe I could make it for a while, no matter what. And if I didn't have this reassurance and encouragement from you, and plenty of it, I hate to say what might happen. It's frightening to be that dependent on someone else, but that's just the way it is with me.

Now, how about you? What is it you want and need from me? I'm gonna have to find out more about this thing called alcoholism. I know so little and want to know so much.

Well, darling, it's late, late, my eyes burn, and I'm exhausted. Hope to God you wake up feeling better about the whole thing.

How I love you!
Your Girl

P.S. I'm going to try my best to reestablish contact with The Man Upstairs.

Love,
Ellen

Mom's tenderness toward Dad melted me. The warmth they found in each other was probably monumental relief from the reality of their lives. The euphoria of pills and alcohol was replaced by the thrill of being in love. He responded to her letters by copying parts of his favorite poems and Bible passages.

Who was I to mock them or declare that their love was fleeting? I couldn't relate to the pain and failure of addiction at that time, and what kind of neediness it meted out. I'll never know what the letdown was or how Mom had disappointed Dad. What exasperated me was that he was her "whole world."

It was this pattern of Mom's that outraged Gram. Gram was able to put love aside and raise her children, which she did quietly, without bravado. That's what she wanted Mom to do. Children need their caregivers to be reliable, and Mom wasn't. She was just too sick.

What about eighteen-year-old Doug who was living with Gram as Mom was writing love letters to my dad? Doug's basic needs were being met by Gram, but the stress of a teenage boy in the same house as Alvin must've been tumultuous. In spite of that supposition, Doug looked "normal" in the pictures, and he still went to prom that year.

Doug, High School Prom

Energy my parents should've spent working through the demons at the heart of their addictions was spent getting it on in X-ray? Rather than focusing on her own reliance on pills, she wanted to learn about the pernicious effects of his disease called alcoholism.

Imagine the super Tweets to the universe that would come out today if some embedded reporter discovered patients were getting it on in X-ray. It was shocking. The mingling was one thing, but how could *that* happen? Mom and Dad were not only getting it on, they were making plans . . . trying to anyway. Mom surely spent hours writing this epic poem to Dad following a major blowout between them.

Davis Does It Again
By Mary Ellen

We were sitting at the table, nonchalantly as could be,
When all of a sudden, he said to me,
"When you gonna get married? Leave this place!"
It was then that my heart began to race.

I thought it might be too presumptuous of me
To assume he might be thinking of we.
So, I really played it cool and endeavored to don
An innocent expression, then,"To whom, hon?"

He went right along with the game you see
As he answered my question with,"Who do you think? Me!"
It seems my fork was suspended with food,
But for some silly reason it didn't taste that good.

Can we make the adjustment successfully
To society from the "penitentiary"?
Will he want me to work or just keep house
And care for him like a loving spouse?

I thought and thought about it, you see.
He finally left, giving up on me.
The poor fellow was waiting for an answer, you know.
You've finally made your decision, now, go!
Off to the smoking room I ran.

Where the H- - - is that man?

Still no Bob.
He's playing hard to get.
Scanned the grounds again.
Aha! Success!

Lying on a bench, relaxed as can be,
How dare him pay no attention to me.
Crept up behind him and kissed the sap,
Then cradled his sweet head right in my lap.

"When you wanna get married and leave this place?"
I fully expected a smile on his face.
But in its stead, he fixed me but good.
"Just forget it," he said. "I'm outta the mood."

Chapter 15

Beverly, Mace

February 2019

After surviving breast cancer, a friend said to me, "Your lady parts hate you."

No kidding, I thought. Maybe I should've been a boy without lady parts. Possibly, my parents might've named me something that didn't cause me the kind of attention I'd always received for being named Kandi. It was never the right kind of attention, usually sexual in nature.

I was scheduled for my fourth surgery to remove suspected endometriosis and ended up at Missouri Baptist Hospital for three days. It was the week of the coldest temps in the Midwest in years. In Chicago, thermometers were reading negative twenty-six degrees. The week before we'd had a foot of snowfall, rare in St. Louis, and it looked like more of the white stuff was about to fall. It was ten degrees.

My hospital roommate was Beverly, a seventy-year-old, grey-headed, saint of a woman whom I immediately adored. Kevin, the tech, gingerly navigated the dwarf-sized room, making his way to the substantial window; at least, we had the window. A glare from the white sky was bouncing off Kevin's shaved head. He looked like a Crossfitter.

He pointed out the shape of our beloved Gateway Arch, which we could barely see through the snows-a-comin' sky. The Arch was closed because of a recent government shutdown.

Beverly and I quickly became "we."

"We are going to watch the football game tonight even though 'we' aren't that into it."

Beverly was the best roomie any unwell person could wish for. We relished talking to each other through the curtain. She was kind and worried about the pain I was in, as I moaned at 2 a.m., and I was genuinely worried about her. She was having her first dialysis treatment.

Even when Beverly complained about being unable to drive, she did it with thanksgiving. She told me she hadn't really had any health problems of significance and reassured me the dialysis was just a little thing she had to do.

When Beverly was sleeping or I tired of *The Golden Girls*, I listened to a self-contained book-on-tape from the library that my thoughtful friend Jane dropped off. Jane watched every Hallmark Christmas movie twice, so I feared these books would be, well, corny. But I had to try. Jane was just as concerned and thoughtful as Beverly and had gone out of her way to bring them to the hospital.

Later, as I lay on my side, staring at the Arch and listening to Jane's bestowal, I began to wonder how narrators for audio books are chosen. Were there auditions? Would I get a vote on who narrated if this manuscript ever saw the light of day? A few chapters in, I wondered why they didn't just get a man to read the male parts? Not that I wanted to take a job op away from a sister, but I could hardly keep from busting out. The reader had a lovely voice, perfect for the thirty- and forty-year-old female characters; but when she read for the husband, it sounded ridiculous. The characters weren't much better. "Here, baby, let me do it."

I just thought, *please, God, tell me my characters have something better to say.*

Beverly and I didn't get below the surface when we talked family, which was great for me. My family's story, if I told the whole truth, would be too much on a dreary afternoon.

Beverly was on the phone several times a day to her son and step-daughter trying to negotiate her ride from the hospital. We were being released on the same day, over a week after she'd been admitted. Beverly first had to have a biopsy, which had been rescheduled from two days earlier.

When I heard "biopsy," I thought maybe she had been downplaying her condition.

Poor Beverly was NPO the night before the biopsy, and guilt panged me as I enjoyed a dismal cafeteria grilled cheese. I knew she smelled it through the curtain.

When they finally came to get Beverly for the biopsy, it took fifteen minutes to maneuver her bed out of the room. Lisa and I had crowded up our side with a tray full of creature comforts—Apple TV, Starbucks cups, and so on. But agile Kevin got it done, and I said bye to her as he wheeled her past me. I wished Beverly the best of luck.

"I hope you don't have to take the bus to dialysis! Good luck!"

I did plenty of thinking about how a few days in the hospital can seem like forever. I pondered what months in an institution would feel like for Mom, and I conjured up scenes whereby she made and lost friends.

How attached I'd become to Beverly after only a few days. Did Mom stay in touch with her people? I bet she always wondered where they had gone and if they had gotten better.

My attitude toward the mystery hadn't changed. I could neither imagine Mom stabbing herself to death nor could I fathom Doug doing it.

Did Mom take a big dip after I was born? Did the stress of motherhood send her over the edge she'd been balancing on for years? By that winter, I was opening up about the book. Every person I told said, "It seems impossible. I just can't imagine someone picking that as the means of suicide."

I still agreed. Suicide by stabbing wasn't even listed in statistics except for the 7.8 percent of suicides counted in the category of "other means."[1]

* * *

AUNT RITA HAD BEEN TELLING me for months that she had some of Gram's things she thought I would want, and I presumed it was pictures. Lisa would love the idea of more photos. Ha! We already had boxes and boxes from my family.

But I loved that about us; we truly did keep everything that had any scintilla of meaning. For our spouses, the amount of space our stuff required was shocking.

Aunt Rita stopped in St. Louis for a quick visit on her way back from a weekend in Crossville, where she'd attended the alumni banquet. At least some of our family still showed up every year. At eighty-two, Aunt Rita was remarkably fit and still driving cross-country.

After she arrived and got her stuff organized in the basement guest bedroom, Aunt Rita brought up a small stack of notebooks. "I thought you might want these."

Maybe writing this book was something Aunt Rita would never understand, no matter how I explained it to her. She'd already expressed, "Gram wouldn't want you asking these questions."

But, Gram also wouldn't have wanted information to be withheld from me. She would've answered any question–if only I had asked. I missed the closeness Gram and I shared. My friends were from loving families, and yet I'm not sure any of them had a parent as devoted as Gram was to me.

Maybe Aunt Rita had a different kind of relationship with Gram. Mom took all of Gram's attention, and after Mom died, *I* took all of

Gram's attention. Understandably, Aunt Rita and Aunt Helen may have felt slighted.

When Rita headed downstairs for more of her unpacking process, I trounced on the notebooks. It was a parade of objects I hadn't seen in decades.

A familiar, faded, maroon ledger was recognizable immediately; it was an epochal item that sat on the Stein Motel registration desk. Gram logged all income from the motel and our two tiny, white rental houses. For fifty-two years, she kept track of these transactions right up until they fell into disrepair and were torn down in 1992.

The first entry was 1940. Ted McMahon paid $48 for two months' rent.

The next item in Aunt Rita's stack of stuff was a blue, spiral-bound notebook in which Gram copied down inspirational quotes and poems.

My favorite: I lose no sleep thinking about my physical condition, but can toss around all night thinking about the ball club. I can do nothing about my physical condition, so the ball club is my sole responsibility.

— Author Unknown

There's a big difference between worrying and thinking. You worry about what might happen. You think to keep it from happening.

— Fred Hutchinson

"I'll lend you for a little time a child of Mine," he said.
   "For you to love while he lives and mourn for when he's dead.
   It may be six or seven years or twenty-two or three.
   But, will you, till I call him back, take care of him for me?"

— Edgar Guest

That poem entitled "Understanding" by Edgar Guest had to be from someone who gave it to her. The first lines were devastatingly hard to read.

Did Carol Sheldon give this to Gram? She'd lost her daughter Susan to leukemia; I struggled to remember the name of another Crossville girl who died. Cancer again. I could recall her image on a tombstone at Stokes' Chapel Cemetery. She was a beautiful teenager with long, dark hair.

The last notebook from Aunt Rita sat on our aluminum topped breakfast table. A smaller, washed-out, red notebook.

In preparation for her death, Gram had reviewed with me every method of record keeping she had stored around our house, but I recalled seeing this notebook only once after her death. I wanted to ask about it in the moment, but it didn't seem like the time. Our family had a lifetime of things to sort through, so I just didn't ask.

The first several pages were blank, then at the top of the fifth page Gram wrote, "Girls' Families." She recorded her methods of travel, including every bus and/or train leg, for every trip she made. There were abbreviations I didn't understand having to do with bus lines or train routes.

Inside Gram's record notebook of travel on the bus

There was little travel noted in the seventies. Gram was home watching out for me. Later entries were simpler. Doug and his wife Celia took me to Six Flags in 1980, when I was eleven and to Busch

Gardens in Florida in 1981. Doug showed me there was a world beyond Crossville, and those trips were exciting beyond imagination.

Gram just couldn't help but write things down.

I've never wasted a brain cell wondering about whether we, the entire family, had OCD, because we showed all the signs.

At the top of the first page that followed a manila divider was written "M.E. and Kandi." The first entry was from 1971. It was an account of my life with Mom.

* * *

IN THE EARLY SEVENTIES, Mom purchased a snazzy, grass-green trailer with white stripes. It was modern and smartly decorated. I'd busy myself on the new, red shag carpet while Mom practiced the piano. Mom took a job working as a cocktail waitress and entertainer for my dad's father, L.E. Davis, at a Ramada Inn he owned, so we moved to a nice trailer court in Mt. Vernon, Illinois. Once in Mt. Vernon, an hour from Crossville, Mom struggled to handle me by herself and make a living for us.

1971   m. E . k.
Oct. 1- m. E. went to Benton to work- K. here
Nov. 12- Moved to Mt. V. in Jvasler-Working Mtu
Dec. 4- Took k. to mt. v.
Dec. 17- She called- we went for k.
Dec. 24-25- m. E. here. Took k.   65 days
Dec.29- Doug- Penny brot. k. back.

M.E. is Mary Ellen; K is Kandi; Mt. V is Mount Vernon;

Each dated line-item was a Mom-related event Gram had memorialized. Hospitalizations, fights, notes on Mom's moods and behaviors. Between October 1 and December 29, I was away from my mother sixty-five of sixty-nine days. Gram counted the days and made a tiny note. Doug and his then girlfriend Penny apparently picked me up on December 29. I wondered if Mom had a date with some man she barely knew for New Year's Eve and called Crossville asking Gram to come and get the toddler who was cramping her style.

I remembered the men she barely knew.

The overmuch of activity recorded on those pages shocked me. So much back and forth for me in 1971.

Aug. 10: M.E. & K ret. C'ville—Mary Ellen & Kandi return to Crossville

Who was Big Jim?

It astonished me that, in a few instances, I saw Alvin's (A.G.) name. I couldn't figure out how Gram sandbagged him into helping. I knew he wasn't completely without obligation to his children, but he rarely availed himself.

So many thoughts entered my mind—I envisaged what it was like for Mom to have Alvin coming to the rescue when she was on her knees, suicidal.

I knew what it was like to cry in front of Alvin. For him, a crying woman was an opportunity to further defeat someone.

When I was a young girl, I would break down after his cruel outbursts, and he would tell me, "You're just like your mother." Bedlam would arise in me. What did this mean? Nothing he could've said would've evoked more pain.

These words should've turned me into a scratching wildcat, but I found his cruelty so absurd I'd snap out of the tears and just laugh at my pathetic reality.

The thought of him anywhere near Mom in her most vulnerable moments made me sick. It was hard for me to understand why Gram would involve him. Gram needed support managing Mom? Was he the only helper she could find? She wanted to keep it in the family?

I considered the motion to commit her to Anna, which I'd seen at the White County Courthouse in Carmi during our visit in 2016. Alvin testified in that hearing that Mom was a danger to herself.

Did Gram, in her savviness, know that two witnesses would be needed to have her committed? Did Gram bring Alvin to our trailer in Mt. Vernon to witness Mom's behavior? She knew the committal process by then.

* * *

AFTER AUNT RITA'S VISIT, I combed through every line in the notebook.

From Gram's first entry in the M.E. and K section—and I counted the incidents and hospitalizations—there were six incidents with Mom between October 1 and December 29, 1971.

I looked it up on findagrave.com. Dad died June 3, 1971. Certainly, that had something to do with my mom's condition that year. Knowing she had another child to raise alone had to be a blow.

The chaos mounted, and I couldn't believe the frequency of Mom's hospitalizations:

1972: 45 incidents or hospitalizations
1973: 64 but with a note that Gram had "missed a few days"
1974: 83 incidents or hospitalizations

Then, there was 1975. I remembered '75. I thought about the late nights I spent with Mom in the lounge of the Mt. Vernon Ramada Inn. I drank luscious, fizzy pink "kiddie cocktails" while she played the piano for the handful of night-capping motel guests. She surely didn't earn enough at the lounge to support us.

As much as Gram loved and cared for Mom, I knew she wouldn't have been giving money gratuitously to any of her children. She couldn't have gotten it by Alvin and wouldn't have understood Mom spending the money on booze or pills.

The very last page of the notebook was astonishing. Gram must've snuck into our trailer when Mom was out, checking to see if she'd relapsed yet again.

Below the list of meds Gram found was a summary of Mom's hospitalizations through 1972.

It was worse than I ever could've comprehended. It devastated me. It relieved me. How could Mom have cared for me? She was so sick. Thank you, Gram, for saving me.

Gram listed Mom's first hospitalization as the month and year of Johnny's death. Maybe she didn't have problems before he died. It made me feel, again, that if Johnny hadn't been killed, Mom might've been not fine but better.

In 1968, she cut her wrists AND had an overdose.
In 1971, she was "sick all summer."

Had Gram torn out the next page which listed '73-'76, or was she just exhausted after she got to 1972 and quit writing?

I showed the list of Mom's meds to my doctor friend.

She commented on the ones she knew by heart. Thorazine (strong anti-psychotic), Norpramin (antidepressant), Elavil (antidepressant), Fiorinal (pain killer), and Macrodantin (antibiotic used to treat UTIs).

She went down the list and then, eruption!

She said, "Mycostatin. That's also usually given for STDs."

I started recalling the little tidbits I'd heard through the years.

"Your mom needed money."

"Your Grandfather Davis took advantage of your mother. Even after your dad died, he wouldn't help her."

And one desperate Sunday, Mom shared with a friend at church, "My father-in-law has lots of money, but he expects something in return. Makes me sick."

Thorazine — Zactirin
Pericolate — Pen G. 250mg-4 daily
Meprobamate — Provera 10mg-1 daily
Norpramin-25 mg. — Norpramin.25mg-3
Macrodatin-100mg-3 daily — Mycostatin-oral
Fiorinal — Eldovil
Datcolax — Chlor tri man 4mg
Dimetapp — Donnatol- Anti-Dic
Supp- distress — Diuvil- fluid

Sept 1958- St.L 2 Mos
Apr.2 1961- St.L.
1961- 1963- No Hosp?
1967 -28 June Clear view- 1 Sept. yet
1967- May 17- June 2- Carmi
1968- Jan.4-Feb 16- ST Hosp
1968- May 11-May 14- Carmi cut wrists
" May- Sept, ST Hosp overdose
1969- Nov. ST Hosp
1970- June-Sept- ST Hosp
1971- C'ville sick all Summer
1972- June 28-Aug 3-ST V. STL
1972- Sept 19- Nov 15- ST Hosp
1972-
Jan.31-Mt.V. — Sept.14. StL, Dr. MtV. amb
Feb 13- ? — Sept 16-MtV. Dr. Peart
Mch 15-20-Centralia — Sept 19-Nov 15- ST.V.
June 20- STL. Hosp 1 day
June 28 -Aug 3- ST.V. STL
Aug 27- Mt.V.
Sept 1- Trans to St.V. Called me Sept 3.
Sept 5- Ret-St.V amb

List of my mom's medications and hospitalizations (Hosp)

My grandfather could have easily helped her. He was a powerful figure in southern Illinois, owning major hotels in Benton and Mt. Vernon.

"Instead of helping her," Gram said, "he gave her that job in Mt. Vernon at the Ramada Inn and paid her next to nothing."

It never dawned on me that the men I remember coming and going from Mom's trailer might've been a specific kind of temporary. Mom had an endless stream of boyfriends. I knew I wasn't supposed to knock on the bedroom door. I would sit in the small living room in the black vinyl chair, sometimes crying, always lonely, and always waiting for Mom and the guy to emerge.

Mom needed more money than what she was making playing piano at The Ramada Inn, and my paternal grandfather, L.E. Davis, facilitated a second part-time job for her as an escort? Did the Ramada play into this? L.E. would've been Mom's first customer, and I knew for a fact he'd pursued a relationship with her after his own son's death. Another reason I didn't want him as a namesake. It solidified my name change decision.

This was a moment of enlightenment, or maybe assumption, I wished I'd never reached. It was nearly the piece of information that made me lie down and forget all about this story. I didn't know if I could take one more horrid detail. I was sick thinking she was that fraught over money.

Mom was a knockout. She had a perfect figure, and when she was well, she was wonderful, vibrant. An exemplary musician. The very first reflection her friends shared, their eyes leaving our conversation and drifting upward, as they thought of the deep feeling with which she played any instrument.

"No one could play 'Moonlight Sonata' like Mary Ellen," they would say, their eyes coming back to the conversation and lingering on me.

That was Mom's resume—music and sensuality. Mom was using the two things she had going for her to get it done. I didn't feel ashamed.

Gram had to know what Mom was up to. She simply would've figured it out, and it must have decimated her. Mom was trying. She had various jobs. She sold Avon. I don't know if she made any money, but we had all kinds of fantastic samples, like the cologne and talcum powder antique telephone. The receiver, tall, skinny and black, held the cologne while the earpiece held the talc powder which was dispensed by shaking the talc through the small holes in the end of the earpiece. I'd spend hours with it, practicing how I answered the phone at Gram's — "Stein Motel, how may I help you?"

We had Avon roll-on perfume called "Sweet Honesty;" bracelets and necklaces; and my favorite, a baby basset hound decanter. Maybe Mom's clients took some nice Avon perfume home to their wives after their appointments.

I wasn't deprived when I was with Mom, or I didn't know I was. At least not when she didn't have a date. We got Fun Meals from Burger Chef. I had no bedtime and slept in the bed with her where she snuggled me tightly all night. I ate and drank anything I wanted at any time, including entire cans of black olives and foamy, green daiquiri mix, sans the rum.

I didn't have to look at the notebook to remember I was constantly being transported between Mt. Vernon with Mom and Crossville with Gram. I remembered one of my triumphant returns to Crossville to Mrs. Candy Flowers' (real name) kindergarten classroom where I popped out of the red and blue pretend hot dog stand to surprise my classmates.

I arrived at school while our class was at recess. "I'm back!"

The kids probably didn't even know I'd left again, but I knew.

My Mt. Vernon kindergarten class was big. I didn't know any of the kids, and I don't remember going to school much. At home in Crossville, Mrs. Flowers played the guitar, and we would scream out the words. "Like a Rhinestone Cowboy, ba-baah-baah!"

I was getting old enough to know that Mom was becoming more unstable and unpredictable. I began to feel uneasy with the strangers she'd leave me with. I knew it was wrong that our neighbor back at the Mt. Vernon trailer court gave her baby boy beer in his bottle.

I missed my friends in Crossville. I missed Gram. I didn't feel safe with Mom anymore.

* * *

As I CONTINUED through the pages of the notebook Aunt Rita had given me, I stopped frequently for some minutes at a time—with my elbows resting on the dining room table and my hands in an almost prayerful position in front of my face. I just had to keep closing my eyes and breathing steadily to decrease my anxiety and heart rate. I was so afraid of what I would read.

I pulled a Faire and poured a delicious, energizing Coke into an icy glass. She liked one cube, but I preferred a glass full of ice.

"Your Mom liked a lot of ice," she would share.

It was probably the first Coke I'd had in a year. It tasted so good. It pepped me up.

After 2013, everything I ingested made me wonder, *Could this be the delicacy that brings back my breast cancer?* Oh well . . . I've got to write a book about a suicide . . . or a murder. I can't worry about breast cancer right now. I made myself laugh out loud.

I'd already looked at all of Gram's entries up to, but not including, 1975. I learned that it was in June of that year that Mom moved our trailer back to Crossville to a small piece of open land between the motel and an old garage that was part of the Stein Station.

On Sunday, August 17, 1975, Gram began documenting nearly every single day.

I noticed the mention of Doug and the word pistol. The more I read, the more pained I became.

I'm certain that it was on the advice of our family attorney, David Stanley, that Gram started making more detailed entries. They were without many of her trademark weird abbreviations.

As the months went on, Gram's script became feverish.

"Released from hosp. 11 a.m. Kandi with M.E."

And then, "Words with Guth" grabbed me. I certainly remembered a day my mom had words with Alvin Guthrel Stein, her father and my grandfather, who Gram often called "Guth."

Aug. 1975
Sun. 17.
   Doug came tonite. Episode here. Doug slept
   here.
Mon. 18
   Row with Bob. M.E. to Carmi Hosp. Ambulanc.
   Kandi here
Tues 19.
   f. to Hosp. M.E. subdued, but got furious. I
   left. called Doug-(Pistol) Kandi here
Wed. 20
   M.E. called-wanted me to Come- I refused.
   furious. Kandi here

Thurs 21-
   Released from Hosp 11 Am. Kandi with M.E.
   words with Guth.

fri. 22
   M.E. took K. School. With her tonite.

Sat. + Sun- 23, 24.
   mad and kept K. with her
Mon. 25
   M.E. took K. School- Slept till 8:30. I brot her
   in 7pm. fed + bathed her. She slept here.

Tues. 26
   M.E. Carmi. working. called from Vintage 9:30
Home 11:30 K. here
Wed. 27
   M.E. to School. f. M.E. K, Pizza tonite.
Thurs. 28
   Gone all day- called fr. Mt. V. 5:15- overnite - K. here

A tumultuous week in 1975, recorded in Gram's notebook

August 1975

ONE HUNDRED POUNDS of rage thudded through the golden, late summer grass toward Gram's house. I could see Mom crying. I sat still on the painted concrete steps outside Gram's door, watching her come. She was in mid-length, white, women's golf shorts and a white, sleeveless V-neck summer top. Gram was sweeping grass clippings from the sidewalk in front of the house. It looked like a tornado was coming.

Gram was unmoved by Mom's agitation and behaved like it was boilerplate mad ole' Mary Ellen. She didn't pay much attention to Mom's approach. Mom's feet hammered up the steps and through the screen door, and then Gram followed her. Each pound of Mom's foot seemed to be releasing some fury inside her. She hadn't stopped to say anything to me. She didn't even know I was there.

I stopped in the hallway between Gram's kitchen and living room and watched Mom, wondering what she had in her hand. It looked like spray paint. Alvin (Guth) was sitting, oblivious, in his green vinyl Lazy Boy recliner, watching a rerun. Mom darted into the living room to her father's chair, raised her right arm, pressing the nozzle on the can, waving it furiously. She didn't speak but her face said it all. Her teeth clenched and nostrils flared. Alvin had been barely able to raise his sun-spotted arms before the wet mist of mace covered his entire face.

"Hell!" he cried.

He pulled his handkerchief from his back pocket and began wiping his eyes and face. He rose from his chair, taking a few steps after Mom, but blinded, he didn't get far.

Having moved in a loop around the house, Mom came in, did the job, and bolted back out the front door running back toward our trailer. I saw Mom stop in the grass and bend over. Her shoulders rose and fell with deep sobs. I stood at the screen door watching, wishing she wasn't crying.

Time immemorial.

Chapter 16

Please, Can You Help Me?

February 2019

I was sitting at my dining room table with my laptop open and my head exploding. I had papers covering every inch of space around me—printed-out emails chronicling my conversations with the Union County Courthouse people the previous September.

In the next pile sat a threatening letter from the county telling Lisa and I we were overdue for the annual testing of our back-flow prevention device.

"Since this test is now several months overdue and to ensure no interruption to water service, please make arrangements to have this test performed immediately."

It had something to do with the sprinkler system, but I had no idea why it needed to be inspected.

Taking a break from her work-from-home gig, Lisa, a contracts attorney, strolled by, still in her plaid pajama pants and St. Louis Blues tee. She was trying to get to the kitchen for coffee, unnoticed, before I stopped her for one of the many reasons I was always stopping her: what sounded good for dinner, did she remember to call her dad, had she given our dog Moose his liver medicine or did I need to do it? I was always interrupting her.

I mused, "I looked up the statute the woman at Anna mentioned, and I just don't see where we need a court order for Mom's records."

I could tell Lisa was in a rush, probably trying to get ready for an important negotiation over billions of dollars or something dumb like that.

"We need to get this figured out, don't we? I should've looked at this earlier. I'm sorry."

Duh, I thought but tried to smile gratefully for the help. Lisa filled her coffee cup and then looked around madly for a pair of cheaters. "So when you talked to the records department, did you cite this statute?"

"No. I don't think I know how to cite a statute and still sound kinda folksy," I told her. "It won't be helpful if I sound like a city mouse."

Lisa looked tired and like she needed a reminder of where we were with the records.

"The Union County FOIA officer and the circuit clerk both thought I was asking them for the records, so I got a 'denial' email. I wrote back saying 'I know *you* don't have the records. They're at Choate or whatever it's called now. They told me they didn't know how to help me. Ringing a bell?"

"Vaguely. Want me to call Choate myself?"

"Yes! You have time?"

Lisa spoke to Angela at Choate, my original point of contact. Because no one had ever initiated a records request, still an astounding idea, Angela didn't really know why we needed the court order, and she didn't have any further details on how to obtain one. Angela suggested we send our question in writing, and she would check with Choate's legal counsel at the state level.

* * *

From: Lisa Burke <Lisaburkexxxx@yahoo.com>
Date: February 28, 2019 at 11:34:28 AM CST
To: Angela.mccxxxx@illinois.gov

Subject: Release of Anna State Hospital Deceased Patient Records

Hi Angela –

Thanks for taking my call this afternoon. You asked that I send my question to you in email so you could get analysis from your legal department.

Here is the question:

It is my interpretation of Public Act 097-0623, that disclosure of a deceased person's health care records is authorized to an adult son or daughter of the deceased person pursuant to a written request if: 1) there is no surviving spouse, 2) no executor, administrator or agent exists and 3) the person did not specifically object to disclosure of his or her records in writing.

If the above conditions are met, can an adult daughter of a deceased person request the records by executing the Authorized Relative Certification specified in the Act without the need to seek a court order? As we discussed, the daughter of the deceased will be visiting Anna State Hospital on March 6 and 7. Due to the age of these records and their storage on Microfilm, we'd appreciate a timely response to this request.

Thank you for your time and consideration of this matter.

Sincerely,

Lisa Burke

It was early on a Monday morning, days after Lisa's conversation with Angela, when Lisa's phone rang from a 618 area code. We were having coffee as Gayle King broadcast that A-list Hollywood actors had paid thousands, maybe millions of dollars, to get their children into Ivy League colleges.

We were nervously hoping for an answer to our emailed question, and Lisa put the phone on speaker.

"Hello? Lisa? When I talked to you Friday, I didn't get any information about the patient. I didn't even get a name when I talked to you. I'm so sorry. I'll need the patient's full name and reason for admission, because, you know, through the years we have housed all sorts of patients — forensic, behavior disordered, mental health of course, even people with tuberculosis at one time, who had to be confined."

I answered, "She was there many times for depression and attempted suicide. Could've been any time between 1948 and 1976."

I gave her the rest of Mom's information including her social security number.

We reminded Angela we were making a visit to Anna the following week and were hoping to know something before the trip, and she told us she'd do her best.

"We appreciate your help."

Lisa hung up the call. "They're just as nice as can be, aren't they?"

"I know."

Now we had to wait for a response from the big boss.

March 5, 2019

I was packing my suitcase to leave for Anna early the next morning when it occurred to me that the only death certificate I had for Mom was the one I had obtained in Carmi in 2016, which was stamped, "For Genealogy Purposes Only."

I felt a panic welling up. If Choate decided to release Mom's records to me, I'd need a certified copy. Springfield, the Illinois state capitol, was an easy drive from St. Louis. I called the Vital Records Department who confirmed that I could get a certified death certificate same-day.

I headed out around noon, stopping at Starbucks for an Americano, then hopping on Interstate 55 north to the Land of Lincoln.

Around two p.m., I arrived at a medium-sized concrete building that had been painted baby blue. They closed at three and through the window, I saw several customers in line ahead of me. I gave the man at the window Mom's information and sat down with the other people waiting for records to be found and printed. Most of them were older, and I wondered if they were getting a death record of a deceased spouse for insurance purposes. I thought of Lisa and calculated how many years it might be before one of us was grieving. Twenty or thirty, I figured, and after the seventeen we'd already spent together, she'd be ready for a break from me by the time I corked off.

What if the solemn man across from me was there because one of his children died by suicide or in an awful car accident?

I was perpetually wondering what tragedy some stranger beside me could be suffering through. Meanwhile, that man would have no idea what disturbing information was on the death certificate *I* was there getting and the ache I was anticipating when I read, again, Mom's cause of death.

Within a few minutes, a crisp, stamped certificate was in my hands. As I took out a credit card to pay, I was perplexed when I noticed it listed Mom's manner of death as "inquest pending."

I questioned the clerk why it might be listed that way.

"That's the decision of the coroner. They probably just didn't let us know what the result of the inquest was."

I wondered if it could have something to do with Mom's life insurance policy. Maybe Gram had lobbied the coroner to hold off on ruling a cause of death to safeguard that I'd get a payout.

I left the office and stopped for my third coffee of the day in downtown Springfield. When I pulled into the angled parking spot in front of the coffee shop, a woman about my age, who looked like she'd been crying, waited for me to get out.

"Please, can you help me? It's so cold. I just need to get on the bus."

My car dashboard told me it was fifteen degrees. I pulled some bills from my back pocket. It was rare for me to have cash. I flipped through looking at a one, a five, a twenty. I deliberated and pulled out the twenty. She saw the bill before I reached her, and she came at me longingly with one of the most tender and earnest hugs I've ever received. The embrace continued on and on while the woman cried and thanked me over and over. She waved at me as she scurried toward the bus station. Her face soaked and red from crying. She could never have known that I also needed that hug. I was tired and frustrated and very anxious about seeing the state hospital.

As long as I live, I will never forget that woman's face. Whether booze, drugs, or a bus ride, I didn't care. I just hoped she would soon be soothed, relieved of her desperation.

On the way out of town, I passed an old brick building with a massive black and white painting of Lincoln. I felt the pride of my home state. The warmth melted within a few miles as I passed square after square of frozen prairie tundra. I imagined what it would be like to walk barefoot through those frozen fields. It seemed like I was always thinking about all the ways people experience pain.

Lisa called to tell me she'd just heard from the Illinois State's Attorney's Office. She'd nearly hung up on the man from the state because he spoke very formally, and she thought it was a robocall.

"I received a forwarded email from Angela at Choate, and I understand that you've written on behalf of Kandi, who is seeking her deceased mother's medical records from Choate Hospital."

"That is correct," Lisa said.

"There is another statute dealing with the release of mental health records that overrides Public Act 097-0623." He gave her the citation. "That statute is what governs rather than the act you cited. The other statute is more restrictive, and we always defer to the more restrictive when making these decisions about mental health records. Therefore, a court order will be necessary."

"And that's why I do contract law and not FOIA," Lisa said when I got home.

I was undeterred by the news. We just had to keep trying. I started dinner, built a big fire, and finished packing for Anna. We were leaving the next morning, and I just knew we'd have better luck in person.

March 6, 2019

There was scarcely a sign of life at the entrance to the Dwight C. Choate Mental Health and Development Center. The campus was sad, dilapidated. The main building, what was once a stalwart, Romanesque structure now looked like it was barely upright.

Carol, Lisa, and I stood staring at the careworn mosaic that had been laid at the entrance to the hospital when it opened. I decided right away I didn't want a tour.

We waited inside the entryway and thought someone might come out of a back office to direct us, but nothing. There was a yellowing, printed sign labeled, "Visitors Must Check-in with Security." We might've stood there all day without being noticed. We could faintly hear the voice of a woman lamenting something "they" were doing.

A room that was once masterfully crafted was now a musty and dirty one, lined with faux wood paneling, circa 1970. The faint voice we heard as we entered was coming from a side office which turned out to be "Security."

I followed the voice and walked into an adjacent hallway, where the wood paneling gave way to a stark stairwell and landing, evocative of *One Flew Over The Cuckoo's Nest*. A woman offered to show us to the records department.

As we walked, I wanted to ask the woman what happened upstairs, but I thought it would sound insensitive, like I was just another person interested in the haunting of Anna State Hospital.

That was actually a thing. I'd seen Anna listed as one of the top ten most haunted hospitals in Illinois by Mysteriousheartland.com.

I had flashes of women in hospital gowns, moping up and down the stairwell, but I didn't see Mom in those flashes. I had disconnected myself, investigating. I'd prepared myself for this day. I was there. I felt strong, and I was ready to get things done, but I wasn't ready to see the patients.

In their faces, I would see my mother and my father. I knew my mind. My mind would create a backstory for each patient I came across and every story would be tragic. I would've concocted that the patients had all been dumped at Choate by an ignorant, cruel family member.

I just needed to remember not to be sad about things that weren't actually happening.

We knocked on the locked door to medical records, and a friendly lady named Nancy opened and welcomed Carol, Lisa and I into the small office.

She held the door and said, "Step on in. It'll be warmer in here. They don't heat the hallways or these open areas. Only heat is in our offices."

The three of us had been sharing looks from our first footsteps into the building. We couldn't believe the decaying condition of the property. It didn't help that it was wintertime.

Carol started to excuse herself to the bathroom. I could tell it was getting to her. She was quiet, looking around at the old, soiled carpet. "I'm just thinking of your mom here."

"I know. I know."

I just couldn't let myself feel more right then.

"I'm okay. Let's go back in," she said.

Nancy welcomed us back into the narrow room. No other staff seemed to be in the office that day.

I told Nancy that she and I had spoken months earlier when she'd told me there were records on my mother. I could tell she wasn't making the connection.

"We've been working with Angela over the last week. She helped us get some questions answered at the state level."

"Ah. Yep. Angela's gone to the courthouse today."

I gave Nancy a little of Mom's story again, that she'd been treated at Anna many times. Referring to the green metal card file cabinet, she pontificated about the records.

"Would this have been a dump and run?"

None of us responded. We didn't understand the question.

Nancy continued, "Would there have been any history given on her when she checked in? Would the family have been involved? Years ago, especially, we didn't have much information on patients because the family dumped them at the curb and took off. Such a stigma."

We were all quiet for a moment as we felt the dismal truth of what she'd said. I tried not to sound incredulous when I told her that my mom had a family who was very concerned and was here many times visiting her. I didn't tell her that I'd had my first birthday party on the front lawn.

Nancy was warm and helpful. Thinking we might sweet talk her, I asked again if we absolutely needed a court order.

"That's what I've always been told. Can't be that hard. We've just never had anyone do it."

"That's so weird," I replied.

"I've worked here twenty years and never seen it." She thought of a nice attorney she knew. "Christian man, Bill Jamison." She thought he could get the judge to do something right away. "Go back out on the road you came in on. Make a right at the four-way. His office is on the left. Judge Bert should be in court today."

Nancy couldn't have been more obliging. It reminded me of Crossville and the general good-nature of people in this part of the world.

We flew out like we were heading to the hospital with a first-time mother in labor. We easily found the attorney's office where we decided I should go in alone to avoid him feeling bombarded by three uppity-looking out-of-towners.

The office assistant caught Jamison in the hallway and conveyed the story I'd just given him. An attractive, very in-shape looking older man about seventy years old came to the counter.

"I could probably help you, but we're really busy right now. Leave your contact information with Dakota, and I'll get in touch with you. It won't be months, but it might be a while."

Bill gave me the name of some other lawyers in town. I got back in the car and started calling.

We looked way too self-important parked on Main in my Volvo, making calls through the Bluetooth system.

In one of the offices, a live person answered, but when she heard the story said, "I'll have to look at the law. I'm not sure."

Carol sat in the back Googling more local attorneys' numbers. Lisa listened from the passenger seat, and I knew what her legal mind was thinking. No one wanted to mess with this because it was probably out of their area of expertise, or they were afraid they'd draw up the papers, and the one judge in Anna wouldn't sign off on it. It wasn't long before we'd called all the law offices, and we needed coffee.

Anna had a quaint Main Street with most of its storefronts occupied. It was lined with beautiful old homes, some impeccably maintained and some worse for wear, but there was still life in that little place. At Kiki's Coffeehouse, Carol and I ordered, and I took a cookie and coffee out to Lisa who stayed in the car to talk to her ninety-four-year-old father about his Jitterbug phone. He'd stolen some foil-wrapped butter pats from the cafeteria in his assisted living complex and then took a nap with the Jitterbug in the same pocket.

"Dad, do you have your hearing aids in?" Lisa screamed through her own phone. "Try and use a toothpick to pick the butter out of the holes in the part where you speak!"

Back inside, Carol was texting with a kid she was tutoring about a research paper due the next day. "Oh my God. He hasn't even started."

We stared at each other, wondering what we should do next. We spent fifteen minutes lamenting the condition of Choate. It was an out-of-body experience in every way.

In a few minutes, my phone rang. It was a young attorney in town who asked me a lot of questions including, "And why do you need to get these records?"

I knew I couldn't say because I'm writing a book about my mother's disastrous life, so I said that my therapist wanted me to check into my family history.

"Of course," he said.

He told me he'd talk to his boss—I assumed an older partner in the firm—and call me right back.

He didn't call back. The partner probably said, "Too much research for too little money."

I was going to have to find another way. Maybe an attorney from upstate who specialized in this type of law.

I was feeling disillusioned and impatient, but nowhere near defeated. I needed to understand the entire arc of Mom's life.

* * *

THE MAKANDA INN and Cottages in Makanda, Illinois, population 540, was situated between Anna and Carbondale to the north. The inn was built by a graduate of Southern Illinois University.

In 2006, in the middle of an impressive career in aviation, Greg Wellman returned to SIU to teach a class and while there, stumbled upon the eighteen acres. Obviously an overachiever, in 2009, he built a small inn and a handful of cottages, using sustainable materials, all locally harvested.

Our cottage was brilliantly designed. It was a total sanctuary. From the cozy sitting area, we discussed the next steps of our research and where in the world we would eat dinner.

"I hope that place wasn't as run down when Mom was there."

I knew there were nearly two thousand patients in the sixties, so surely it was in better shape.

"When they first opened, it was totally self-sufficient. They had gardens, livestock . . . I think it was all run by patients as part of their therapy."

"It is so dismal now," Carol said.

"Wouldn't make anyone want to get well."

We heard about a pizza place in Cobden a few miles down. We had ten miles of gas and Cobden was nine.

Lisa and Carol were a nervous wreck. They'd rather have been stranded on the worst street in the worst city in America, versus a breakdown on a dark country road.

I was at peace. I knew someone would come along and help us if we needed it.

"Watch for deer," I reminded Lisa.

We made it to Cobden, got gas, and had a drink at the bar in a pizza place called "Downtown Abbey."

We loved the name. We promptly connected with the pregnant bartender, asking about the Mexican grocery down the street and hoping she could explain the school's mascot, the "Appleknockers."

"The orchards," the bartender told us. "There's a village of Mexican workers south of town."

We hadn't changed much, America. It was another form of the Sundown Law, just directed at a different group of people. The orchard bosses needed the labor but were unwilling to pay a wage that would allow the migrants to live in town. I could picture decomposing trailers probably provided by the orchard owners. Likely plopped on some random piece of property.

"What are you thinking about over there?" Lisa prodded me.

I joined in with the chat about the school's mascot.

The bartender, Jill, shrugged and said, "I have no idea what an Appleknocker is. Someone said they used to hit apples around like a baseball back in the day."

We left without an answer about Appleknockers and drove back to the cabin with our pizza. We were immersed in the dense, spectacular Shawnee National Forest, so it wasn't surprising that my phone went straight to voicemail when a woman named Susan Werner called.

"Hello, Ms. Davis, this is Susan Werner returning your call about getting your mother's medical records from Choate. My number is 618-555-2525 or 618-... "

She paused and a background voice filled in the rest of the numbers she couldn't think of or didn't know.

* * *

I AWOKE TOO EARLY the next morning and stared at the massive, perfectly milled, golden timbers holding up the ceiling of our cabin bedroom. I grabbed coffee and sat down on a cushy couch looking for the determined woodpecker I was hearing outside. The main room of the cabin was clad with gorgeous custom windows. I was thrilled to be hearing signs of life after such an icy, snowy winter. The cabin was warm, peaceful, and uplifting–a total contrast to Choate.

My whole quality of life sat in contrast to Mom's and Gram's: indulgent vacations, my own stable family with Lisa and Moose, and

I'd had a rewarding career as a chef. I was the luckiest unlucky person.

Lisa and Carol joined me in the living room, and we did some more sizing up of the masterful workmanship of the cabin. Eager to return Susan's call, I set an alarm for 8:00 a.m., which seemed like a reasonable time. I watched the minutes, and at 7:58 turned off the alarm on my phone and dialed Susan Werner's office. I laid out the story once again, and then Susan thoughtfully talked with Lisa about possible strategies. Susan was willing to give it a try.

She told us to meet her at her office at 10:30 and to bring the certified death certificate.

A WHITE STANDARD poodle named Louie met us at the side door to Susan Werner's office. We walked into the aging home expecting to see Boo Radley. But the inside was filled with interesting furniture and modern artwork. A minute woman with a tailored suit, heels, and short, highlighted auburn hair led us into the parlor of the old Victorian. Carol shoved me in the shoulder and pointed at Susan's heels. They had a little, blue pom pom on the shoe's upper. We smiled at each other.

Despite the pom poms, I could tell she would mean business when she met with the judge about our request at one o'clock that day.

There was no time to chit chat. She talked about the law she was going to cite in her petition and told me I needed a good reason for asking for the records.

"I could get a letter from my therapist declaring it would be beneficial to my treatment."

"Good. You're leaving tomorrow?"

"We'll stay as long as we need to."

I knew my therapist Joan would agree to write the letter if I could just reach her in-between sessions.

Twenty minutes later, Joan's letter arrived in Susan's email inbox. Susan told us to come back at 12:45, and she'd have something for me to sign before she headed across the street to meet with Judge Bert.

We hurried back down to the action of Main Street. Carol found a little storefront that advertised "Chinese Buffet." It smelled wonderful and warm. We gobbled down a plate full of fried deliciousness and were clearing our plates from the table when we heard, "Great minds think alike!"

It was Susan's admin grabbing lunch for the office. She must've known a shortcut back because the massive house already smelled of egg rolls when we walked back into Susan's office.

"She's upstairs," she yelled from a back room. "Go on up."

I signed an affidavit certifying that I was Mom's next of kin, and Susan frantically flipped through pages of complicated law.

"Well, crap. I see now that we have to put Choate on notice. So nothing will happen today. I'm asking that the records be released to your therapist instead of directly to you. I think we have a better chance if we ask for that."

"It's been like fifty years. I can't believe a judge would say no."

She looked up from her papers with sincerity. "I'll let you know."

I could see the courthouse through the window as I walked out of Susan's upstairs office and down the wooden stairway. Louie the poodle and I walked together back into the admin's office to pay for Susan's work.

You know that moment of hesitancy right before you buy something big? Will this massage chair give me the results I'm looking for? I've tried so many other things. It probably won't work. Before I knew it, the transaction was complete. Susan was our only hope.

MY HALF-BROTHER, Mark, on my dad's side, lived in Carbondale, just a few miles from Anna. Carol, Lisa and I met Mark for breakfast the morning after we'd been at Susan's office.

"I don't know how long Mary Ellen and Dad were married. Not long."

"I visited them sometimes in Evansville in their little house. I liked it there. I helped them take care of you, and your mom would buy me piano music." The piano was a beautiful symbol to our family and almost everyone played because, well, what else are you gonna do in southern Illinois?

"What were they like together?" I asked Mark.

"Well, I mean, not good. Dad would go on about her. 'She's back on those pills again.'"

"Was he sober for a while after he and Mom got out of Anna?"

"Yeah. He was, actually. He seemed to be doing well," Mark said. There was a noticeable sadness in his voice.

I laughed to myself. Conversely, I'd heard from Aunt Rita that Dad was sneaking shots of Lavoris during his marriage to Mom. My half-brothers had their hopes dashed by Dad so many times.

"Did you know Doug?" Carol asked Mark.

"A little." He paused, seeming lost in thought. "You know, I've thought about this. Doug never seemed the violent type. He really didn't. He was always friendly. I know he drank a lot, but he never seemed aggressive or mean."

"I never heard him even raise his voice," I said.

Mark's wife Renee appealed to our common sense. She'd been an ER nurse, "I just can't believe your mom could do that to herself. I've seen a lot of terrible things but never anything like that. When I think about how Doug died . . ."

"It's hard to believe. Was Mom ever violent?" I asked Mark.

"Tell her about Florida and the mustard," Renee suggested.

"Well, your mom and Dad split up, and Dad went to Florida to manage an apartment building Grandpa bought in Treasure Island." Our grandfather L.E. had properties all over the place. "I think Dad was considering getting back together with my mom. But he was still off and on with Mary Ellen, and she drove all the way to Florida by herself with you."

Mark quietly told the rest of the story.

"Dad left the apartment for something, and while he was gone, Mary Ellen got mad at him and just destroyed the place. Cut up his clothes, ruined all the carpet. There was mustard and ketchup all over the walls."

Mom never raised her voice to me—not even a little bit, and I never witnessed violence other than her attack on Alvin with the mace.

There was obviously a lot I was too young to remember, and Gram's note mentioned a pistol and other incidents with mace. Mark's story made me more curious about Mom's diagnosis.

Chapter 17

Do You Know Where You're Going To?

S uicide by self-stabbing is extremely uncommon, constituting only 1-3 percent of suicide attempts. Surprisingly, the mortality associated with this kind of wound is low. Most people cannot follow through. There are only a few case reports of it in the U.S. National Library of Medicine.[1] And on the flip side of the coin, the *what in the world happened coin,* Google told me that between 1976 and 1999 there were 1,083 incidents of matricide with "argument" listed as causation.[2]

> *Myth:* Suicide is a selfish act.
> *Truth:* Suicide isn't about living or dying.
> It's about not wanting to be in pain today.

I don't know what I was hoping to find out by reading the statistics, but maybe I just wanted to know the odds of one scenario over another. At a rate of 50,000 or so suicides a year, suicide significantly outweighs the probability of matricide, even a suicide by stabbing.[3] When I saw in Gram's notes the frequency of Mom's hospitalizations during 1975, I knew that anything was possible, even other scenarios I hadn't entertained.

But I also had very clear memories of the day Mom died, May 19, 1976. I was almost seven. As a highly sensory person, certain landscapes are bookmarked—a phone call, emotions running high, a tug of war, eternal regret.

May 18, 1976: Faire's Story, The Day Before

If anyone is more tired than I am today, they're too tired. I'm tired from worrying about Kandi. Tired of sweeping rain water out of the basement. I'm tired of cooking for Alvin. I'm tired of wondering if Mary Ellen will finally do herself in by the time I wake up in the morning. She's not even trying to earn just a little bit of money and is talking about selling her car. I told her I'd pay her to help me with the garden, and she says she can't do it. She's just too tired. The drugs turn her into a zombie. She slurs like Otis, the town drunk.

Kandi gets herself up on her own, gets dressed for school, and fixes her own breakfast. She tells me when her mother is "mad" or "on the couch."

Mary Ellen says she's in pain. Tells me her teeth hurt. We've been to the hospital five times this month. She's found a Dr. Feelgood down there. She goes into such hysterics when she's out of pills. Sometimes we drop Kandi off at Maxine's, but often K just comes with us at all hours of the day and night.

Mary Ellen had some good days last fall. She's in a good humor when Dick Symke calls and tells her he will be coming for a visit. Dick has to work out how to get there without his wife knowing.

"He's leaving her," Mary Ellen tells me, but half the time he doesn't show up for their dates which sends her into her darkness.

She sold some Avon last week. The order came, and I helped her sort it out. She delivered it last night and told me she stopped at The Vintage to "work." Thought she might sell a few things. Got home at 11 p.m. K stayed here, and I got her to school this morning.

Mary Ellen is still in bed, and it's nearly noon. I'm of the mind to go try and get her up, but we'll end up in a fight. I tell her, "For heaven's sake, Mary Ellen, you'll feel better if you just get up and do some work. When it's summer and humid and my arthritis is at its worst, I have to get up and around. I feel better when I move and you would, too!" Then Mary Ellen gives me a bawling out, tells me I don't understand, and that she's going to go back to Mt. Vernon and take Kandi.

I've nearly lost my will to help her. She's been this way for thirty years. I'm worn out.

May 20, 1976: Kandi's Story, The Day After

"Kandi, what did you and your mom do on Tuesday?" The town cop sat beside me in the slatted wooden swing, which hung from the old washhouse behind Gram's sister, Aunt Maxine's, house.

It was early on a sunny May morning, and I was worried about missing school. Mrs. Price would be wondering where I was and how I could miss the last days of first grade.

Officer Spencer continued to question me. "Who picked you up from school on Tuesday?"

"Mom."

"Did you go straight home?"

"We went home, then we rode bikes. We were racing. We rode all the way around the driveway a bunch of times."

"Do you know how long you rode bikes?"

"Mom stopped and said she wanted to go home. We had to walk our bikes through the grass." I wasn't sure if I should tell them she was crying.

"We stopped in the grass. She was sad. She asked me if I knew she was sick, and I said I did, and she was hugging me for a long time."

"Did you go inside your house?"

"Yes. I watched *The Electric Company*."

"Your Gram said you went somewhere in the car."

211

"To the liquor store in Carmi with the big windows. She bought twelve beers. I counted them on the way home. They were on the floorboard in front of my seat."

"How did your mom act on the way home?"

"I think she wasn't very happy. We were singing a song on the radio. It's from a movie with Diana Ross. We saw it."

I sang it for them. It was a sad sounding song. *Do you know where you're going to? Do you like the things that life is showing you? Where are you going to?*

"Did you see Doug when you were in Carmi?"

"No. Mom said he was with his friends."

"You didn't see him when you were in Carmi getting beer?"

"No."

"What happened when you got home?"

"Mom started drinking the beers, and I was happy because she said I could make our supper. She told me how to do it."

"When did you walk over to your Gram's?"

"When 'Donny and Marie' came on. Gram called, and I got to answer. She wanted to know what we were having for supper, and I said that we didn't make it yet. She asked me where we'd been and what Mom was doing. She wanted me to come over."

"Do you know how many beers your mom had by that time?"

"I don't know."

"And you're sure Doug wasn't there?"

"I didn't see him anywhere."

"What about your granddad, Mr. Stein?"

"He was at the farm, Gram said."

"What was your mom doing when you left?"

"She started to cry again when I was putting on my shoes." I felt badly about what I was going to say next. "Mom said she would make me a kiddie cocktail, but I just wanted to go to Gram's. She told me we could go to the Dairy Queen after supper."

"Did you see your Mom again after that?"

"No." I started to cry a little. "She died."

May 19, 1976: 4:00 a.m., The Day Of

No one gets up in the morning expecting a catastrophe. No one wakes up thinking this is the day — the day you will revisit for the balance of your life.

It was a catastrophe long predicted. Gram's tired body climbed out of bed in the wee hours that morning, looking across the expansive yard, past the massive oak tree where Mom and I had stood with our bikes the previous day. Where Mom asked if I knew she was sick.

Gram saw a light in our trailer. It was just so out of the ordinary for Mom to be up that early.

Gram walked through the dewy morning grass in her canvas Keds. Usually she'd walk down the long sidewalk to the motel, take the walkway past all the motel rooms, and then arrive at our trailer parked next to the motel. Gram liked the exercise and didn't want the grass to stain her white sneakers, but she was in a hurry that morning.

In darkness, she navigated our living room, running her hands along the black vinyl couch, likely tripping on my toys. She walked through the kitchen, feeling the wall of the hallway as she made her last few steps to Mom's bedroom. She was weak-kneed—it was too quiet.

Gram could make out the silhouette of Mom's body on the bed. She placed her trembling hand on Mom's arm. Ice cold. I imagine that she lowered herself to the carpet. In the silence, she knelt, alone, in the darkest hour of her grueling life, and she sobbed out of sorrow and shock and deliverance.

May 19, 1976: 8:00 a.m., Kandi's Story, The Day Of

Bright morning sun streamed through Gram's bedroom window. The alarm hadn't gone off. I was late for school and remembered I didn't have any school clothes at Gram's. The voices whispering in the kitchen were recognizable. Aunt Maxine noticed me rounding the corner. "Here she is, Faire." She had to say it loudly enough for Gram to hear.

We had all kinds of company, which was usually exciting, but not that day. Whatever the reason, it was bad. Granddad was sitting at the table (he would usually be fishing by now), then Aunt Maxine, Mom's friend Minnie, our neighbor Emma Vogel, and Reverend Phillippe who sat in the chair closest to Gram.

In small towns, the local pastors did more than minister to the spiritual needs of the community. The reverend can be called upon to do the worst kinds of jobs. They are sometimes the only ones who know the mechanisms that drive function or dysfunction in the family. They know all the bad stuff.

"Kandi, baby," Gram said. She pushed her chair out from the kitchen table a little bit and slid over to leave me half of her seat. She squeezed me. That was our usual morning routine. Then, she'd tell me to go wash my hands and gargle with Listerine, but she didn't mention it that day. "You're not going to school."

I was disappointed. It was going to be a special end-of-the-year game day.

"The preacher is going to talk to you for a minute."

I was worried. I'd never talked to him on my own. Reverend Phillippe was a sweet, gentle man. We shook hands with him on Sundays as we exited the church after the service. He would bend over, making himself level with my eyes. He had soft hands.

Sometimes, when he came to our house for surprise visits, Mom would say, "Oh, the preacher's a callin'!" and she would giggle. But she liked his visits. He would stay with her for a long time while I watched TV, and at the end, he said a prayer. I wondered what his house looked like, and sometimes, I wanted to go with him.

As I sat with Gram that morning, Reverend Phillippe reached across the table and held out his hand to me. We were going to say a prayer together. I was hoping maybe I could go to school after all, when we finished. He led me into the living room. I could hear the busy highway and was distracted by noisy morning sounds. The man at the weigh station down the road came on the loudspeaker and told an eighteen wheeler, "Go ahead."

Reverend Phillippe stared at the carpet, and I bowed my head. He was still holding my hand, and it was soothing. "Dear Lord, please bring us comfort on this sad morning. Shine your light on Kandi and her family during this sad time. Let us all be grateful for the quietude that Mary Ellen will find in your arms. Help me to counsel them with love and understanding. Amen."

I said amen, too. He kept his head down and continued to hold my hand.

"You are a good girl, and this is going to be hard for you to understand. I know how much you loved your mother. You know she was sick, don't you?"

"Yes. She told me."

"She was very sick last night. She's in a better place where there is no more pain. She has passed away, Kandi, and now she's in Heaven."

I knew what he meant, but I couldn't think about what he was saying.

"Do you want to ask me any questions?"

"No."

We sat together for a minute. When we stood up, I went into Gram's tiny library and sat on a small stool. I found the ViewMaster I'd left on the floor the night before. I held it to my eyes and flipped through the images. I thought about never seeing Mom again. I missed her when I was away from her.

Then I thought about staying at Gram's every night, and my sadness softened.

We buried Mom beside Johnny. A Carmi pharmacist, a friend of our family, sang "Bridge Over Troubled Water." He'd counseled Mom through many moments of panic when she was crying, pleading for pills.

It was a beautiful service, I heard. Gram decided I shouldn't go and asked our neighbor to take me to the Evansville Zoo. Mom didn't look like herself, and Gram thought the open casket would frighten me.

Cards and letters poured in from family and friends who knew Mom when. They were an assurance to Gram that she'd done her best, the most any mother could do.

Dear Faire:

There isn't much I can do at this time to ease the pain and terrible hurt you are experiencing. I'm sure that you are all suffering, including Doug and Kandi. But being a mother, my heart has been with you. Kandi is too young to really know just what losing her mother will mean. But, I'm sure she is old enough to know that her young life has suffered a loss.

Faire, I know that you've been a good mother to your girls, a loving and caring mother. So please don't blame yourself for things that you weren't able to change. You are not only a good mother to your own but to me too growing up. And I'm sure you were to all of your girls' other friends along the way.

When I last saw Mary Ellen, she gave me a picture of Kandi and promised me one of Doug. She looked tired that day.

I'm going to remember how beautiful and happy she looked on her wedding day when she married Johnny in 1949.

Eleanor

Chapter 18

Healing Touch

March 2019

Affter eight hours of writing, I just couldn't keep thinking about Mom. I'd work all day with her pictures strewn across our table. When I stopped for the night, I'd turn them all upside down. I didn't want to see them until I had to the next day.

Mom and Me

I needed something to comfort me—mulling it over for hours on end, looking at the last picture of Mom and me. I stared at pictures of the bundles of brilliant flowers sent in her memory, a huge arrangement with a "First Grade Class" banner. I reread the notes from loved ones, to and fro.

(One Copy – 5/23/16)

We are very thankful to you, our good friends in this church, for your many acts of kindness during our troubled days. But what is even more comforting to us is your compassion and understanding

We are very thankful to you, our good friends in this church, for your many acts of kindness during our troubled days. But what is even more comforting to us is your compassion and understanding toward Mary Ellen.

~Her family

My therapist Joan suggested a form of Healing Touch to help me with these difficult days. "It is the process of a healthy, strong person passing their vitality, love, and compassion into you. Literally. As strange as it sounds, the science tells us it can be very healing. Think about it."

Sweet Reverend Phillippe had been performing a sort of Healing Touch with me. When we sat together on Gram's couch, and he told me Mom had died, he held my hand, infusing me with comfort. Maybe he had become a bishop, or was he still pastoring a small church somewhere in Illinois? Maybe he'd be one of those lucky people of a certain age who was Google-proof.

To my surprise, I immediately found an online article and knew it had to be him. A bold headline read, "Injured Pastor Returns to Metro-East Church," and a short paragraph explained that the good reverend had sustained serious brain injuries when he fell from a twelve-foot ladder while on a mission trip to Honduras. His church raised $70,000 to bring him home and pay for his medical expenses.

What a cruel turn! Then, not just one brain injury, but "injuries." Why have one when you could have more? How cherished he must've been for his congregation to raise $70,000 to bring him back to the states.

I was prone to over-empathizing with other people's misery. I had enough of my own misery, and taking on other people's grief was a real problem.

Dubious, I tried Joan's suggestion of Healing Touch. I got myself to a better place, and spring was coming.

It was time to move on with my research. I cleared my mind and started back on May 18, 1976, and Doug. I was *sure* he wasn't at the trailer before I left for Gram's.

WHEN MOM DIED, Doug was working in St. Louis selling shoes and also as a model. He appeared in an ad, posing in front of a KMOX helicopter, the station being one of the most widely recognized AM stations in the Midwest because of its affiliation with the Cardinals.

Doug came around regularly in reaction to Gram's summons. He was also partying hard, and although classy in dress and manner, he was a wild child.

Doug with the KMOX helicopter

He was the smartest guy in the room, patently well read, and you wouldn't have known he was sipping straight gin from the giant cup he refilled from the trunk of his car. He always smelled like expensive cologne—not liquor. I don't remember him slurring words or passing out. The women thought he was handsome. I just thought he was cool.

Doug

Doug didn't wear a helmet on his Kawasaki, the fastest motor-cycle being made, and in '74, after a night of drinking, laid it down on the interstate near the Poplar Street Bridge in St. Louis.

Gram logged his accident in the red notebook from Aunt Rita, right above a line saying Mom was in "bad shape."

I couldn't think of any length of time when Gram had it easy.

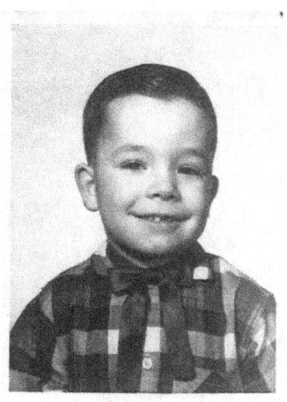

LINCOLN
SCHOOL DAYS 55-56

Doug, Kindergarten

Doug's precious childhood school pictures made my stomach hurt. Johnny's family wanted him and could've given him a good life. Aunt Helen and Aunt Rita were teenagers when he was born and mothered him like their own little baby.

If they could've done something, they would have. Were they all in fear of what extreme, maybe violent thing Mom might do if they called social services?

Doug had been so deeply hurt by Mom—the abandonment, the feeling of being cast aside and replaced by some flavor of the month guy, the worrying she might take one too many pills.

What if Doug's and my roles had been reversed, and I'd been the older sibling, watching Mom try to raise him? A train wreck unfold-ing. If I saw Mom neglecting him when he was inconvenient, but then pulling him to her bosom when she needed the security of the one love that was reliable, I might've easily resorted to vigilantism.

And maybe Doug did. Maybe he believed he was giving Mom the only remedy that would give her lasting peace . . . death.

Gram's grandchildren

August 22, 1976: Three Months After Mom's Death

There was no warning that my two-month slumber party with Gram was about to end. I learned how my future was determined in a draft of a letter from Gram to Doug's beloved long-time girlfriend. Gram adored Penny and hoped she'd be Doug's salvation, but Penny had given up on Doug.

Dear Penny,
 We thank you so much for the beautiful flowers you sent for Mary Ellen. The pretty

222

green bowl they were in, I shall keep for Kandi.

Since I feel you are concerned about K's future, I'll tell you. She is with us for the summer, but Janet is her guardian, and when she and her family are here in August, they will take K home to Powell, Wyoming.

She is looking forward to moving. Janet has three boys—seventeen, thirteen, and eight. I think K will fit in well.

Remember me to your mother. I think of her often and hope she is adjusting to life without your dad.

And, for you, Penny, and your husband, I wish you the very best. Thank you, again.

Sincerely,
Mrs. S.

I was looking forward to moving? News to me.

Gram and me, the morning we left for Wyoming

We posed for going-away pictures on the morning we left for Wyoming. Gram was sixty-seven, but between losing a child, her arthritic hands, and the horn-rimmed glasses, she looked considerably older. No more warrior-pose. Gram became hardened by the kiln effect of Mom's illness, but that fire was out now. It just didn't relieve her.

Mom's death was the worst kind of fait accompli because it wasn't over and never would be. The way it ended, the ashes from that fire would never go out. Gram needed rest and peace, but she wasn't getting it. She mustered up a smile, trying to convey her Healing Touch to me, but how could she have had anything left to give?

That photo didn't show the face of a child who wanted to leave home.

Mom made plans for me in the event of her death, something Gram made her do with Doug twenty-five years earlier. My educated guess is Mom didn't want her kids to be reared by Alvin, so Gram wasn't in the running to be my permanent guardian.

I have no memory of leaving down the gravel driveway away from Gram's house, to drive the thousands of miles to Wyoming. Once we were loaded up and began ticking through the miles, my sadness became tempered by the excitement I felt about a big family, complete with a mom and dad and three brothers. It was something from a movie.

Settling in Wyoming and adapting to this new life wasn't easy for anyone. Jack was nearly the same age as I was, and we fought. He got stuck with me in his room, which couldn't have been fun for him. At night, I was homesick, and I cried quietly in my bed.

For Aunt Helen, just the workload alone must've been overwhelming. Add a grieving child to the stress of regular life, and I'm sure Aunt Helen was exhausted and at a loss as to how to help me.

The two older boys, Patrick and Matt, assumed the role of older brothers with valor, and Jack eventually came around.

"Hey, that's my sister!" he said one day on the schoolyard when some kid broke my pricey prescription eyeglasses.

It lifted my heart beyond explanation. I was needy, and despite the beautiful mountains and my new family, I was being crushed by loneliness because I still knew that I was an orphan, and it showed on my face in my new family's Christmas card.

When the holidays came, Gram flew from Evansville, Indiana, to St. Louis to Denver to Cody, Wyoming. We stood outside the chain-link fence and watched Gram gingerly walk down the six or eight steps from the tiny plane onto the tarmac of the one-gate airport. We were looking for her quilted maroon coat—the winter coat she'd been wearing for twenty years.

Me and my cousins in the Christmas card

Between the logistics of getting there, the cost, and her fear of flying, I can't believe she made it. But there were never any miles or weather or mechanical failures that ever kept her from getting to her kids. Gram knew I was struggling and needed to see my new family situation for herself.

Me looking very serious on Christmas Day

No child should be that serious on Christmas Day.

After the holiday, I watched plaintively as a heartsick Gram left on the plane in her maroon coat. I thought maybe Gram would take me back with her to my familiar hometown, to our house, and to my friends, but she didn't.

Gram boarding the plane

Gram stopped in Denver to visit Aunt Rita who told me, thirty-five years later, that Gram cried throughout her visit. Gram might as well have been my mother, and we all know how it goes when a mother has to give up her child and has no choice in the matter.

* * *

THAT SUMMER, we made the long trip back to Crossville from Wyoming, for our once-a-year visit and the annual Crossville Alumni Banquet, a twenty-plus hour drive, straight through. I hadn't performed well in second grade after being separated from the three most influential people in my life—Gram, Aunt Maxine, and my mom. While we were home, Aunt Helen sat on the double bed, an old frame and mattress from the motel, with a thin avocado green bedspread.

"Do you want to stay here with Gram?"

It was difficult for me to tell Aunt Helen how I felt. So I didn't elaborate, but also didn't hesitate when I answered Aunt Helen's question. I so desperately missed Gram. Aunt Helen wanted a girl, but I have to wonder if the thought of going back to doing laundry for three children instead of four might have been a relief. She would never have complained about the extra work.

Now eighty-five, Aunt Helen has never whined about a single thing in her whole life. When I visited her, she told me that she was very happy to take care of me that year and wouldn't have had it any other way. What a kindness.

* * *

GRAM HAD the pictures of my 1977-going-away-day framed, and they hung in the hallway between the kitchen and living room for the next twenty-three years.

Time passed; I became a teenager. I wonder now if Gram positioned them in that hallway so that she could oft be reminded we had to tolerate each other because the alternative, separation, was worse.

In one of many contentious teenagers versus the elderly exchanges, I yelled, "You're not my mother!"

"Well, I'm the only mother you've got!" she replied.

I wish I could apologize. It was a hurtful thing to say. What a wonderful mother she was to me.

Chapter 19

Return to Sender

1977

G ram and I took our seats in the nosebleeds. Afraid of heights, Gram took forever getting up the steps with her pocketbook and popcorn. Once the show started, I was out of my seat, arms flailing up and down. The colorful anime of the scene was magnificent.

It was the Barnum and Bailey Circus.

We were so frantic in anticipation of the high-wire act that none of my three friends nor I sat still in the back seat on the way; no seat belts, one of us was on the floor board and one of the others climbed up in the crevice of the back window.

Gram just laughed. She'd been bored while I was gone.

It cost $125 to legally move my guardianship from Aunt Helen to Gram, and it came out of my own checking account to our attorney, David Stanley.

Gram wrote a slew of checks on August 22, 1977: the first to David for the legal work, $21 to Mrs. Shoup for math tutoring (Gram knew I was behind in all subjects, especially math), and $4.05 to the school for lunches through the end of September. Twenty cents a meal.

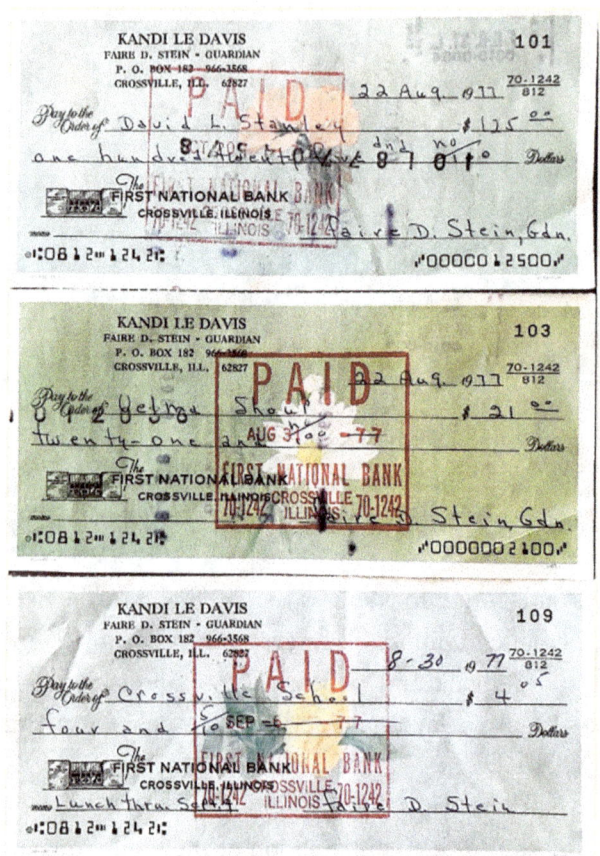

At the end of my first summer back from Wyoming, Gram got down to business. The average life expectancy for a female in 1977 was seventy-two years. Gram was nearing seventy years old, and therefore, started training me for my life beyond her lifetime.

"When your mom died, people were generous. You have money in a checking account in your name."

I interrupted Gram.

"Can I have an Easy Bake Oven?" I questioned her excitedly.

"We need to save it for your schooling," and she continued. "I'm entitled to a stipend from the state as your guardian, but I'll cash the check and keep it for you as spending money for ball games or Fall Festival. Then Grandad won't know what we're spending."

* * *

"THOSE KIDS DON'T HAVE what you have," Gram insisted.

I was irritated by the economically disadvantaged kids in school, not because they were poor but because I thought they were irresponsible. If they missed a Christmas concert, I just couldn't understand how they could do that to the rest of us and to the music teacher.

"You've been to Cherie's house."

"Yeah. I wish we lived in an apartment. It's cool."

"She lives in subsidized housing. Those families live there because they need help. Cherie might not have anything to wear for the Christmas concert."

* * *

"DANCING IS A SIN, AN ABOMINATION!" the preacher said. "Even if it's just the cake walk. I've never even danced with my wife," he boasted.

Many in the congregation had been "dancing" around the cake walk circle at Fall Festival, gambling a quarter per cake giveaway. There were at least five beautiful desserts given away every year, so some sinners spent a whopping $1.25. Heading home, Gram modified the morning message: "Methodists generally don't believe in those crazy ideas. He should be worrying about something other than the cake walk." She liked to teach me about how common sense and religion could hold hands.

Putting the dishes away after Sunday lunch, she said, "Damn!" She was exasperated over the utensil drawer that became stuck in the open position if it got off its tracks.

It was the first time I'd heard her curse, and I was engulfed with the genuine fear that she could go to hell.

When I finally told her why I was brooding, she laughed as if to say, "We've got bigger fish to fry, kid."

I was fixated on what could happen to her and where I would go. I prayed that she'd live till I got out of grade school.

* * *

"COME OVER HERE!" Mrs. Desper, our tough loving, cackling, paddling, preaching junior high English teacher called me over to her desk after class. I thought she was going to reiterate one of her mantras like, "Not is never, ever, ever a verb, Kandi."

I also thought I could also be in trouble for talking in class and would be writing sentences all night. Again.

However, she clasped my arms and turned me to face her. I nervously looked up at her. I hoped no one noticed her talking to me. Classmates already thought I was her pet, and I didn't want anyone disliking me for it.

"You know, if anything ever happens to your Gram, you can live with me."

I started to cry and couldn't respond. I never forgot her magnanimous commitment.

1978

When Grandad set out for Evansville, intent on buying himself a new Chevy, Gram was furious. "You have a truck! Now a new car? You're something, Alvin. Pearl doesn't like the truck? Do you know when we bought my Pontiac?"

He sat on the bed he shared with only himself, pulled on his cotton undershirt, and buttoned a white collared shirt.

"It was '62. I said I was leaving this place if you didn't get me a new car, so you came home with a used one!"

Grandad snickered and walked out.

I know Gram fretted from the moment he left, wondering how she'd follow through on her threat. I expect she could've been cleaning a motel room when she started counting the years he'd been carrying on with Pearl, but was too angry to do the math.

Uncle Joe wasn't the one who had to cook and clean for Alvin and run this whole place when he counseled Faire a lifetime ago to "work it out."

She knew the year Uncle Joe had intervened. It was '54.

"Calm down. It'll be alright."

I can imagine Gram putting her head down and crying, embarrassed by her histrionics.

"Where will you go if you leave?"

It would have been a sincerely posed question from Uncle Joe.

"I can stay with Mother and Maxine. It could be like old times!" she laughed, a sad sort of laugh.

Uncle Joe shook his head, acknowledging the option.

"Do you think Alvin would have that? You over here and him over there? The motel and everything else falling apart? He couldn't manage for one day."

I'm sure Gram chortled, imagining the satisfaction of him scrambling.

"I'm not afraid he'd hurt any of us. I don't think he'd take on the whole family, but I'm afraid he'd leave you destitute, Faire."

Every ten years when Gram had had enough and came to him, Uncle Joe worried over what he would advise.

"Can you find a way to have your own life? Stop angling to leave. Let him go off with her, and you find yourself some peace and quiet in your crosswords and your reading."

"He's making a fool of me. Everyone knows where he's off to when he gets his Sunday suit on."

Uncle Joe paused. Honestly, he'd never had a bit of use for Alvin.

"If we are truly Christians, we will pray for him. If we want to be practical, we will just ignore him. It's you I'm worried about. None of this is upsetting Alvin. He can't even imagine that you're here with me now, crying. He is so cruel to you. I don't know if he realizes it or not, but he does everything he can to demean you.

"You deserve better. But I'm afraid if you try to divorce him, he'll leave you with nothing. You'll spend the rest of your life being bitter because you're the one who made all that money through your hard work, and you'd have none of it at the end of the day. When you can't do it anymore, and that's got to be soon, because I swear you're gonna work yourself to death, Faire, you just quit it! Just stop doing everything around there. He'll never put you out on your ear. He wouldn't know how to feed himself, for one thing."

Twenty-four years after that first talk with Uncle Joe, I think Gram was truly about to give out. The motel was on its last leg. The white plaster was falling off in large pieces from the north and south sides of the building. The water fountains didn't work anymore, and the swing set Johnny helped them build was now too old looking to excite any of the children who stayed overnight. And that was just the tip.

The rental houses were in such disrepair. They attracted disadvantaged tenants with a lot of problems Gram couldn't solve. Despite trying, she could never keep out of it. When the renters in the apartment above the station tied their dog up with a heavy chain and didn't feed it, Gram snuck chicken bones to the dog in the middle of the night.

The same couple were gone for days, and Gram asked the children what they'd been eating. When the kids responded, "Ketchup sandwiches," She walked up the sidewalk to the station with bologna sandwiches and wet washcloths for them to wipe their faces and hands.

Gram snuck another tenant, Vicki Low, money to get away from her abusive husband. Vicki left him but also left her children. Gram was sick over it. Her internal maternal warrior couldn't fathom Vicki's decision.

* * *

WHEN WE WENT to my softball games, Gram and Aunt Maxine preferred to get to the ball field early so as to get their lawn chairs set for a good view of all the positions. Gram was bored with tee-ball and was relieved when I graduated to something more competitive.

It was still slow. She liked the power of baseball, the snap of a fast pitch in the catcher's mitt. She'd never played any ball. It wasn't even a thought for women when she'd been a kid, but baseball was just everything she held dear—memories of her dad, competition, good-looking guys, and hard work.

After one particular game, I came back from the concession stand with Funyuns; a grasshopper, a mixture of fountain sodas including Ski, Nehi Orange, and Pepsi; and popcorn for Gram and Aunt Maxine.

We watched a little of the older girls' game.

"Stay around and watch the older girls, and you'll learn something," our coach told us.

I was intimidated by how hard the pitcher threw and how hard Coach hit the grounders at them during warm-up. My sidekick, Robin, was already playing with the older girls. She was being groomed to catch, and Robin had such a powerful arm. She busted a hole in the pitch-back right after she got it for her eighth birthday.

We headed home after the third inning. We walked in the doorway of the living room, just as Grandad let out a big laugh at his program. Gram marched over to the console TV in the corner and turned down *Sanford and Sons*. Grandad continued a conversation he had started before we had left for my game. "I bought you a car," he said. "You can go pick it up."

She waited for Alvin to say, "Boy, I got you, didn't I?" But he continued to try and watch *Sanford and Sons* and ignore Gram.

"Are you kidding me or not?" she asked him.

"Call 'em," he said and handed her a business card.

Gram dialed the number for Kenny Kent Chevrolet.

"Yes, ma'am. And I'll be here until 8:00 tonight."

"Kandi, call your Aunt Maxine. Let's go pick up the car."

We drove to Evansville in record time. The smell of the brand new candy-apple red Nova was some combination of vinyl and treated carpet, and Gram had never smelled anything quite so wonderful. It might as well have been a Cadillac.

"I just need you to sign the invoice," the salesman said as they wound through the showroom to his office.

I think Gram wanted to see what Grandad paid for the vehicle — how it compared to the cost of his. She saw a checkmark next to the Impala, and the salesman then checked off the Nova and handed her the pen.

She focused on a third line item:

```
Nova, Wondrous Red, 4-dr, $3,702
Impala, Burnt Orange, $5,471
Silverado Pickup, Sunset Tan, $5,282
Tax $ 722.00
_____

Cash Sale Total: $15,177.75
```

Gram nearly choked. Alvin actually bought himself *two* new cars. Gram piled all the things from the Pontiac in the trunk and would have to organize it all in the morning. She spent the first fifteen minutes of the ride stewing about what she'd say to Grandad. But it didn't last. The new car was more than she'd expected from him.

The sun was setting over the New Harmony, Indiana, bridge, the last leg in the journey back to Crossville. No one was coming, so Gram drove down the middle of the narrow, old, metal structure and stopped to pay the fifty-cent toll.

Gram carefully pulled into the carport. She calmly walked into the house, set down her pocketbook, went to the restroom to wash her hands, and stepped into the living room to the side of Alvin's chair.

"I'm putting a closed sign out in the morning. I'm through with the motel. I've done enough."

1979

When Doug finally married an elementary school teacher, Gram thought he'd been rescued from booze and late nights. Celia was a lovely person and encouraged Doug to invite me on their summer vacations.

Gram needed a break from me. She loved me more than life, but it was surely exhausting to have a ten year old who never stopped talking.

I would get so excited before Doug picked me up that I couldn't sleep for days. I'd tell all my friends that my big brother was taking me to Florida.

"He looks like Big John," I would announce.

Big John, the giant, dark-haired Dudley Do-Right-looking statue man, sat in front of the grocery store in Carmi.

Doug showed up one summer in a new Ford Bronco 2. I couldn't wait to get inside. He held a plastic cup between the legs of his terry cloth shorts. Gram didn't know it was gin, but I did. Driving, Doug's left elbow would rest on the door as he nervously twirled pieces of hair in his left hand. Elton John was on the radio.

Doug took me to the ocean, put me on roller coasters. Celia eventually bought me my first bra and explained to me the concept of underarm deodorant. We played catch, went to Chicago where I fell in love with the gold coast of Lake Michigan. We saw the impressive Museum of Science and Industry and The Shedd Aquarium.

Doug bought me my first real bike — a pink Huffy dirt bike that I rode until the thick foam seat fell off. And my first real stereo — a Soundesign turntable with big, loud speakers.

* * *

Gram with Doug's son

"IT'S A BOY!"

Doug called from the hospital to tell Gram she was a great-grandmother.

After the baby was born, Doug's visits were less frequent. Maybe the stress of fatherhood was causing him to turn to alcohol more than usual. He was distant and moody.

Doug and his son

I visited over the Fourth of July. The backyard was full of people I didn't know, partying the night away—something I'd never seen. I was lonely and nervous, and I just wanted to go home.

* * *

GRAM WORRIED about what extreme chore Grandad might have me tackling. "Be careful with her, Alvin," she would command.

From the time I was seven or eight, he had me doing all kinds of work, ranging from greasing the joints underneath the Impala to climbing on the roof of the house to clean out the gutters. Gram was terrified he didn't have the car safely on the lift or that the ladder he set up wasn't exactly secure. In summertime, I went along on his morning trips to the farm. He would flash a rare smile and hum while he chewed a piece of sassafras between his teeth. The pickup rolled over chunks of large white gravel, and pieces jumped up from the dust smacking the side of the truck.

"Boy, oh boy. Shewie." He hated the nicks the gravel made in the paint of the Silverado.

Our one-hundred acre farm was wedged-shaped, the front half taken up by small ponds for fishing and open grazing land for livestock, which Grandad had long since given up on.

The wide entrance to the overgrown grassy driving lane was blocked by a six-foot high gate trimmed with a barbed wire top and a "Keep Out" sign.

"Open up the gate."

I'd run cheerfully up to open the heavy lock and release the weighty chain. The chain itself was half my size, and it took a minute or more to wind it out through the lattice of the fence and then lay it on the grass. The fifteen-foot long gate was wobbly on its hinges and dug into the unleveled ground. Alvin drove through, and I closed the gate behind him, bouncing excitedly back toward the cab of the truck. Then we traveled down the rugged lane, past the old salt lick, to the big barn. Grandad slid open the rugged wooden door to the usual smell of catfish food.

Gram said she couldn't think of a time when Grandad couldn't eat, and fried fish was one of his favorites. He filled one of his ponds with channel catfish and did all he could to fatten them up.

"Fill it up good, and throw it out there. Then come back for more."

The fish food pellets landed on the surface, between the lily pads and cattails, and catfish mouths immediately surfaced to engulf them. I'd go back for more.

I loved the smell of the barn and the routine of putting our small boat in the pond to drift around and explore. Grandad baited my hook and handed me the little cane-pole to lower into the murky water. By 10:00 on those sticky morns, he would've soaked through his overalls and soiled the white handkerchief he used to wipe his brow. We'd pull the tin boat up off the shore, turn it face down, and Grandad would sit on an old wire spool while he put the tackle back in its box.

Once home, Gram would put lunch on the table and maybe she'd delay it a bit, just to show Grandad she still had a will of her own. After our meal, Grandad would get the fish ready to freeze. He killed the poor things by pounding them in the head with a hammer, something no one could watch, and then with great pride, gutted them and filleted them out.

1980

"Mrs. Stein, can we talk to you in the hallway?" The medical staff wanted to talk to Gram.

"Kandi is finished with the surgery. There was a problem."

This was supposed to be a simple procedure—a very minor nasal surgery. I'd spend one night at St. Mary's in Evansville and then go home. The nurse went on with her explanation of what had happened instead.

"One of the recovery nurses noticed Kandi looked blue in the face. She aspirated the cotton packing that was in her nose. It's lodged in her trachea. They're doing a tracheotomy right now.

"She was without oxygen for many minutes. We think five or more. We don't know what she will be like when she wakes up. There may be brain damage."

Gram called Aunt Rita, frantic over how she would care for a disabled child. Nothing was ever easy for Gram.

I spent three weeks in the hospital and now wear a CPAP as a reminder of the tracheotomy that caused scar tissue.

"Sue them, Faire. Take that doctor for everything he's got. He was negligent."

"No," she'd say. "No one's fault. Just gotta be thankful it wasn't worse."

1981

"Boy, your granddad is something. He tried to shoot me last night!" Kevin Schmidt was a distant cousin. "I went fishing down there. Granny said it'd be okay with Alvin. I climbed the fence, and was just trying to catch something for dinner. He's a bad shot, though."

The whole eighth grade class heard. I don't know why I cared. Everyone in town could name things they'd seen or heard about Alvin through the years.

It was the eighties, and it was an all-out Cold War at home. We would sit mostly in silence at the kitchen table during supper. Gram was never happy at mealtime. She was tired and didn't herself ever care much about food, other than maybe a piece of pie and a good cup of coffee. I was *always* unhappy with the offering. I picked and complained about the meat of the day, which I considered to be either too chewy or too slimy, making it an even more thankless job for Gram.

It was a bad combination of moods. The dynamic should've been studied by psychiatrists. Gram would talk to me but never to Alvin.

She rarely looked at him. Gram was minding Uncle Joe's advice and considered the topic of "Alvin" to be completely triturated.

Grandad mostly looked at his food. The reason, I don't know—self-loathing, disinterest—it was impossible to tell what went on in the mind of a person who spoke less than five total words a day.

I think Grandad must've been a slow eater. Gram and I would be finished, have our dishes washed, and leave him there. She'd be in her bedroom recliner, watching *The Wheel* before Alvin got to dessert.

As the sun would go down, the house was dark, with Alvin controlling even the light switches. It was absent the warm glow of a lamp or fireplace that gets one through the endless Midwest winters that Gram and I hated.

People would drive by and say, "I thought no one was home."

Having a teenager in the house complicated the wretched environment.

Nearly eighty, Alvin began to suffer mini-strokes and was in and out of reality. He believed there were workmen atop the water tower downtown—he would watch these imaginary men for hours. I had sympathy for him. Although, whatever effect the strokes had on his brain didn't lessen his propensity for turning everyday situations into some dramatic rampage.

My friends were afraid of him, and he didn't change just because we had a guest. I was constantly embarrassed by his meanness, and I'm shocked other parents let their kids come over. I suppose they knew we were safe enough with Gram around.

I came home one day to find one of my teachers sitting at our kitchen table. Somehow, she knew Grandad had a shotgun and had probably heard gossip that he was losing it. She was worried about our safety.

What could Gram have said in response? "Oh, he'd never get his shotgun out. He'd never do anything that crazy."

1984

The Nova was our escape. We'd zoom out of the driveway, gravel flying. On those many evenings when we needed sanctuary, we would head out in our new four-door. Gram's sister, Aunt Maxine was always up for anything. We'd pull up; I'd hop out of the car and walk right in the back screen door, scaring her half to death. "Wanna go for a drive?"

As she gathered her pocketbook and sweater, Aunt Maxine would sometimes decide to bring along a recent edition of *The Carmi Times,* if it was a newsy week.

Gram and Maxine were serious devotees, enthusiastically awaiting the paper at three-ish every weekday.

One was quick to phone the other to say, "It's here."

Getting *The Times* was kinda like getting *The Wall Street Journal,* but not exactly.

"Local News" was recounted of course by locals. It would be filled with: "So-and-so's daughter, who now resides in Champaign-Urbana, visited last weekend. For dinner, the family enjoyed pot roast and Betty's apple pie."

Or: "Sophomore Bulldog basketball sensation so-and-so suffered a broken ankle helping his paternal grandma, Barbara Nielsen, clean up her basement. We wish him a speedy recovery and hope they were finished before he was injured!"

Gram liked to know where people who "made the paper" lived. We could easily find their addresses in the phone book, which she stored in the black, plastic organizer that rested on the floorboard between the front seats of the car.

The Nova was like Gram's little office. Gram stored other vital items in her car:

- Windex, name brand only
- paper towels
- eye glass cleaner

- Crossville phone book
- Carmi phone book
- Rag—always a piece of a pillowcase or sheet because they didn't leave streaks on the windows. The fabric would often be stamped "Stein Motel"
- Sunglasses (the "slide over the frame" old-lady kind)
- Wintergreen Certs
- Freedent gum, the kind that didn't stick to dentures
- Kleenex, a box in front and one in the rear window

Gram enjoyed driving past the houses, inspecting the yards, visualizing all the goings-on that had been reported, judging if she thought they had money or not.

I was mortified by this. I would lie down in the back seat so that I couldn't be recognized and ask her questions about why we were so nosey.

"Why do you care?" I'd ask her.

"I like to see where people live. They have no idea who we are. We're just Crossville bumpkins."

1986

Five hundred and twenty. I tried to calculate how many ball games and concerts Gram and Aunt Maxine escorted me to between '77 and '87.

"You're keeping them young," people told me.

Nearly every one of the eighty-seven students at Crossville High School played a sport. We usually had about what we needed to field a team and no one to spare.

I was a cheerleader, played volleyball and softball, was in the band and choir and all the plays.

And that was just school. Church brought a whole other litany of appearances. Not to say that I was good at all of these things. It was just what we did to keep the activities going.

Gram and Aunt Maxine loved every minute of it except volleyball.

"I don't understand it."

"Do you want me to explain it to you?"

"No. I just don't like it."

But she was still at every single game—she and Aunt Maxine, showing up in their slacks and blouses and making their way up the old wooden bleachers, their pocketbooks hanging over their arms.

There would never be more than five people rooting for us.

We fielded a surprisingly competitive softball team that practiced starting in January with games beginning in March and continuing throughout the summer.

Faire and Maxine showed up sometimes before the team arrived on the bus, pulling the Nova up (still spotless inside and out) into the perfect spot—close enough to see the action but far enough down the line that a foul ball wouldn't find itself meeting the hood of the car.

At away games, when there wasn't parking near the field, they'd carry their aluminum, webbed-seat lawn chairs behind the backstop, look for an even spot in the grass, and set them up where they could call balls and strikes themselves.

It was the week of the Alumni Banquet and everyone who'd moved away was back in town. Our softball team was chasing a ticket to the state tournament.

The yearbook photographer caught Gram's consternation. She may have been more devastated than I was when we lost 6-0.

Gram at a ballgame

The late writer Patrick Seil called it a David vs. Goliath confrontation. We had thirty-seven female students, and with no class system at that time in Illinois, we were playing schools ten, twenty, thirty times the size of Crossville High School. We'd already faced and beaten Mt. Vernon, an AA school.

246

David finally ran out of pebbles Monday afternoon. And, when the end came, the Tigers and their fans showed what class is all about. There were no tears, no complaining, just sportsmanlike applause and handshakes, and words of congratulations. Coach David Lee presented the trophy and said afterward, "It's really something for a school the size of Crossville to go this far," he said as the end drew near. "I'm sure that doesn't mean much to them now, but it will someday." There are bigger schools and teams with more talent — but none with more heart.

* * *

WHEN STEVE SANDERS, the son of Gram's first cousin, became an anchor of the noon news broadcast at WGN out of Chicago, Gram and Maxine were glued to the TV every weekday from twelve to one. Gram analyzed his choice of ties and probably wrote letters to his parents about which ones she preferred. I blame Steve for what happened to Gram and Aunt Maxine.

The Cubs. There were no lights at Wrigley until 1988, so for four years, the games followed Steve's newscast. St. Louis games weren't viewable in our market, so that's what happened to Gram.

She left the winning St. Louis Cardinals, who'd already had one World Championship in the eighties, for... the ... Cubs.

They had never, at that point, NEVER won a World Series.

Gram would apply a massive coat of Absorbine Jr., a stinky green arthritis liniment in a glass bottle with a felt dabber tip, and pour herself a half glass of Coke with one, only one, ice cube, and she'd watch every pitch. She was hot for Ryne Sandberg, the second baseman, and thought The Bull, Leon Durham, first baseman, was the best she'd seen.

Harry Caray captivated her with his weird way of slurring from either beer or a just a genetically large tongue. His sidekick was Steve Stone, a cigar smoking, level-headed baseball aficionado. Back when Gram was still a Cards fan and listening to them on the radio, Caray was the color commentator for the Cardinals but was fired in 1969, after he began messing around with the wife of Cardinals owner, Gussie Busch—as in Anheuser-Busch. Caray went to Chicago and got back into the business for the White Sox until '81, starting with the Cubs in '82. Obviously a risk taker. Cardinals to Sox to Cubs. Caray could've been murdered by any number of fans.

1987

It was the middle of the night on the evening before I left for college, when Grandad's summoning whistle startled me out of a dead sleep. I went to the top of the stairs and saw him motion for me to come down. He sat down in the chair nearest the stairwell. It took him a while to speak. He started to cry. I was half-awake and couldn't believe no one else was witnessing this moment of tenderness.

"Why don't you stay around here? You could go to school in Carbondale."

I'd planned on majoring in music and was going back to Wyoming where there was a good jazz program near Aunt Helen.

His tears stunned me, and I was so caught off guard by this big ask that I couldn't even respond. "Your gram will be awfully lost without you here." It was the only time he had *ever* had a conversation with me. He'd communicated in demands.

"Make me an egg sandwich."

"Shut that light off!"

I'd never received so much as a "Happy birthday," let alone a gift, and never saw him give Gram a single present, card, or even a verbal acknowledgment on any holiday.

It's hard to believe, but that's how it was.

In the morning, with my car all packed up, Aunt Helen told him, "Dad, we've paid her tuition."

Gram probably never heard that story, but she would've wanted to. Like me, she was always looking for something good in him.

Grandad died of complications from a stroke in November of 1987, three months after I went to college.

February 2019

"How did Alvin treat you, Kandi?"

Carol, Lisa and I were still in southern Illinois for the Anna visit and had just come from Susan Werner's office

Alvin holding baby Kandi

My sister-in-law, Renee, my half-brother Mark's wife, was asking about the latest on this book when Alvin's name came up. He wasn't my favorite subject. "He was old. I could outrun him. When I was

249

little, he wasn't so bad. There are some pictures with grandkids where he was smiling." I spoke casually as I told the story. My Alvin issues were too much to let myself feel.

Lisa suggested, "Tell her about the horse."

Aunt Maxine's husband, John, was a livestock broker for local farmers, and he took his big truck with the fenced-in bed to the auction house in Vienna, Illinois. Uncle John purchased livestock on the farmers' behalf and delivered it to them. I was eight or nine and loved the loud rolling call of the auctioneer, as he pressed the cheap, scratchy-sounding microphone against his lips. After hours of the valuable animals being circled through, the auctioneer paraded out the leftovers meant to be pets. Uncle John and I once brought home a baby goat, one time a squealing piglet, and sometimes, ponies.

One sad, little pony named Anne had no intention of being ridden, and back in Crossville, she darted skittishly around our farm-land. She sensed she wasn't safe. Grandad's strategy was to chase her in his pickup. I thought we'd get close, and he'd stop the truck, so I'd be able to snag the reins, but he didn't stop. He laughed as the truck went thud into her side.

Anne made a run for it one morning, passing our truck and running out the gate of the farm onto the dusty gravel country road. Grandad sped after her, *Dukes of Hazard* style, as she turned into an overgrown old church cemetery. We bounced down the rocky lane into the uneven grass, and Anne became penned against a fence. Grandad's truck surged into her repeatedly. I couldn't say a word. I didn't *have* the words.

He told me he was giving Anne to the farmer down the road. When I asked to visit her, Grandad claimed the farmer had put her in a pen with some full grown mares who'd trampled her to death.

More likely Alvin lost his temper and pulled out his shotgun or possibly finally did her in with the truck.

I began to despise him. Like my mother, I wasn't very good at hiding it. There was a look Grandad had when he came after me. He would follow me into my room and shove me against a wall or trap me behind a door, smashing me against the opposing wall. He would pinch and slap. Do whatever he was able to do as an elderly man. I was never seriously injured—physically.

Like all bullies, Alvin thrived on making fun of people. If I stayed on the phone with a girlfriend long enough to get on his nerves, he'd pick up the receiver in another room and mock my conversation in a high-pitched girlish tone. The embarrassment always made me cry, but I attempted to ignore him for long enough to finish the phone call. If I didn't hang up soon enough, he'd jerk the handset from me and slam it down.

Severely hearing impaired since her sixties, Gram never heard the commotion.

"I hate you!" I would scream at him.

Gram and I were suffering, and I didn't have the words to ask for help.

Grandad and His Garden

I arrived at a teenage church youth group party one night very shaken by Alvin and locked myself in the bathroom with a small plastic knife we were supposed to use for our dinner. I began scraping my arms with the knife, not attempting to do real harm, but as a cry for help. Someone would ask me what happened, and I'd tell them it was Alvin. A wound would give me an opening, but the marks were too benign for anyone to even notice, let alone make a connection to Alvin. I considered giving myself a black eye but chickened out.

A new level of hostility arose when I caught him forcefully squeezing Gram's arm during an argument. He was on the verge of hitting her in the face but stopped short and retreated to his recliner to watch boxing.

Crying and shaking, I yelled, "Don't touch her. I will kill you!"

I meant it. How peaceful and sane life would be without him. Alvin didn't apologize or promise it wouldn't happen again. As victims, Gram and I never called the town cop, later dropping the charges. We just dried our eyes. Gram would pat me lovingly and say, "Let's go."

We'd leave the house for a drive, usually straight to the Dairy Queen where we'd eat our feelings. We'd be gone for hours and hours.

Chapter 20

I-Urndit

1989

Three years after Alvin died, Gram bought herself a new Oldsmobile and thought of a clever vanity plate, I-URNDIT, but she worried about the extra cost and what people would think.

College was going well for me, and although Crossville had closed its schools and there were no ball games to see, Gram still had the Cubs.

Instead of nights at the hospital with Mom, Gram was enjoying Scrabble games. It's noteworthy that her protective maternal demeanor evaporated as soon as we started keeping score. She liked nothing better than to be at the kitchen table with her family, secure in the framework of her kitchen, Coke, and homemade party mix.

When Gram turned eighty, Aunt Rita and Aunt Helen flew home and surprised her, something she hated—surprises. They filled the kitchen with classmates and close friends. She rarely socialized—didn't take the time and couldn't hear well enough to converse, but she enjoyed that day. It was probably the only birthday party she'd ever had.

* * *

GRAM never much cared for Christmas after Mom died. She wanted the tree down by Christmas afternoon. Her lack of enthusiasm was disappointing to me. Why couldn't she sit still long enough to enjoy *It's a Wonderful Life,* or why didn't she want to experiment with new recipes for Christmas dinner? She'd prepared hundreds of obligatory meals and got no lift from thinking about gourmet food the way I did.

"Aunt Rita and I think we should have a non-traditional Christmas meal. Something different." I screamed through the phone from the tiny front bedroom of my college apartment. We were tired of ham and decided we'd make a glazed pork loin.

"Sounds good to me. If you two are cooking, I'm happy." I brought friends home from college who were amazed at Gram's agility and vibrancy at eighty-one. She was driving, taking care of a good-sized house, but had finally hired someone to mow the yard. She didn't think about selling it at all. And I'm sure she still utilized the window, gazing out of it with the same faraway stare, going over it all, wondering what she did wrong.

It was the day after Christmas. Gram was in her bedroom, watching football. I sat down on the stool in front of her chair, positioned so she could read my lips which she was adept at. She took off her headset that had been rigged up, so she could hear the TV. We could've been talking about a trip to Evansville, or maybe she was telling me about things she needed help with. As she looked at me, I saw the corner of her mouth slowly drop, and the rest of her face became drawn. I could tell she couldn't feel what was happening to her.

"We gotta go," I screamed to Aunt Rita. We grabbed Gram's coat and purse, and she walked herself to the car.

It was years before interventional stroke medications existed.

The world picked the worst person it could think of to make immobile, but Gram battled hard. They rehabbed her in the hospital, helping her speak audibly and walk. Once home, she was religious to her exercises and walked laps around the house daily. For two years, she cared for herself with Aunt Maxine assisting her when necessary and Aunt Rita making frequent long trips home to help.

And then it just didn't work anymore. It happened so slowly, the atrophy, but eventually Gram was unable to even take herself to the bathroom, and she required twenty-four-hour care.

The fell swoop of circumstance had crashed down on her once again.

Chapter 21

Idea Unfelled

July 1997

"The doc told me I was trying to drink myself to death, but that I wasn't doing a very good job." Doug said. "It's been thirty days, and I don't even miss it."

Doug, now forty-eight to my twenty-seven, had been in critical condition—nearly died.

It was daytime, and Doug was lucid. His late-night calls were usually tearful ramblings. He'd give me his version of why Celia had left him and why he wasn't allowed to see his son. Then suddenly, "Mom loved us, you know. She was a good mother."

He sounded like that little boy with the sweet face.

For years, I avoided talking to him. My pain from the past was curdled and stuck somewhere in the pit of my stomach. I was making my own way in the world, working seventy hours a week teaching at a massive suburban school, managing a cast of eighty kids involved in huge musical productions. I couldn't think of anything except whether the pancake makeup on Jane Eyre was going to make her look sallow, in a cool way, or just dead.

"All I want to do is eat candy," Doug told me on the phone. "I've quit smoking. You know I lost my job. That's how bad I was."

He spoke like someone in recovery with a twenty-five-year coin, talking as if it was all behind him. "I can't believe how good I feel."

I wondered who would take care of Doug while he recovered, and if he had any sober friends to lean on. How would he get to meetings? Did he need money? *I should go*, I thought.

I talked to friends about it. "I don't know if he wants to see anyone. He's been really sick. He'd tell me if he wanted me to come," I theorized.

Truthfully, I had a vacation planned, and I didn't want to cancel it. I was tired. I deserved a vacation, and I hadn't seen Doug in years. I couldn't remember when he'd been to see Gram.

I sent Doug a box of candy, wrote him a note of encouragement, and went to Mexico. My visit was an idea unfelled. When I landed back in the states, Doug was MIA. I followed up with another letter.

October 1997

Dear Doug,

Just wanted to drop you a line and check in. I'm not sure what's going on but just wanted you to know I'm thinking about you. There is a lot of football on today, so I wonder if that's what you're doing.

I was in Crossville last weekend for the big Fall Festival. Aunt Maxine and I walked up with our lawn chairs. You know how she loves to people watch and get in on "the scoop."

The parade consisted mostly of politicians, John Deere tractors, and a few Shriners here and there. I went home long before Aunt Maxine did so, no telling what kind of mischief she got into after I left. Gram was fairly confused and not much interested in talking. She did get pretty excited about a chocolate shake I brought from the Rotary stand.

Teaching is fine, and I have small classes this year. So far, no problems to speak of and that is something to celebrate.

I hope that you're doing OK. You know that I think about you but am unsure about how to help. You know where I am, and you know that I love you.

Kandi

I got no response to my letter, and I feared Doug was drinking again.

October 31, 1997

"We should do something tonight! It's Halloween." I was trying to convince my friend Sheryl, not a costume kind of person, that Halloween was a worthy holiday.

"It just kind of gives me the creeps," she answered.

"We don't have to go to a haunted house, but we should do something." In my opinion, Halloween should be a high holiday.

While we considered our options, I checked the Call Notes voicemail on my home phone.

"Kandi, it's Aunt Rita. I need to talk to you. Call me as soon as you can."

There was another message shortly after the first one. She must've tried to reach me at school, too, but I'd left as soon as my last class was out. Sheryl was asking me questions, but I couldn't come up with any words. It was Gram. I knew it. I was afraid to return Aunt Rita's call.

It's the worst feeling in the world. You just know someone has died. Time stands still, and you think, *Here it is.* When I called back, she gave me the news.

"It's Doug. He shot himself on the balcony of his apartment."

* * *

Myth: People often make a cry for help before they commit suicide.

THE AUTOPSY SHOWED Doug was riddled with pancreatic cancer as a result of his years of drinking. He had no chance of recovery, no insurance, no access to the solace of hospice care. I'll never know if the cancer drove him to suicide. It may have driven the timing, but I'm not sure if it was the impetus.

The guilt paralyzed me. I got through the remainder of the school year and decided on a leave of absence from teaching. My tank was empty.

I didn't say goodbye to students or staff. I just knew they were all thinking, *Aren't her parents already dead, too?*

Our family decided on a quiet graveside service and buried Doug next to Mom and Johnny. We lied and told Gram Doug had died of cancer. We couldn't bring ourselves to give her the rest of the story. Aunt Maxine's son, Rob, a wonderful man of enviable character offered words of logic and comfort, but we were all guilty. First, Mom, and had we just let it happen again? Couldn't we have, at least, made him comfortable at the end? He was a victim in the truest sense of the word.

But we didn't know. We just didn't know. I still felt culpable.

And now *you*, the reader, know what I know.

What guilt was Doug trying to allay with the evergreen essence of gin? The explosive finale to his life was a huge certitude in the overall fact pattern surrounding my mom's death.

I never wanted to write a crime novel. I only wanted to know the facts, and knowing what truth I knew and what I could piece together required me to consider that my brother had killed our mom.

Chapter 22

Please Take Notice

March 2019

L ife was rolling along for me in St. Louis. I hadn't heard a word since I'd met with the attorney Susan Werner in Anna two weeks earlier. I had no idea where things stood with Mom's medical records. Susan's email responses were too hurried and obscure to follow.

One spring morning, I walked down our steep, blacktop driveway to retrieve the mail and stepped back into the kitchen where Lisa was figuring out her breakfast.

"What is there to eat?" Lisa asked me from the kitchen.

"Cereal."

"I don't see cereal. I only see granola."

"Granola is cereal."

"Oh."

I sorted through the mail and held up an envelope from Susan Werner announcing we had been assigned an upcoming court date.

```
PLEASE TAKE NOTICE that on March 27, 2019, @
1:00 p.m., or as soon thereafter as counsel
may be heard, I shall appear before the
Honorable Judge Bert, or any judge sitting
in his stead, in the courtroom usually occu-
pied by him of the Union County Courthouse,
Jonesboro, Illinois, and then and there be
present for a hearing. DEFAULT JUDGEMENT MAY
BE ENTERED IF YOU FAIL TO APPEAR.
```

After so much effort, we were finally getting somewhere. Leaning over a bowl of granola, I began to worry about what questions the judge might ask me in front of a courtroom of strangers.

* * *

April 2019

On the day of the hearing, I explained to Lisa, "I'm just trying to manage my expectations." We were each sorting through clothing for something simple, nothing intimidating or too cosmopolitan.

"Manage expectations about what's in the records or about what the judge decides?"

Moose was on the bed barking for our attention.

"What the judge decides."

Lisa continued, giving me her thoughts on a theory she'd been mentioning since our original trip to Anna. "I'm telling you, this judge could be thinking about whether he might be setting a prece-dent. If he allows this, he could potentially have to hear a lot of cases about this same thing, and he may not want to do that. It could involve cases statewide. This could be a big deal."

"So weird. Of all the things I'm trying to do, setting a legal prece-dent isn't one of them. How would anyone know a precedent had been set? No one has ever even made a request for records."

"Well, Choate may not know everything that goes on. People may have made appeals to the judge, but he never agrees to have the records released."

"We could be overthinking this. Maybe our experience could somehow make this process easier for all the other families. All those postings online from people who couldn't figure out the process," I told her.

I was in the shower, and Lisa poked her head into the bathroom, talking as loudly as she could over the exhaust fan. "I'm going in the courtroom with you, OK?"

"Yes. I want you to."

"OK. Just making sure that's what you wanted," she said sweetly.

She'd already made the decision for me that if and when we received the records, she would read them first. I was so grateful for Lisa, that day and every day. Even after nearly twenty years, we were still so happy together.

I had drunk several cups of coffee before showering and was vigorously giving myself all kinds of advice as I washed with the new grapefruit shower gel I'd gotten from Amazon. *Seem responsible and together but not intimidating. Seem like you're affected by it but not too affected by it. And don't say how Mom died. He'll think you're looking for a scapegoat. Wear real deodorant, not the natural stuff. And don't wear Birkenstocks.*

I put a little extra food in Moose's bowl and hit the road for the two-hour drive to the Union County Courthouse. "Pretty day for a drive," Lisa said, and I thought of Gram, of course.

* * *

INTERSTATE 55 SOUTH OF ST. Louis is bordered by picturesque bluffs with sleek faces like El Capitan. They are followed by low lying flatlands. Oversized trucks with men and women sporting orange and camouflage passed us. Near Cape Girardeau, in the Missouri Bootheel, a view of substantial ridges, almost small mountains, marked the horizon. Three inches of bright green wheat were popping out of the dirt.

We crossed into Illinois via the Bill Emerson suspension bridge spanning the mighty Mississippi which barrels up along the border between Missouri and Illinois. Emerson was a Missouri politician known for his successful recovery from alcoholism and his openness about his struggles.

We passed a number of ramshackle domiciles on the highway between Cape Girardeau and Anna. In Crossville, we called these areas the "bottoms"—areas near rivers, prone to flooding, where land is cheap. Nearing a village called Ware, we noticed two single wide trailers about twenty feet apart crudely adjoined to a long, narrow livestock barn. The entire unit, which looked like it might've been welded together, appeared to be a compound for general living purposes, and I didn't want to know what else.

A progressively thinking farmer had planted a field of lavender that grew into a lovely purple carpet, breaking up the monotony as we traveled the last five miles.

The courthouse was surprisingly modern and seemed brand new. A huge American flag was flying on a sky-high, shiny metal pole. We parked in a spot next to a seventies conversion van covered with bumper stickers telling everyone this guy was really into ham radio and ham radio clubs and ham radio stations.

"Is that Susan coming?" Lisa said, looking down the road from the second floor of the courthouse. "I can't tell if that's her. How old do you think she is?"

"Seventy?" I guessed.

"I hope I'm not towing a briefcase that size when I'm seventy."

"This will be no big deal, right?" I prodded.

"No big deal," Lisa reassured me. "I doubt you'll have to say anything. If you do, I'd just say that you are in therapy and that having your mom's records would help you in your treatment."

"It'll be fine. I'm just going to say whatever comes to mind," I blurted out and waved my hand, diminishing the whole thing.

Lisa looked at me like that was a terrible idea. "He may not ask you a thing," she said.

I wasn't exactly nervous, but I wasn't exactly *not* nervous either.

"Do we know if someone from Choate is showing up?"

"Susan hasn't told me anything," I explained.

"Yeah. Well, $500. Small potatoes."

"Lord, I'd do it for $500," I exclaimed. I thought about the difference between the hourly rate of an attorney compared to the rest of the real world.

"I'm just glad we got someone to do it." It brought me back to why we were really there.

Susan rushed out of the elevator in heels and a sharp pantsuit. She pushed out a fake smile. I introduced Lisa, and Susan smirked at her but didn't shake her hand. Susan needed some customer service training. She was warm and affectionate to her standard poodle, Louie. Maybe it was homophobia, but that was never my first thought. I couldn't imagine how anyone could hate Lisa and me.

"Judge Bert will be starting in here in just a minute. Choate isn't sending anyone."

As Susan continued to explain, she walked toward the courtroom door, shoved it open, looked back at us, and very quietly said, "I have the subpoena, and Bert already signed the order. He didn't care. I've got nine things on the docket in here, so I gotta go in."

Lisa and I looked at each other but didn't speak. We sat in the church-style, nicely padded pews at the back of the room and waited.

"Look how chatty she is with people she knows. You're an outsider," Lisa commented.

"I'm not an outsider. I'm an insider! Anna is five times the size of Crossville. She just doesn't know I'm an insider. I can't believe how unfriendly she is to us."

"She's schmoozing the clerk. See. The clerk holds the key to the kingdom, so she'll be nice to her."

Susan was laughing and telling her some engaging story.

The judge entered, and everyone hopped to. A friendly, forty-five-year-old bald man waved to everyone in their seats.

"OK. Sit down. Sorry about the delay. Let's get through this quickly here."

He looked down at the papers and called two cases whose people weren't anywhere to be found. A couple who was divorcing came forward. The bailiff asked the woman to step behind the line that was drawn between the judge and the regular people.

"Miss Allen, you are supposed to be providing a financial statement today. Do you have that for me?"

"No, I don't, Your Honor. I'm still waiting on some papers."

She was a thin, dark-haired woman who was probably twenty-five but looked forty-five. Some of her teeth were decaying and blackened.

"Do you need some help with it? I think we have people who can provide that."

"No."

"OK. Can you absolutely get this form taken care of by the next time we are here?"

The soon-to-be ex-husband spoke. "Your Honor, it's been two years since she attempted suicide."

The judge quickly and sternly admonished him for bringing up a topic so sensitive and unrelated to the financial matter.

I felt sorry for all of them—the woman because she was a mess, the husband because the judge yelled at him, and the judge because these people were all driving him crazy.

Lisa leaned over and said, "Judge Judy."

The husband walked out shaking his head at the judge and his ex-wife.

"Davis," the judge read off his document.

Susan waved me up, and I walked to the front, being careful not to cross the line in front of the judge. Susan approached the bench, and we both watched as he read through the papers, looking down and then looking up at her.

"He wants me to look through them?" the judge said to Susan.

She looked at him and shrugged. "I don't get it either."

"So, they'll send the records to me, and then I'll send them on?"

It was a question and a statement.

"I suppose so," Susan said.

The judge never looked at me. Susan never looked at me. In forty-five seconds, it was over. I turned back at Lisa, hoping for some direction, and she waved me out of the courtroom.

"I'll tell you what's going on," Lisa said as she grabbed my arm walking out. "Sounds like the attorney for Choate wants the judge to review the records before he releases them to you."

Susan gathered her things and met us in the hallway outside the courtroom where she verified what Lisa told me.

"It's the strangest thing I've ever heard."

"Do you know why?" Lisa asked.

"The attorney for the state is just stupid, no clue what he's doing," Susan said under her breath.

She fished through a file and handed me a copy of the motion to release the records granted by the judge. I saw the date.

"Choate will get them together, send them to the judge; he probably won't really look at them, and the clerk will send them to your therapist."

Susan didn't look up from the folder to say goodbye or shake hands.

Lisa and I sauntered to the elevator with the feeling of *Wow. That was so weird*. We waited until we were outside to ask each other why it was necessary to drive two hours when she apparently knew the judge had signed the order prior to the hearing.

"Seems like she isn't very interested in your case."

I got my tennis shoes out of the back seat of the car and put them on. Lisa pulled out her laptop, so she could get back to work. We looked at each other for a minute still, stunned that it was over already and then, before getting on the highway, drove through the Dairy Queen and ordered Gram's usual.

Chapter 23

Seventy-Five Days

May 2000

Near the end of her life, Gram spent seventy-five days in a skilled care nursing facility. It was hard to tell how much she was comprehending, although I believe she knew where she was.

It was seventy-five days more than anyone should spend in an unfamiliar place at the end of life, but the women who'd been caring for her told us Gram's legs had become so weak, they practically had to carry her to the bathroom.

"I'm sorry you have to do this," she would say, teary, thankful.

Aunt Maxine visited every day making sure Gram had everything she needed. I visited every other week. Should've been more, but I was too self-absorbed to understand the loneliness of old age. I'd walk into the "party" room, a large open space with a piano, crafts, and about six folding buffet tables. Gram would be all alone in a wheelchair, her eyes closed and her chin resting on her sternum, wheezing from her most recent fight with pneumonia. She simply looked broken. It was pitiful.

She'd been asking me for a long time, "Why am I here?"

I didn't know the answer and respected her too much to give her a glib response.

On August 14, 2000, Gram passed away in her bed from complications of pneumonia. She was ninety-one.

I was so lucky. I'd prayed for her to live until I was out of junior high, then high school, and she made it until I was thirty-one.

Gram probably still wasn't sure I was going to be okay, and I can guarantee she continued cogitating about it. Did I stay in touch with friends and family? Did I have good health insurance? Would I ever get married?

It wasn't the kind of finale Gram deserved. In this era of long but crappy-at-the-end lives, I don't think many people have the sort of final days they deserve.

Don Prince, Ph.D. (Gram liked to tease him about his title), our Crossville cousin, gave the eulogy. He was the same cousin who hadn't given her credit for being one of his influential teachers. Don went over each stage of Gram's life, referring to her hardship, but talking about her little known achievements.

Afterward, people came up to me and said, "I didn't know Faire went to college," and, "She was like a civil rights pioneer, and no one even knew."

I was happy and sad. Few people knew what kind of heroine Gram was because she didn't need them to know. A quiet warrior.

One of the grandkids said, "Someone should write a book about Gram. She was so cool."

Aunt Maxine followed Gram's lead, in the literal sense, almost every day of her life. Whether it was the suggestion of a drive, where to shop, what to watch on television, or who to root for when it came to baseball, she was the consummate little sister.

Gram told me once, "Being the older sibling requires sacrifice." And she laughed. "For Christmas one year, Mother and Dad gave me a toothbrush and an orange, but Maxine got two new pairs of shoes!" And she laughed some more.

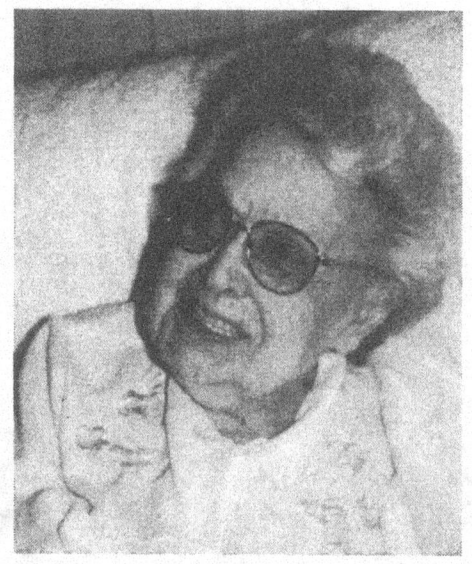

Faire DeLain Stein
January 12, 1909 - August 14, 2000

Gram became more serious then, stating, "She's not as strong as I am."

No one was as strong as Gram was.

We sold the whole of Stein's Corner—the northern tip of the property, where the filling station had once been, all the way to the edge of the weigh station which bordered the yard of the southern-most rental house.

Gram told Aunt Helen and Aunt Rita that I was to have anything I wanted from the house. It was unfair, but they'd gotten used to me getting all of the sympathy and attention.

As I loaded up the U-Haul, we said goodbyes to Aunt Maxine.

"Don't forget about me," she said.

I didn't forget about her. Aunt Maxine had been an ever-present anchor for me, and we couldn't have managed Gram's care without her devotion.

Maxine DeLain Randall and Faire DeLain Stein, 1946

Gram hadn't been her only charge. At eighty-six, Maxine was among the younger of her group of friends and one of the few still driving, so she filled her days with errands for old people.

One rainy September day, she set out for Paul's pharmacy in Carmi, the same Paul who sang at Mom's funeral. Midway between Carmi and Crossville, a brutal storm pounded down. Determined to finish her task, she continued along the seven-mile drive to Carmi.

"KANDI, Maxine's had an accident. I was driving by and saw her car. The preacher was there. He saw us and pulled over. She didn't suffer. We prayed with her." It was my childhood friend who still lived in Crossville. The state police explained that the storm had caused a driving rain and that even a younger person wouldn't have been able to see well enough to drive, so it was no wonder she crossed the centerline. She met a full-sized van head-on.

Aunt Maxine was buried on September 11, one year and one month after Gram died.

The woman driving the other vehicle was wrought with emotion when she approached Aunt Maxine's son, Rob, at the visitation.

Rob hugged her. "You can't imagine how my mother would've felt if she'd lived, and you had died. You have nothing to be sorry about. And, she would've been a terrible patient if she'd been the one injured," he joked.

Rob showed us all how to handle tragedy with grace and compassion.

Chapter 24

You're Just Like Your Mother

October 2019

"**K**andi, I think you need to go to the hospital. I know you're scared, but it's just for a few days. We need to get you stabilized, so we can figure out what's going on," my friend, a behavioral health care professional, advised. "You can come in tomorrow."

I hadn't slept one second in fifteen days. Not one second. I was severely depressed and sobbed uncontrollably.

It had happened. My lifelong fear was being realized. I was my mother. I'd been perfectly willing to tell the dirty secrets of my parents, but now it was me.

Over a period of fifteen years, I'd tried to manage multiple cervical and lumbar disc herniations and that caused constant nerve pain in my legs. I'd strived to fix it through hundreds of hours of therapies, MRIs, and so much money. I'd had PT, chiropractic, massage, acupuncture, did yoga, prayed a lot. When the therapies stopped providing relief, I had become reliant on tramadol, Flexeril, gabapentin, and sometimes narcotics.

My closest friends were medical professionals and warned me that tramadol was not the non-narcotic pain reliever it was billed to be, and when they learned that I was taking a daily dose of 4800 milligrams of gabapentin, they were worried sick. They knew just enough about my parents.

"They told me at the pain clinic that I could add more milligrams of gabapentin as needed for pain, but not to go over 4800."

It sounded like a lot to me, but I was no doctor. And I was miserable.

A surgeon suggested a lumbar fusion. I couldn't wait to get on with my life. I'd be able to do all the other things on my life list—more sections of the Appalachian Trail, go back to work in a kitchen (the thing I loved most in the world).

I hated not being able to move. But I had no idea what was coming my way.

I had the fusion and began the year-long recovery process. No bending or twisting or anti-inflammatories for one year. That meant no tying my own shoes and no wiping my bottom in the traditional way, as that meant twisting. It was a very difficult recovery.

Three months after my surgery, I was still in pain, but it was time to be off the meds. I had to do it. The surgeon's office advised me I could discontinue all of it without any major side effects. I stopped the gabapentin, the muscle relaxants, and began to taper off the hydrocodone. But I'd received bad advice. When I stopped the meds, my body rebelled.

"Women don't come down with severe depression in middle age for the first time," the doctor told me in the hospital. "It's gabapentin withdrawal. It's a miracle drug for nerve pain, but it can really mess up your nervous system. You just went off it too quickly. Your body will adjust."

After two months my depression and insomnia persisted, and the psychiatrist told me, "We aren't sure. I've talked to the other doctors in my practice. None of us have ever heard of anyone being on 4800 milligrams of gabapentin a day. It's new territory."

My friend Patty helped get me into an outpatient psychiatric program. Many days, I could barely get myself to walk into the building. Tales of chronic and debilitating depression from other patients ignited my fears.

"I just got out of the hospital. But, it's only my third time this year, so that's pretty good for me."

"I've been suicidal since I was a teenager. I've had at least one suicide attempt every year. "

"They're going to try Prozac this time. Before that I was on Remeron, Lexapro, Cymbalta."

"My mom has depression. My aunt has depression. We all have depression."

Over and over, the stories were the same. Years of hospitalizations and ongoing misery with the occasional year where things weren't so bad.

Oh, God. I had coped for forty-nine years. With my parents, how did I ever think I could escape the inevitable? But, I had never felt this way. I'd had situational depression, particularly after Gram's death. This was different. This was crippling.

Sixty days became ninety, and I was a little better. I started to believe the doctor that maybe I wasn't my mother. At 120 days, I was better still. At almost eight months, I was much closer to normal.

I was humbled. I was ashamed. I felt ignorant and naive. I'd let my guard down.

"Hey Kandi, it's Joan. So, I received your mom's records in the mail today. Quite a lot here."

I picked up the records from Joan, my therapist. I gave the fat envelope from Susan Werner to Lisa, asking her to hide it. I was still recovering from a major depressive disorder and didn't want to trigger myself. Months of conversations with Joan prepared me to read them, but I needed to settle myself first. Within a few weeks, I felt ready. Lisa organized the records by dates of admission and pulled out the most significant pages for me. The first page was proof of my mom's first admission date. This was before Johnny's death. One question answered. Johnny's death was not the source of Mom's plummet.

Additional notes proved the enormity of her disease.

1957 Admission, Anna State Hospital

Onset: In September, 1957, the patient was admitted to Deaconess Hospital in St. Louis, Missouri. She had been depressed for six months prior to admission and began taking drugs during this time.

Diagnostic Staff Report: Acute Brain Syndrome related to Drug Intoxication

Reason for Admission: Patient was brought to Anna by the deputy sheriff and a neighbor. On arrival, the patient was confused and disoriented. In a few days, she regained her emotional balance and proved to be a frank, intelligent, and truthful biographer.

The patient's mother and son were equally valuable and seemingly objective as informants. Their information was largely identical to that which we obtained from three different hospitals, where patient was treated. Her history indicated emotional instability and a tendency to have recurrent depressions.

Quoting patient: "I was taking, at one time, up to twelve dextroamphetamine tablets daily and wouldn't sleep for three or four days."

During her current hospitalization, patient has been on minimal doses of tranquilizers or no medication regimen. In spite of this, the patient retained her emotional stability.

1968 Admission, Anna State Hospital

Onset: This is the patient's fifth admission to a psychiatric facility. In previous hospitalizations, she has received electro-shock treatments as well as insulin shock treatments.

On December 31, 1967, the patient's son came home late and found his mother completely confused. She imagined there were people in their home and talked to them. The day of her admission she believed was Christmas Eve, and she acted very childlike in her anticipation of Christmas.

Patient has been on heavy medication for several years. Shortly after her last discharge, she began dating a man who traveled to various churches photographing the members. She had an affair with him believing he was divorced and would marry her. He was opposed to her drug usage, and when her prescriptions ran out, she did not have them refilled. A week later, she learned that the man she was dating had reunited with his wife.

The informants feel the combination of the patient's withdrawal from drugs and the disappointment about her boyfriend contributed to her present condition.

1968 Admission, Anna State Hospital

Reason for Admission: The patient was found unconscious in her apartment by her mother about twenty-four hours prior to her transfer to Anna State Hospital. Patient was semi-comatose upon arrival.

Mental Examination: For years, this unhappy and probably self-centered woman has been going from one to another depression. Resentment toward her father was noted and discussed. In a way, she refused to grow up, and each time as life disappointed her, she turned toward herself without trying to cope with it.

The informant, the patient's mother, says patient was very lonely after her return home from her last hospitalization and that most of the patient's friends avoided her because of the stigma of having been in Anna State Hospital.

Patient has made three serious suicidal attempts in the past six years.

1972 Admission, Anna State Hospital

Reason for Admission: "They handcuffed me, and I became very angry to put it mildly. Yes, I was hostile. I've been to this shit-hole so many times. I am getting worse and worse. I want to get well. I have a three-year-old daughter. I want to take care of myself and my daughter...I can't stand my father. I hate him. I don't like my daughter to be in that kind of environment."

"My fourth husband committed suicide by taking an overdose of pills." The patient began to cry and asked to be excused, saying, "I don't want to think about it."

I thought Dad had died of alcohol poisoning. Accidentally. This hurt. But, it was different.

It was sadness for my dad's other children that enveloped me. They knew him, had memories. I had merely a hollow feeling around the word "father." Nothing there. I'd grown up in Crossville, not knowing much about the Davis's from Eldorado, thirty-six miles away. Without the strong ties that bound me to Mom, it fell flatter than it should've. Detached and weary I was.

Chapter 25

She Was Crazy, Though

2019

Lisa and I and four friends had just hiked thirty miles of the Appalachian Trail, which wasn't even a sliver of its totality. We were driving through the hills of Tennessee on our way back to St. Louis.

"Where do you think those other hikers are by now? Think they made it to Garenflo Gap? Can you imagine how soaked they are?" My friend reminded us of how much rain the women had endured.

"Whose idea was this. . . Kandi!!!!" Lisa looked at me lovingly.

We'd been unplugged a few days. Voicemail notifications started dinging, as our SUV emerged from a beautiful Tennessee valley.

"Kandi, this is Tim Given," said a man with a low voice and a slow drawl. He spoke carefully.

It had been over a month since I sent a letter to Tim in Carmi, and I was worried I'd burned a bridge. Tim was Doug's childhood friend, probably one of Doug's last remaining friends when he died. Tim came to the gravesite for Doug's burial in 1997, and made impromptu visits to Gram during the twelve years she was house-

285

bound. Gram was proud that Tim became the mayor of big ole Carmi and still had time to stop and speak to little ole her.

In my quest for information, Tim came to mind. I thought for a long time about how to ask him if he thought Doug could've been involved in Mom's death without giving him an anxiety attack over his breakfast cereal. This was a real concern.

I felt guilty about the shock it could bring about and knew if I were retired, I wouldn't want to get involved in any research about a crime that *may* have occurred some forty years ago.

But I knew that people talked. "Is that where it happened?" and "Do you think *he* did it? She was crazy, though. She could've done it to herself." And without a doubt, Tim had heard things.

People have no idea the power of the word "crazy."

* * *

Dear Tim,

It has been so many years. I've thought of you when I've been in Crossville and wondered if you were still mayoring. Gram appreciated your visits and was proud of your rise to fame.

I'm still in St. Louis, as I have been for years. All is well for me, personally.

It's hard to know how to transition into the reason for this letter. I apologize if what I share here is shocking and ruins for you what might've been a nice day. Maybe it won't be so surprising.

You know Mom died by suicide. Doug was twenty-five. He was the last person to have seen her alive — a heavy burden to carry, and it took a tremendous toll on

him. He was already badly bruised after his unpredictable childhood.

I WENT on to tell Tim about finding the inquest article in 2015 and that the transcript of the inquest had supposedly been destroyed in a flood. This was according to the clerk at the courthouse.

Somehow, I found the nerve to ask Tim directly.

> Did Doug ever mention to you anything about the
> night Mom died? I'm wondering if in a sentimental
> moment, he might've hinted at anything?
> I'm not looking for vindication. If Doug had any
> culpability, it's moot now. I only have sympathy for him
> and how difficult his life was. I'm seeking the truth,
> so that I can achieve some level of clarity and closure.

* * *

IT WAS unlikely there would be any big aha moment when I talked to Tim, but I still believed that somebody, somewhere, knew something.

Lisa opened her resting eyes and said quietly to me, "Tim just may not remember much. It has been so long."

It took me another few miles to get my nerve up, and then I dialed his number.

* * *

AFTER WE CHATTED FOR A BIT, Tim remembered what he could. "He was wild, you know. That motorcycle of his, he drove it like a bat outta hell. And your mother, what a sweetheart."

"She just let him do whatever he wanted. No curfew. I knew she had some problems with prescription drugs, ya know, because Doug told me, but I never saw that."

I smiled, relieved that he hadn't seen her when she was low. "I know. She was fun," I said. What a dumb thing to say.

"As far as the other stuff, Kandi, he never mentioned anything to me. I never knew how your mom died specifically, other than that it was suicide. Doug never talked to me about her death."

"Gram found her," I revealed to Tim.

"I didn't know that. That's awful. What an image she lived with."

* * *

Tim texted me a few days later.

"I go up to City Hall every once-in-a-while. I'll ask the coroner to look around for those documents again. I'll be in touch."

Two weeks later, when the inquest was the last thing on my mind, my phone went DING.

* * *

September 2019

On September 10, 2019, at 2:02 p.m., I received a message from Tim Given that would mark one of the most significant moments of my life.

It was World Suicide Prevention Day.

We were traveling to Florida with Jane and Jill, two of the close friends with whom we'd hiked the Appalachian Trail and the same Jane who'd brought me the silly book during my hospital stay. The four of us had just landed in St. Pete for vacation when Tim's text came through.

"I just heard from the coroner. He is going to call you. He might have something. His name is Christopher Smith—a swell guy."

We were all the way to the rental car before I even mentioned the text to the others. Smith found "something". I thought maybe he'd searched Mom's name and downloaded a divorce decree . . . or four. I was working on a final chapter for the book that was going to offer no fulfillment to the reader. No good ending.

We arrived at our little Florida bungalow when a call from area code 618 came through.

"Hi, Kandi. I did some digging for you," Chris said. "The previous coroner was in office thirty-seven years, and I'm still sorting through records. Many of the files from the 1970s were destroyed, but I had some boxes in my office closet. I found a transcript from the inquest held after your mother's death."

I was in such disbelief. The only exclamation I could muster was, "Wow."

"I have it scanned in, and I'm ready to send it," he told me.

The entire exchange lasted no more than thirty seconds.

I gave him my email address.

* * *

"Are there towels up there for you guys?" Lisa hollered upstairs to our guests, Jill and Jane. She was zipping around the place, making sure everything was just so.

She returned to our bedroom and noticed my face.

"What? What's going on? You're scaring me. Did you do something to your back?"

"That was the White County coroner. He's found the inquest in the closet of his office. He's emailing it right now."

Her eyes were wide and frozen and unblinking.

I walked into the kitchen for a glass of water. I was bracing myself to read about the knife.

Would this be nothing or would this be big? Closure or confusion? Worthwhile examination or small-town faux investigation? The level of apprehension I felt was like nothing I'd experienced. I was anxious to hear what jurors thought about the circumstances. I'd always just wanted facts. I needed desperately to settle it within myself. When the thin cardboard disc of slides went into my internal View Master and the imaginary, sepia tone crime-scene photos appeared in succession, I wanted them to be fact-based. The truth couldn't have bludgeoned me more than forty-three years of wondering had.

I heard a ding from my email. Lisa took my phone from me and opened the email attachment.

INQUEST

September 10, 2018 at 3:15 PM

From: coroner@whitecounty-il.gov

To: Kandace Davis

Attachment: Davis_1976_inquest.pdf 2.13MB

Please let me know if I can be of further service to you. I hope this helps in finding what you want.

Blessings,

Chris Smith

White County Coroner

"It's ten pages," Lisa told me.

She put on her cheaters and looked up at me, waiting for me to give her a cue.

"Would you just read it to me?"

She smiled at me gently and began.

Inquisition into the Death of Mary Ellen Davis, May 28, 1976, Held before Mr. Thomas Wilson, Coroner of White County, Illinois

(Jury duly sworn by Mr. Wilson)

290

<u>Mr. Wilson:</u>

Gentleman of the jury, witnesses, and others present, this is an inquest into the death of Mary Ellen Davis, white female widow, forty-four years of age, address, Crossville, Illinois. This is neither a civil nor a criminal trial procedure, merely an inquest into the cause of this woman's death.

ALVIN STEIN

A: Witness, after being duly sworn testified as follows:

Q: State your full name?

A: Alvin G. Stein.

Q: Your age?

A: Seventy-two.

Q: Your address?

A: Box 82, Crossville, Illinois.

Q: Your occupation?

A: I do a little farming and run a little motel and do a lot of grass mowing.

Q: Mr. Stein, on May 19th, did you have reason to be in your daughter's trailer, Mary Ellen Davis?

A: No.

Q: Were you called to that trailer?

A: You mean when they found her dead?

Q: Yes.

A: I was that morning.

Q: Were you also there May 18th?

A: No, I went over to the trailer, and Doug was sitting in there, and I talked to him through the door, but I didn't go in.

Q: Doug Myers. Is that the deceased's son?

A: Yes.

Q: Where is Doug employed at?

A: Some shoe company in Chicago, Rickens & Company, I think.

Q: On May 19th, when you went in your daughter's trailer, would you tell me and the jury what you found?

A: Well, the day before, she had been awfully mad and everything, and my wife had been staying away from her. She had got to my wife about as much as she could stand. So, my wife noticed that night after Doug left that she hadn't seen any lights on over there, and about 5:30 the morning of the 19th, my wife got up and woke me up, and she met me in the hall and said I bet Mary Ellen has done something last night. She said I didn't see a light all night. I hadn't been in her trailer for a good while because she and I didn't get along. My wife wanted me to go over there, and I hesitated. I wanted her to go, and she did.

It wasn't but a minute then before she turned and came back, and I could tell by her walk that something was wrong, and she told me that Mary Ellen was gone. I couldn't believe it, so I said that I would go myself. I went on over there and felt her shoulder, and she was stiff and cold. My wife called Bernard Sturm then, and I didn't notice the knife in her then.

Q: Would you tell the Jury the position of the body, and where it was located?

A: She was in her bed in the bedroom with her
hands folded with the covers pulled up, so that
you wouldn't notice the knife.

Q: Has Mary Ellen been depressed for quite some
time?

A: Oh yes. Off and on for years. We've tried to
do everything we could.

Q: Has she attempted to take her life before?

A: Yes, sir. She sliced her wrists and different
things.

Q: Has she talked about taking her life?

A: Yes, about three days before this, she called
her mother from a hospital in Eldorado and told
her mother that she wished she was dead.

Q: Is there any doubt in your mind that she
killed herself?

A: Yes, I think she killed herself.

Q: Do you think the wound was self-inflicted?

A: Yes.

Jury:

Q: Did you recognize the knife?

A: I have never seen the knife.

Mr. Wilson:

This is a statement from the deceased's son, Doug
Myers, he could have been here tonight, it would
have been a hardship. This is dated May 27th,
from Crossville, Illinois. It reads as follows:

I arrived in Crossville about 6:00 p.m. on
Sunday, May 16th, for a visit with my mother,
Mary Ellen Davis, and my grandparents, Mr. and
Mrs. Alvin Stein. I had called my grandmother

previously to tell her that I was coming. I
called my grandmother because my mother had been
in the hospital in Eldorado, and this is why I
called her instead of my mother. This irritated
my mother, so by the time I arrived, she was in a
bad mood. I did eat supper with her that night.

The following day, May 17th, I spent little time
with her, as I was in Carmi most of the day.
Tuesday, I made no less than a dozen attempts to
talk with her at her trailer. Each visit was
short, as she made little sense. We were quarreling because I was concerned over the care of
my half-sister, six years old, Kandi Davis. I
felt that she should be sent temporarily to stay
with my aunt and her family in Wyoming.

During one visit to the trailer, my mother got
out some liquor and said that she guessed she
would just get drunk. I knew she had already
taken Valium, and she was already thick-tongued
from that. I was so disgusted from that, that I
took a bottle of pills from her purse and flushed
them down the toilet. This infuriated her so much
that she tried to squirt me with a bottle of
mace. I took the mace away from her, and she
pulled the buttons off my shirt. After this incident, she spent the rest of the day in bed.

Later when I went back, she was talking on the
phone. When I came in, she was saying, "My name
is Mary Ellen Davis. I don't know if you remember
me or not, but you treated me a couple of months
ago. I have to hang up now." I then checked the

notepad, took the number down. She was calling to Dr. M. in Evansville. The last time I went to her trailer trying to talk reason with her, it was to no avail. The last thing she said to me was, "You get out of this trailer and never come back." I then went to my grandmother's house to tell her I was leaving and then left for Chicago. The time was approximately 6:30 on May 18th.

The note was signed by Doug Myers and then notarized by Maxine Randall.

BOB RANDALL

A Witness, after being duly sworn, testifies as follows:

Q: State your full name?

A: Robert C. Randall

Q: Your age?

A: Seventy.

Q: Your address?

A: Crossville, Illinois.

Q: Your occupation?

A: Livestock dealer.

Q: Were you related to Mary Ellen Davis?

A: She was my wife's niece.

Q: Did you see Mary Ellen Davis on May 18th?

A: No.

Q: Would you tell us about what happened on May 19th, what happened from the time you received the phone call to the time the authorities arrived?

A: On Wednesday morning the 19th, the phone rang about 5:30. My wife got up and answered the

phone, and her sister Mrs. Stein said that there
was something wrong with Mary Ellen, and she
wanted us to come down. At that time, my wife
developed a bad nose bleed, and I told her to
take care of herself, and I would go.
I went down and went over to the trailer and met
Mr. Stein, and he told me that Mary Ellen was
gone.

I went on over to the trailer, went in, turned
the light on, and could see that she was gone. I
felt her arm, and it was as cold as ice, and
raised her eyelids, and her eyes were yellow. I
noticed her arms kind of crossed, and one little
finger was sticking up. I could just barely see
it and wondered why, so I pulled the cover back,
and the finger was against the knife which was
still in her chest.

Q: Could you tell us the position the body
was in?
A: She was lying in bed.
Q: Was Mary Ellen depressed a lot?
A: She was depressed most of the time. When she
wasn't, she was as nice of a girl as you could
find anywhere, but she got the alcohol or those
pills in her, couldn't anybody be around her.
Q: Have you and Mary Ellen ever had differences?
A: Yes, she tried to spray me with some mace one
time, and I got her down and took it away from
her, and I thought she had gone on home, and
after a while, she came back and tried to spray
me through the screen door.
Q: How long has she been like this?

A: About twenty-two years.

Q: Half of her life?

A: Yes.

Q: Is there any doubt in your mind that she took her own life?

A: I think she killed herself.

Q: Any more questions?

WITNESS EXCUSED

BILL ABBOTT

A witness, after being duly sworn, testified as follows:

Q: State your full name?

A: William H. Abbott.

Q: Your age?

A: Forty

Q: Your address?

A: Carmi, Illinois

Q: Your occupation?

A: Sheriff of White County, Illinois.

Q: On May 19th, were you called to Crossville?

A: Yes.

Q: And what was this occasion?

A: I was called to the trailer of Mary Ellen Davis.

Q: What did you find?

A: I found you, the coroner, Bernard Sturm of Grayville, Dennis Campbell, Mr. Stein, and Mr. Randall.

Q: Do you want to tell the jury the position you found the body in when you arrived?

A: She was laying in bed with a housecoat on. She was covered up.

Q: Did you take these pictures?
A: Yes, I did.

MR. WILSON SHOWS PICTURES OF DECEASED TO THE JURY

A: The deceased was laying in bed, looking very neat and composed. When we removed the covers, we found the right hand gripping the knife still in the chest, just below the rib cage.
Q: Is this the knife?
A. Yes, it appears to be.
Q: Sheriff, in your investigation, did you find any evidence pointing that this would be anything other than suicide?
A: No, I didn't. We checked the surroundings over and found that everyone seemed to be intact.

<u>Mr. Wilson</u>
The pictures are self-explanatory. The pictures do indicate that she was dressed for bed. She was lying in bed. She was pronounced dead at the scene, by Bernard Sturm, funeral director of Grayville and Deputy Coroner of White County.

Q: Did you know Mary Ellen Davis prior to this?
A: Yes, I've known her since 1967. I was Deputy Sheriff at that time and had occasion to have dealings with her since I've become Sheriff.
Q: Have you known her to be depressed?
A: Yes.
Q: Have you known her to take alcohol and drugs?
A: Yes, I have. Prescription drugs.
Q: Any further questions?
WITNESS EXCUSED

The knife which we have here was taken from the body of Mary Ellen Davis. It was apparent that she had made two other attempts to stick the knife in herself. The first few times, she just pricked the skin, hitting gristle. It's tough there. The last try she went in where it was soft and no bones. When I arrived, I found the same things that the Sheriff found, and in my mind, there is no doubt that it was anything but suicide. We found no evidence of foul play.

The testimony points to the fact that Mary Ellen Davis was depressed. Her father and uncle testified to the fact that she did use drugs and alcohol, and she was very depressed. Blood tests were made and are not back yet. If they should show later that this test turns up anything other than alcohol or a mild drug, the inquest will be reopened.

Gentlemen of the jury, this constitutes the evidence in this inquest. It will be your duty to deliberate your findings, and if possible arrive at a verdict as to the case of death, whether you deem it to be accidental, suicidal, homicidal, or from natural causes; whether the blame should be placed on the part of anyone concerned. When you have reached a verdict, you will report to me, Coroner of White County, State of Illinois. You gentlemen now retire and deliberate in privacy. Copy of Verdict Attached.

* * *

VERDICT OF CORONER'S JURY

```
STATE OF ILLINOIS
   White County,
   In the matter of the Inquisition on the
body of MARY ELLEN DAVIS, deceased, held at
CARMI on the 28th day of MAY A.D. 1976.
   We, the undersigned Jurors, sworn to
inquire of the death of MARY ELLEN DAVIS on
oath do find, that she came to her death by
```

SUICIDE.

IT WAS several moments before either Lisa or I spoke.

We had so many more questions. No one saw a light on at Mom's house immediately after Doug left? What did Alvin and Doug discuss "through the door" that day? The random question of where Doug was employed. Seemed unrelated.

I let out a sad chuckle. Alvin. His wife and a terrified mother asked one thing of him, and he failed.

"My wife wanted me to go over there, and I hesitated. I wanted her to go, and she did."

Of course she went! Pathetic. But, reading his words, I felt a tinge of tenderness for Grandad. I can't explain why.

Why wasn't Gram called to testify? Could Mom have pulled the covers up over her hand in order to prevent Gram from having to see the knife when she found her?

Most concerning, did the coroner lead the jury to a particular conclusion in his summary before sending them off to deliberate in private?

Sheriff Abbott had seen every phase of Mom's progressive illness, including Doug's years of suffering. He'd seen Mom at her worst, which must've influenced his testimony. Abbott had seen what Mom's illness had done to our family.

What a memory that man had. What the sheriff recounted to me on the phone in 2015 was identical to his testimony from 1976.

* * *

NEIGHBORS AND ACQUAINTANCES see the nice car and expensive vacations and wonder what kind of worries someone like me would have. Life is now dotted with first world annoyances—my drowning corn plant in the dining room or annoyance over getting dark meat instead of white with my grocery delivery.

It's true. My biggest daily decisions are which $12 bag of gourmet coffee to buy. But, we don't know what others have on their minds.

My daily moments are never without Mom. As I grind the beans and get the coffeemaker set for the next morning, I glance at the set of gleaming, stainless steel knives hanging on the magnetic rack, and Mom appears, on her bed, with a knife in her chest.

The imagery is fleeting, but it makes regular appearances. I've spent the last twenty-five years as a culinary professional with knives in front of my face for hours, every day.

Halloween has never been the same after Doug's suicide on what had been one of my favorite holidays.

Accidents: I think about Aunt Maxine and how terrified she must've been for those few minutes she sat, crushed behind the steering wheel of her car.

My thoughts turn to Gram when I think of women I know still today who stay with their abusers because they can find no way out.

Some days, I am reminded of my own past and question how exactly do I keep my childhood, this story, from interfering in my future? I find myself desperate to make sure that what happened to my then family doesn't happen to my now family—me, Lisa, and Moose.

The potential for anxiety, depression, or any mental illness doesn't just live homeless on the streets of San Francisco. The possibility lives in all of us. I try not to get vinegary when ignorant people start with their fear-based reasons as to why they think it's hooey-phooey. It always comes from folks who've never had one minute of counseling. Not that things would've turned out differently, but if medication and psychotherapy had been availed, utilized, we might've coped. Doug might've lived. Silence is deadly.

The suicide epidemic in America is so unsettling to me, particularly the suicides by children and teens. I give hateful stares to parents who I see treating their children badly. I just can't keep myself from getting involved.

I saw a young father dragging his two-year-old daughter behind him down the sidewalk in front of Walgreens. She was dawdling, so he began pulling her along by her arm while he talked on the phone, oblivious. The little girl was dirty, her shoes were way too big and falling off, and she had no coat on. She was doing her best to keep a hold of a thirty-two-ounce bottle of soda, presumably carrying it for her dad, but it kept slipping through her tiny hand. He had no idea she was whimpering while her knees buckled, and her little feet dragged the ground.

As they got closer to the car, he hollered at her, "Get in there. Come on, let's go."

I snapped and rolled down my window. "Why are you screaming at her?" I yelled at him.

He responded with, "Shut up, bitch!"

I drove home, told Lisa, knowing she'd scold me.

"I hope he doesn't take it out on her," she said.

I've stopped getting in fights at Walgreens, but Lisa still fears I will one day come home from the store with a child who doesn't belong to us.

"And what would be wrong with that?" I say.

Kids just need one person who loves them more than anything in the world. Doesn't matter who loves them. Just that they do.

* * *

FIFTEEN MINUTES after hearing Lisa's calm voice read the ten pages of the inquest, I felt a resolution, a peace that stayed with me throughout the evening. Hearing about the knife was agonizing. But, somehow, I was better.

In the hours before bed, I felt an understanding I hadn't felt before. Mom did it herself. I was sure. After two tentative attempts, she went deep with the knife. What was she thinking about in the minutes remaining as she bled out? I'd like to believe she was thinking of me and Doug. I choose to believe she was not in great distress. I choose to believe she was resigned to it and felt not life flowing from her, but lightness flowing into her like an injection of sunshine straight into a major artery.

I wonder, was she maybe even smiling? No different than the Kevorkian departure of a patient with ALS — incurable, brutal, relentless. After a twenty-two-year debilitating illness, Mom put on a beautiful red nightgown and took a trip with the angels.

* * *

September 11, 2019

Dear Gram and Mom,

Hello again. So, there it is. The story decoded. Now, how do I make something good out of such pain? The moral? A beautiful, haunted woman; a long-suffering mother; a barbaric suicide; a wounded child. Addiction, grief, or the strength of women? It could be about how enough love can save a child from any hardship. Or about the security that a strong sense of community provides.

You'll be happy to know the change in me on the morning of September 11, 2019, was more than I predicted. I was so often preoccupied with the past. My brain can finally rest.

Mom, I've told some stories that are unbecoming of you. These were decisions I didn't take lightly and when I told the world, it was for the purpose of showing the level of desperation you were feeling. I hope you understand.

I'm so sorry.

Sorry you felt you had to tell people you were okay when you weren't. I wish you'd had a place to safely share your feelings . . .

Sorry the doctors at Anna claimed you cried for "no reason." Those words would never be used today. The body cries as a release, and you had a lot of things to cry about:

- For your misfortune in losing Johnny when you were twenty-seven
- You were ill in a time when you had no real diagnosis and no long-term treatment plan. I believe you could've been struggling with bipolar disorder, but it wasn't even a thing then
- No one believed you were sick
- Gram's strength made you feel weak
- I called you a cry baby

Gram, you're annoyed because you never wanted this amount of attention, but people needed to know about the fabulous Faire Stein from Crossville. You'll just have to get over it.

I hope people see that acquiescing when it comes to choosing a spouse can have generational consequences.

I resented you for smothering me, and consequently, I couldn't wait to get out of Crossville. Now that I know the extent of Mom's illness, I understand why you hovered.

Thank you for so many things:

Thank you for teaching me how to suffer with a gracious heart,

Out of the Night that Covers Me

for being the original Atticus Finch,

for never saying one bad word about my mother,

for not taking it easy on me,

for telling me, "Take what you want, but eat all you take,"

for climbing the basement steps twenty times a day, doing my
laundry when your arthritic back was killing you,

for making me go to church on Sunday night instead of hanging out
at Pizza Hut. I needed to learn how to sit still and listen,

for teaching me that you can judge the character of a person by how
he treats those beneath him,

and finally, for teaching me that a drive can cure almost anything.

I miss you so much.

Now, back to Scrabble, you two.

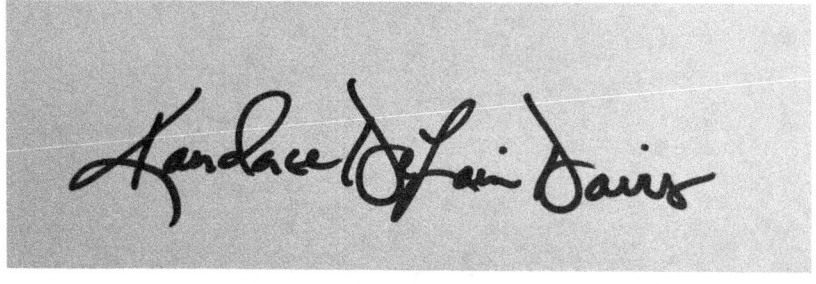

305

Epilogue

At the eleventh hour, in the editing of this book, information came to light about a disturbing turn of events at The Anna State Hospital, now known as Choate Mental Health Center. Multiple investigative articles cited reports from the Illinois Department of Human Services's (IDHS) watchdog office, revealing horrifying examples of cruelty, abuse, and poor care of patients.

An IDHS inspector wrote that in October of 2017, two Choate employees had broken a patient's arm and bragged about getting away with it. The staff boasted about bullying other employees to keep them from reporting abuse.

Several nurses told an investigator that it was common practice to force patients with pica, a disorder in which people feel compelled to swallow inedible objects, to dig through their own excrement to determine whether objects they swallowed had passed. The investigation was triggered in the spring of 2022, when a facility monitor noticed a patient leave the restroom with a bag of feces.

In possibly the most disturbing report, the inspector general cited two nurses for neglecting a terminally ill patient. In the days before the patient died in July 2021, one of the nurses failed to properly manage his pain, and the other failed to notify a physician that the patient had lost twenty-one pounds in one week. These failures of staff caused him to experience emotional distress and tremendous discomfort, according to the inspector general's review.

These reports, relating to events that occurred between 2017 and spring of 2022, come following of a series of news stories documenting widespread and repeated failures at the Choate facility. The investigative series by ProPublica revealed a culture of cover-ups at Choate, later confirmed by inspector general reports. The news organization uncovered employees obstructing investigations and lying to avoid consequences in abuse and neglect cases.

In November 2021, a Choate technician was found to have retaliated against a patient who wet himself after the tech rejected his request to use the bathroom. The employee made the man mop up the urine and tossed his personal letters in the bucket of dirty water. When questioned by an investigator, one of the patients who witnessed and corroborated the event began to cry and said he "was tired of being abused."

At the time of print and following numerous grand jury indictments, the state has announced plans to "repurpose" Choate and move patients to other facilities. This transition is taking place with the help of the Southern Illinois University School of Medicine.

Notes

12. A Free Flow of Tears

1. Browne and Finkelhor, 1986; Paolucci et al., 2001; Santa Mina and Gallop, 1998
2. *Psychiatric Times*, Effects of Childhood Trauma on Depression and Suicidality in Adults, Karen Wagner, MD, PhD

14. Hope You Get Out Tomorrow

1. Drugaddictiontreatment.com
2. http://theconversation.com/weekly-dose-valium-the-safer-choice-that-led-to-dependence-and-addiction-59824

15. Beverly, Mace

1. https://afsp.org/about-suicide/suicide-statistics

17. Do You Know Where You're Going To?

1. Misiak, Piotr, Sławomir Jabłoński, Katarzyna Dziwińska, and Artur Terlecki. "A Very Unusual Case of Attempted Suicide." *American Journal of Public Health.* June 30, 2016. https://www.ncbi.nlm.nih.gov/pmc/articles/PMC4971271/
2. *Journal of Interpersonal Violence.* December 2007. https://journals.sagepub.com/toc/jiva/22/12/
3. McKeown, Robert, PhD, Steven P. Cuff, MD, and Richard M. Schulz, PhD. "U.S. Suicide Rates by Age Group, 1970–2002: An Examination of Recent Trends." *American Journal of Public Health.* October 2006. https://www.ncbi.nlm.nih.gov/pmc/articles/PMC1586156/

Acknowledgments

Thank you to my many "parents:" Aunt Janet, Aunt Ruthie, Dorothy and Paul Burke, Minnie Coston, David and Marcia Coston, Jerri Davis, Teresa Hon, Claire and Don Prince, Robert Prince, and Bob and Jenny Warden.

I am forever indebted to Nina Furstenau and Carol Voelker-Brandt who spent hours assisting me with this eight-year project. With little to nothing in return, they helped research and edit this entire story, multiple times. Without you, I don't think I would've persisted. You advised me, laughed and cried with me, and went through hell with me. I adore you eternally.

To my best mates, thank you for the love and encouragement: Sheryl Bonsett, Dr. Elizabeth Cavanagh, Dr. Mona Etchison, Marie Freise, Piper Fuhr, Rachel Coston Gollaher, Jill Hoy, Julie Kellogg, Robin Warden Mick, Kim Micke, Kenda Morado, Patty Morrow, Jane Small, Dr. Angie Tripp, and Jill Wehmer.

Thank you to my therapist, Joan Brackmann, MA, who helped me face this story.

Thank you to my publisher, Margo Dill, at Editor 911 Books, for taking on this manuscript. I felt completely safe in your hands.

To the people of my tiny hometown of Crossville, Illinois, your support has uplifted me beyond words.

Thank you to the late Jimmy Gaines, of Carmi, Illinois, your assistance proved to be of incalculable value.

Thank you to Barry Cleveland for your legwork in finding important documents.

And to my wife, Lisa, who loves a great mystery but probably never thought you'd be involved in investigating one, thank you. I'm sure you didn't realize what you were signing up for when you chose a parentless adult-child with unresolved trauma. This project was no picnic for you. Through many dark days and shocking moments of discovery, you were unbreakable. You were the logic against my emotion. You were advisor and attorney. You were the Official Hugger. Sometimes, that was the only thing to be done.

"You chase all the ghosts from my head.
You're stronger than the monster beneath my bed."

~*The Indigo Girls*

About the Author

Kandace Davis began her career at a large, suburban St. Louis school district where she taught English and theatre. In 1999, she moved on to a twenty-five year career as a chef and founded the award-winning St. Louis food company, Cha Cha Chow. The company was thrice named by The Daily Meal, NYC, as one of the top food trucks in America. Kandace and Cha Cha Chow have been featured in the *St. Louis Business Journal*, *Sauce Magazine*, *Feast Magazine*, and *Show Me St. Louis*.

In 2013, Kandace was nominated and accepted into Les Dames d'Escoffier International, a philanthropic organization of women leaders in food, fine beverage, and hospitality. She has served on the board of her local chapter.

As part of her work to help provide healthy food to underserved communities, Kandace is a supporter of Earthdance Organic Farm School and Mutual Aid St. Louis. During the coronavirus pandemic, Kandace helped facilitate the adoption of sixteen St. Louis families, soliciting donations from the community and personally delivering groceries weekly.

Kandace has participated in local events supporting the Nation Alliance on Mental Illness, the Black Lives Matter movement, and as a breast cancer survivor, The Breast Cancer Fund. Having begun her career in education, Kandace devotes time to the children in her life and strives to be a loyal and loving advocate for them.

Kandace stepped down from Cha Cha Chow in 2018, freeing up her days to work on this book she had long wanted to write. She and her wife Lisa enjoy hosting friends and family on the patio, hitting their favorite restaurants, watching the Cardinals and Blues, hiking, traveling, and watching *Downton Abbey* for the millionth time.

www.ingramcontent.com/pod-product-compliance
Lightning Source LLC
Chambersburg PA
CBHW061137120626
46546CB00005B/1819